Friedrich Schlegel's Lucinde *and the Fragments*

——— ◇ ———

The photographs of Friedrich Schlegel
and his wife Dorothea Veit are used by
permission of the Freies Deutsches
Hochstift, Frankfurt am Main, and the
Staatsbibliothek der Stiftung Preussis-
cher Kulturbesitz, Berlin, respectively.

——— ◇ ———

Friedrich Schlegel's Lucinde and the Fragments

translated
with
an introduction
by
Peter
Firchow

UNIVERSITY OF MINNESOTA PRESS · MINNEAPOLIS

Published in the United Kingdom and India by the Oxford University
Press, London and Bombay, and in Canada
by the Copp Clark Publishing Co. Limited, Toronto

Library of Congress Catalog Card Number: 77-161440
ISBN: 0-8166-0624-2

——— ❖ ———

The translation of *Lucinde*, the *Fragments*, and "On
Incomprehensibility" is based on the critical edition
by Hans Eichner in volumes 2 and 5 of the *Kritische
Friedrich-Schlegel-Ausgabe*, published by the Ferdi-
nand Schöningh Verlag, Paderborn. Permission to
use this edition has been granted by the
editor and the publisher.

——— ❖ ———

For Evelyn,

WITH UNFRAGMENTED LOVE

Preface

Lucinde has been translated into English once before, in 1913 by Paul Bernard Thomas as part of the German Classics series.[1] Though its rather Victorian vocabulary tends to be annoying at times, Thomas's translation is, from a strictly stylistic point of view, a good one. Even so, it contains a number of faults which make it ultimately unsatisfactory. Besides its relative inaccessibility, its most obvious inadequacy lies in the omission of two of the most important sections of the novel, the "Allegory of Impudence" and the "Apprenticeship for Manhood" — in other words, more than a third of the novel. Although there is no direct statement to the effect, it is probably safe to assume that Calvin Thomas's observation in his introduction that Lucinde "now and then . . . passed the present limits of the printable in its exploitation of the improper and unconventional" accounts for the omissions. And the same moral delicacy very likely is to be blamed for the further omission of brief passages within the sections of the novel which were translated. One of these in particular illustrates how mistaken and even

1. Friedrich Schlegel, "Lucinda," trans. Paul Bernard Thomas, intro. Calvin Thomas, in The German Classics (New York, 1913).

self-defeating such a policy of omission can be. The passage in question occurs just as Julius is about to make love to Lucinde. Fully translated it reads, "Can't I feel if you're as passionate as I am?" which Thomas renders as "'May I not feel * * *.'" If anything in this speech could offend one's moral sensibility, it is these three asterisks.

The present translation does not follow such a practice of omission. In the terminology of sensationalist book blurbs, it is unexpurgated: its basis (and that of the *Fragments* and "On Incomprehensibility") is the recent critical edition by Hans Eichner. I have also included an English translation of the prose sections of the proposed continuation of *Lucinde*, but not of the poems because the order in which they were meant to be read cannot be determined with any accuracy.

I am, of course, aware that this rendering of *Lucinde* and the *Fragments* is by no means perfect. My apology for at least some of the imperfections must be that a translation can by its very nature never be perfect, or, to revise Schlegel's dictum on the Romantic novel, that there can never be such a thing as a perfect translation, but only translations forever trying to become perfect. The problem with translation is that, do what one will, even the most closely equivalent words in different languages still connote different things, a problem complicated in this instance by the frequent deliberate vagueness, ambiguity, and "confusion" of Schlegel's style. The great temptation in such cases is to put "order" and "sense" into the confusion and ambiguity, in short, to "improve" upon the original. I have tried to resist this temptation. My aim throughout has been to get at the original as closely as is possible in a different language: to capture something of the same sentence rhythms and to reflect something of the same quality of the language without resorting to anachronistic modernization.

My thanks at this point are due to the Horace H. Rackham School of Graduate Studies of the University of Michigan and the Department of English of the University of Minnesota for financial assistance in the immigration, to Professor Raymond Skyrme

Preface

and Professor David Haley for advice in the naturalization, and to Professor Hans Eichner for his help in the indoctrination of this *Lucinde* in English dress. If, however, despite all this effort, she and her fragmentary brethren still remain foreigners, the fault is mine alone.

Contents

Friedrich Schlegel's Lucinde *and the Fragments*

Introduction

Lucinde is an unusual book written at a time of unusual books and unusual events. In 1799, the year of its publication, the French Revolution was taking its first militant steps into Empire, and a new literary and philosophical movement, as yet unnamed, was also preparing to march against the old establishment. For Napoleon, it was supposedly a struggle of the liberal French armies against the restrictive forces of the conservative world; for the Romantics, as they came later to be called, it was a war against the rational, neo-classic conception of art and life, symbolized by the French authors and philosophers of the seventeenth century. Though *Lucinde*, un-like, say, Wordsworth and Coleridge's *Lyrical Ballads* of 1798, represents only a small battle in this great Romantic war, the novel is nevertheless noteworthy for its intensity, and for the lessons in strategy it provides, because its leader was one of the most famous, brilliant, and aggressive strategists the whole movement possessed.

When *Lucinde* was first published, most of its public realized that it was an unusual novel, but only in the sense that it was un-usually bad. Still, the book was not wholly without enthusiastic ad-mirers, even quite eminent ones. For example, Friedrich Schleier-

Schlegel's *Lucinde* and the Fragments

macher,[1] Schlegel's old friend and former roommate, was moved to publish in 1800 a collection of fictional letters, *Confidential Letters on Schlegel's Lucinde*, in which most of the prevalent hostile attitudes toward the novel were taken up and refuted. And another friend, the philosopher Fichte,[2] declared in September 1799 that *Lucinde* was one of the greatest productions of genius he knew, and that he was about to embark on his third reading of it. But these and some few other favorable reactions were not enough to stem the tidal wave of hostile criticism that threatened to inundate the book completely. Friends and philosophers might console Schlegel, but they could not rescue his book from general condemnation.

The hostile contemporary reception of a literary work of merit is, of course, no unusual occurrence; on the contrary, it is one of the clichés of literary history. What one generation rejects, the next accepts; what one generation throws into the garbage pail, the next places on the dining-room table. As Kierkegaard perceived, one's generation and the public are not merely often, but usually, wrong.

The cliché, however, has not held completely true in this particular instance. Although, in Germany at any rate, the public in the twentieth century has at last given wide acceptance to *Lucinde*, the critics have been more slow and grudging in their approval. The reasons for this critical hesitancy are complex, but the very fact of the hesitancy probably indicates how much ahead of its time *Lucinde* actually was.

At the very beginning it appeared almost as if *Lucinde* was

1. Friedrich Schleiermacher (1768–1834), German theologian and philosopher whose *Reden über die Religion* (*Talks on Religion*) (1799) was one of the chief reasons for Schlegel's writing his *Ideas*.
2. Johann Gottlieb Fichte (1762–1814), German philosopher, whose early thinking was an extension of Kant's ideas but who later moved toward a much more mystical position. His best known works are *Bestimmung des Gelehrten* (*Vocation of the Scholar*) (1794), and *Über den Begriff der Wissenschaftslehre* (*On the Notion of the Theory of Knowledge*), dating from the same year, but expanded in subsequent years.
(A word about the footnotes: No strict rule of annotation has been followed, but in general those names which might seem unfamiliar to the English-speaking reader have been briefly identified.)

Introduction

meant to be taken out of time entirely, as if, in fact, the novel would be completely forgotten. Friedrich Schlegel himself may have been partly responsible for this temporary oblivion. When in 1823 he came to edit and publish his complete works, he omitted *Lucinde* altogether. By that time Schlegel, grown old, Catholic, and conservative, no longer approved of his period of youthful radicalism and exuberance. But what the aging Schlegel perhaps wished to eradicate from the memory of mankind was resurrected six years after his death by an artist and critic who was still young, exuberant, and radical. In 1835, Karl Gutzkow[3] issued the second edition of *Lucinde*, and it soon became one of the basic texts of the Young Germany movement of which he was a leader.

The second edition of *Lucinde* forced a smaller re-enactment of the original battle of 1799. Ironically, the most notable hostile critical reaction came from Heinrich Heine, himself a quasi member of the Young Germany movement, as well as a sometime Romantic. In his extended essay "The Romantic School" (1836), Heine discusses the career of Schlegel and gives a brief analysis of his novel. He begins by asserting that *Lucinde* is "ludicrously Romantic," and he concludes — alluding to Schlegel's Catholicism — with the remark that, though the Mother of God may be able to forgive Schlegel for having written it, the Muses never will. Six years later, another writer of considerable reputation, Kierkegaard, made an even sharper attack on the novel, charging that it denies the spirit for the sake of the flesh, that it aims at naked sensuality, and, finally, that it attempts to eliminate all morality.

Succeeding nineteenth-century critics by and large mirror these condemnations of Heine's and Kierkegaard's, usually with more scholarship if less wit. Rudolf Haym, the author of a long work bearing the same title as Heine's essay — and, though first published in 1870, probably still the most comprehensive study of the early Romantic movement in Germany — calls *Lucinde* an "aesthetic

---

3. Karl Gutzkow (1811–1878), German novelist and dramatist, best known for his novel *Wally, die Zweiflerin* (*Wally, the Doubter*) (1835), which marks the beginning of "Young Germany."

Schlegel's *Lucinde* and the Fragments

monstrosity"; his contemporary, Wilhelm Dilthey, in his biography of Schleiermacher, considers it self-evident that this novel is "morally as well as poetically formless and contemptible." It is only with the coming of the twentieth century that more liberal and favorable critical views began to be expressed, most significantly by Josef Körner, Paul Kluckhohn, Wolfgang Paulsen, K. K. Polheim, and Hans Eichner.[4] However, even these views have not been able to prevail wholly, in part perhaps because they themselves have often been halfheartedly maintained. Josef Körner, for example, though tracing the origins of *Lucinde* with a good deal of sympathy and scholarship, still comes to the conclusion that Schlegel did not achieve in it what he had hoped, and that such form as *Lucinde* displays is ultimately due to chance. Wolfgang Paulsen, who is even more overtly sympathetic and who expends much ingenuity in an attempt to prove that *Lucinde* is not formless, nevertheless feels compelled to assert that the third part of the novel is undeveloped and incompetent. Only Paul Kluckhohn, in his study of eighteenth-century and Romantic conceptions of love, Hans Eichner, in his introduction to the recent critical edition of *Lucinde*, and K. K. Polheim in his afterword to the Reclam edition of the novel, evaluate it in anything like a wholly positive way. But even these favorable or ambiguously favorable modern criticisms are balanced by others that are almost unambiguously unfavorable. The novelist Ricarda Huch, for example, does not even bother to disguise her contempt; for her *Lucinde* is an artistic miscarriage, formless, pretentious, and dull.

4. Josef Körner, "Neues vom Dichter der *Lucinde*," *Preussische Jahrbücher*, 183 (March 1921), 309–330, and 184 (April 1921), 37–56; Paul Kluckhohn, *Die Auffassung der Liebe in der Literatur des 18. Jahrhunderts und in der deutschen Romantik* (Halle, 1931); Wolfgang Paulsen, "Friedrich Schlegels *Lucinde* als Roman," *Germanic Review*, 21 (October 1946), 173–190; K. K. Polheim, "Nachwort," *Lucinde* (Stuttgart, 1964), pp. 110–118; Hans Eichner, ed. and intro., *Dichtungen* (Munich, 1962), vol. 5 of *Kritische Friedrich-Schlegel-Ausgabe*, under the general editorship of Ernst Behler. Hermann A. Korff's *Geist der Goethezeit*, vol. 3 (Leipzig, 1949), contains a brief and interesting analysis of *Lucinde*. Korff sees *Lucinde* as the book on Romantic marriage par excellence, but thinks little of Schlegel's artistic ability.

Introduction

The question that naturally arises out of this brief and partial review of *Lucinde*'s critical reputation is, why should anyone bother to read this novel? If past and present critics have been so nearly unanimous in their condemnation of it, what is it then that makes this book so unusual? One answer, perhaps, is contained implicitly in the question itself. For surely a book must be unusual when, after all the charges that have been leveled against it, it still insists upon being read. And *Lucinde* does insist on being read: today it is probably the best known and most popular novel to come out of the German Romantic movement.

The primary reason for its continued vitality is not far to seek. *Lucinde* was the cause of one of the most notorious literary scandals of the early nineteenth century, for it was thought to be a pornographic novel. Pornography, as modern literature so amply testifies, is usually a profitable commodity — but in this respect as well *Lucinde* was unusual, since its first edition definitely did not sell well. Nevertheless, the reputation of being a dirty book, fostered by numerous more or less puritanical critics, has stayed with *Lucinde* to the present day and has no doubt increased its readership. A recent German edition, for example, is copiously illustrated with woodcuts of nude figures in various positions. But, as is so often the case, the illustrations have very little to do with the text. *Lucinde*'s reputation for frank sensuality has been greatly exaggerated; by present-day standards, it is very mild indeed. There are no four-letter words and hardly any graphic description of any sort (let alone sexual). Like the traditional Hollywood movie, there is a fade-out at all the crucial moments, and, for the rest, the sexuality is kept very vague and, to use one of Schlegel's favorite words, allegorical. No doubt *Lucinde* has been a disappointment to many of its readers.

Basically, there are two reasons why the virtually innocent *Lucinde* got such a wicked reputation. The first of these can be traced to the social and hypocritical phenomenon of a double morality, a dichotomy which *Lucinde* was designed to attack. It is highly probable that that mythical entity, the average reader of the late eighteenth and early nineteenth centuries, was not significantly more moral than the average reader of the twentieth century. As an examination of even a small city like Weimar will testify, the moral behavior of the upper (and, therefore, reading) classes was open to considerable censure from a Victorian point of view (as Thackeray did censure it later). Furthermore, any good bibliography of the period will quickly prove that there was no lack of genuine pornography, and that any dearth in the German supply could easily be supplemented from the French. No doubt many a German reader savored his curious and erotic little volume in private while he condemned *Lucinde* in public for overstepping the bounds of decency. And he could do so without any real sense of contradiction because ordinary pornography was thought of as nothing more than an amusing and stimulating trifle – it was usually unpretentious and did not presume to be taken seriously. But *Lucinde* clearly presumed to be taken seriously, both as a work of art and as an attempt to revise the existing code of moral and social conduct. Most pornography was published either pseudonymously or anonymously. Not *Lucinde*: its title page boldly proclaimed that it was written by one of Germany's foremost literary critics. What by contemporary standards should have been a private concern, an anonymous, naughty triviality, had become a matter of excited public discussion. That is one reason why the publication of *Lucinde* constituted a scandal. What is acceptable in private is not always acceptable in public.

A further cause can be traced to an even more serious breach of this distinction between private and public morality. Schlegel presumed to use recognizably real people and events as the models for his fictional characters and actions. To anyone who knew anything of the lives of Schlegel and his then mistress, Dorothea Veit, it was obvious that Julius was a thinly disguised Schlegel and Lucinde a thinly clad Dorothea. Schlegel had violated another, even more inviolable social taboo: he had admitted the public into his own bedroom. And not merely admitted, but welcomed it in. That was not just scandalous; it was unheard of.

II

Since *Lucinde* is partially and consciously an autobiographical novel — and a roman à clef — it is obvious that to understand and appreciate it as fully as possible, one needs to know something of the life and thinking of the author, enough, at any rate, to make the relationship of *Dichtung* to *Wahrheit* comprehensible.[5]

Friedrich Schlegel was born in Hanover on March 10, 1772, the youngest son of a Lutheran pastor, Johann Adolf Schlegel. His parents had originally intended him for a business career and had apprenticed him to a Leipzig banker. But in 1790 Schlegel, unhappy with this life, persuaded his parents to allow him to study law at Göttingen, where his brother, August Wilhelm (1767–1845), was pursuing classical studies under the famous philologist Christian Gottlob Heyne.[6] It was at Göttingen, one can safely say, that Schlegel's intellectual life took its rise; and it was there as well that the two brothers began to forge the intellectual alliance which was later to exercise such an enormous influence on the course of German and European literature. With the elder brother initially providing the guiding hand, they undertook together extensive aesthetic and philosophical studies which contributed to Friedrich's deepening interest in Plato, Winckelmann, and the Dutch philosopher Hemsterhuis.[7]

5. There is no comprehensive biography of Schlegel. However, *Friedrich Schlegel in Selbstzeugnissen und Bilddokumenten*, ed. Ernst Behler (Hamburg, 1966), is much more than the collage its title suggests. It is an interesting and intelligent ordering and occasional discussion of the salient data of Schlegel's life, and it also contains a brief survey of his general critical reputation. The closest thing to a full-scale biography is Hans Eichner's *Friedrich Schlegel* (New York, 1970), which is, however, limited by the scope of the Twayne Series for which it was written. Even so, it is unquestionably the most thorough and coherent account of Schlegel's life available in any language.

6. Christian Gottlob Heyne (1729–1812), German classical philologist and archaeologist. He was not a narrow pedant, but considered the study of grammar and language as a means not as the end of philology.

7. Johann Joachim Winckelmann (1717–1768), German archaeologist and aesthetician. His most important work, *Die Geschichte der Kunst im Altertum* (*History of Ancient Art*) (1764), made him a European celebrity and helped shape the Grecophilia of nearly every major German writer of the late eighteenth century. François Hemsterhuis (1721–1790), Dutch aesthetician

9

Schlegel's *Lucinde* and the Fragments

Around Easter 1791, Schlegel left Göttingen for Leipzig, where at first he continued to study law, but gradually began to devote most of his attention to art history, philosophy, and literature. It was during this period of his life (1791–1793) that he met Friedrich von Hardenberg, later to become famous under the pseudonym "Novalis," as well as one of Schiller's patrons, Christian Gottfried Körner,[8] and Schiller himself. But despite these new friends and acquaintances, his closest intellectual ties were still to his brother, who was now in Amsterdam. The brothers maintained an intensive and searching correspondence, and Friedrich confided to August Wilhelm the various stages of a progressively more serious spiritual crisis. The cause of this crisis — portrayed in *Lucinde* in the section entitled "Apprenticeship for Manhood" — seems primarily to have been Schlegel's growing inability to reconcile his idealism with the reality he saw about him. Secondarily, it may also have been the result of a kind of — possibly sexually induced — self-disgust, complicated by considerable financial difficulties. August Wilhelm (who seems to be the distant friend to whom Julius holds out his arms in the "Apprenticeship") was able to help him with money, but Friedrich's moods of depression were partly relieved only when, in the spring of 1793, he decided to give up law and devote himself entirely to the study of philosophy and literature. A more complete recovery followed shortly afterwards, when, in the summer of the same year, he undertook to act as a kind of guardian to his brother's mistress (and later wife), Caroline Boehmer, who was staying in a village near Dresden. Caroline — Julius's first great love in the "Apprenticeship" — was one of the most intelligent, exciting, and charming women of the age, and

and moral philosopher, whose unsystematic Neoplatonism appealed to a number of German writers.

8. Friedrich Leopold, Freiherr von Hardenberg (1772–1801), German poet and novelist, often thought of as the prototype of German Romantic poets. Best known for his *Hymen an die Nacht* (*Hymns to the Night*) (1800) and the unfinished novel *Heinrich von Ofterdingen* (1802). Christian Gottfried Körner (1756–1831), distinguished Saxon jurist and intimate friend of Schiller; also the father of the patriotic poet Karl Theodor Körner (1791–1813), who died in the wars against Napoleon.

was obviously good social and emotional medicine for the moody Schlegel.

About this time Schlegel began to devote himself to an intensive study of Greek literature. Inspired by the example of Winckelmann and influenced by the brilliant criticism of Johann Gottfried Herder,[9] he had great hopes of doing for Greek literature what Winckelmann had done for Greek art. That he was never able to realize these hopes can be accounted for in part by his need to supplement his meager income through rapid and frequent publication, and in part (if one may judge by his later performance) by his chronic inability to complete any of his major literary undertakings — *Lucinde* included.

In the essays from this early period (1794–1795), Schlegel is, though with considerable qualifications, a classicist.[10] In discussing the literary achievement of classical antiquity, he generally adheres to the neoclassic party line, repeating, for example, the old cliché that the value of the ancients lies in their striving for the typical, the universal, and the beautiful. He deviates, however, from neoclassical convention in his attempts to contrast the direction and practice of modern literature with that of the ancient. And, in so doing, Schlegel begins to reveal an unseemly interest in modern

9. Johann Gottfried von Herder (1744–1803), German critic. The "Coleridge" of Germany, Herder was one of the seminal minds of his time. Together with Goethe, he was a leader of the *Sturm und Drang* (Storm and Stress) movement, and his writings on comparative philology, mythology, anthropology, and philosophy of history, though frequently obscure, are full of brilliant insights.

10. For Schlegel's critical theory and its development, see particularly Hans Eichner, ed. and intro., *Charakteristiken und Kritiken I (1796–1801)* (Munich, 1967), vol. 2 of *Kritische Friedrich-Schlegel-Ausgabe*. The present introductory essay owes a considerable debt to Eichner's lucid analysis of Schlegel's criticism. Also helpful are Oskar Walzel, *Romantisches* (Bonn, 1934); Benno von Wiese, *Friedrich Schlegel* (Berlin, 1927); K. K. Polheim, *Die Arabeske, Ansichten und Ideen aus Friedrich Schlegels Poetik* (Paderborn, 1966); and the previously cited works of Haym and Kluckhohn. In English, the best studies are probably Hans Eichner, "Friedrich Schlegel's Theory of Romantic Poetry," *PMLA*, 71 (1956), 1018–1041, as well as his *Friedrich Schlegel*; Victor Lange, "Friedrich Schlegel's Literary Criticism," *Comparative Literature*, 7 (Fall 1955), 289–305; and René Wellek, *The Romantic Age* (New Haven, 1955), vol. 2 of *A History of Modern Criticism, 1750–1950*.

literature which was eventually to move him to a critical position in many respects quite the reverse of the classic.

This interest in modern literature grew more apparent in the following two years (1796–1797). Though still largely adhering to the neoclassic critical principles, Schlegel during this time wrote almost solely on modern subjects. Publishing chiefly in Reichardt's[11] journals (first *Deutschland*, later *Lyceum der schönen Künste*), Schlegel wrote extensive review essays on Schiller's *Musenalmanach auf das Jahr 1796* (an annual poetical almanac) and on Schiller's journal, *Die Horen* ("The Hours"), as well as three further essays, on F. H. Jacobi's novel *Woldemar*, on Georg Forster,[12] and on Lessing. These essays began to bring him something approaching national fame and, in certain circles, notoriety.

Reputation, despite Shakespeare, is usually paid for: in Schlegel's case, the price was Schiller's enmity. Schiller, who had been rather annoyed by Schlegel during the few encounters he had had with him, was enraged by his biting reviews of his work and responded by severing all personal contact with him and by including several satirical lashes at him in his and Goethe's series of epigrams, the *Xenien*. Schlegel did not respond to the personal element in these attacks; he merely wrote an unfavorable review of Schiller's journal, the *Musenalmanach*, in which the *Xenien* had been published. And he probably acted wisely in not doing so, for, although he had irredeemably lost any chance of gaining Schiller's favor, his reputation was not so secure that he could afford to offend the Weimarian Jove, Goethe.

During these years, Schlegel was groping toward a way of defining the essentially "modern" in modern literature. In his earlier writings, particularly "On the Study of Greek Poetry" (written

11. Johann Friedrich Reichardt (1752–1814), German composer, musicologist, and publisher.
12. Friedrich Heinrich Jacobi (1743–1819), German philosopher and novelist, whose unsystematic philosophy Schlegel admired but whose attitude toward marriage, particularly as stated in *Woldemar*, he deplored. Georg Forster (1754–1794), German author, accompanied Cook on his second expedition, and wrote well-known and perceptive travel books.

Introduction

1795; published 1797), Schlegel had contrasted modern with ancient literature and had arrived at the conclusion that modern literature was concerned primarily not with the beautiful but with what he called the "interesting," meaning thereby that the modern writer was prepared to sacrifice beauty to a didactic, philosophic interest. Furthermore, the modern writer generally was more realistic, more devoted to portraying individual rather than general nature: he was, in Schlegel's terminology, "characteristic." The modern writer also, unlike the ancient, strove for originality and gave free play to his imagination, and, in doing so, developed an individualistic mannerism; consequently his works were, to Schlegel, "fantastic," "individual," and "mannered."

The causes for these differences Schlegel saw as residing ultimately in the differences between ancient and modern civilization. Greek civilization seemed to him "natural" — that is, primarily instinctual — whereas modern civilization was "artificial," or rationally controlled. However, as a consequence of its instinctuality or sense-orientation, Greek civilization was cyclical: it could and did achieve perfection, but only an instinctual perfection, limited and finite. Modern civilization, on the other hand, being controlled by reason, could and did err, because reason errs. Nonetheless, reason could by its very nature always find its way back to the right track, and therefore opened up the possibility of an eventual perfection *without limits*. But because this was a process or a kind of dialectic, no modern work of art was perfect, though every modern work of art was on the way to perfection. Ancient civilization and art, in other words, were static and perfect; modern civilization and art were progressive and imperfect.

Schlegel's ostensible reason for writing these early classicist essays was to bring about a reform of modern literature whose tendencies toward the "interesting" he found deplorable. Though he clearly recognized that, given the inherent character of modern civilization, it was impossible and even undesirable to reshape modern literature according to the model of the ancient, he still hoped for a kind of fusion of modern progressivism with the ancient ideals of beauty and calm repose, a fusion whose beginnings he already thought to perceive in Goethe. Schlegel's classicism, then, did not advocate a servile imitation of ancient practice and rules, but a revivification of modern literature by an incorporation of classical ideals.

Though the analysis of modern literature contained in these early critical writings already adumbrates the later doctrine which came to be known as Romanticism, Schlegel was not yet prepared to take the decisive step. This step — or, rather, leap — could be taken only after he had determined to his satisfaction not merely what was modern, but what was *essentially* modern. What Schlegel wanted to do, beginning with the fall of 1796, was to find a concept and a word that would enable him to distinguish what he considered the false tendencies in modern literature (e.g., French pseudo-classicism and Richardsonian realism) from those which were true and good. In the course of the following year, Schlegel gradually formulated a theory which would allow him to do this.

In July 1797, Schlegel had moved from Jena to Berlin. There he entered into an intellectual society centered on the salons of Rahel Levin and Henriette Herz, and frequented by men like Schleiermacher (the Antonio of the section in *Lucinde* entitled "Julius to Antonio") and Ludwig Tieck. It was at this time that Schlegel also read the aphorisms of Chamfort which had been the subject of a recent and favorable review by his brother.[13] It was this reading of Chamfort that gave Schlegel the idea of writing aphorisms or, as he called them, "fragments" of his own. Schlegel by this single stroke managed not only to turn his greatest weakness, his chronic fragmentariness, into his greatest literary virtue, but also to lay the foundation for his immortality — which, however, has also, perhaps with a certain poetic justice, been fragmentary. It was these fragments which, of all Schlegel's writings, made the greatest impres-

13. Sebastien Roche Nicolas Chamfort (1741–1794), French courtier, dramatist, journalist, and revolutionary, now primarily remembered for his *Pensées, Maximes, Anecdotes, Dialogues*, posthumously published in 1796 (German translation, 1797).

sion on his contemporaries, and it is for these — and for *Lucinde* — that he is chiefly remembered.

During the brief period between 1797 and 1800, Schlegel published three collections of these aphoristic dicta, the first two under the rubric *Fragments*, the third with the title *Ideas*. This last collection, first published in 1800 but the direct result of thought and work reaching back to 1798, is particularly interesting for *Lucinde*, because here, as in the novel, Schlegel is primarily concerned with working out the theoretical and practical aspects of his new religion. In fact, the *Ideas* can perhaps best be seen (and understood) as a fragmentary mirror of *Lucinde*, though not a broken one; it clearly reflects his increasing religious awareness and his desire to be the prophet of what he terms the "religion of man and artist." To be sure, the *Ideas* is also interesting in itself; it is perhaps the most finished, the most polished of all his collections of fragments. But at the same time it is probably also the most incomprehensible, since it is the best specimen of what Schlegel in a subsequent moment of ironic inspiration called "the dialect of the fragments." Perhaps for this reason, it did not make and has not left behind much of an impression. And the very fact that Schlegel published no more fragments thereafter indicates that they may have been a kind of dead end: the *Ideas* did not lead to further ideas.

This is not true of the *Lyceum Fragments* (1797), and certainly not true of the second and largest collection, the *Athenaeum Fragments* (1798).[14] The real impact was made by this latter series: the *Lyceum Fragments* served only as an appetizer to this much richer intellectual repast. The *Athenaeum Fragments*, like its contemporary across the Channel, the *Lyrical Ballads*, constitutes a landmark in the development of modern literature; and, rather curiously and possibly significantly, it is also a joint production, with one author doing the lion's share of the work. In the case of the *Athenaeum Fragments* it was Friedrich who was definitely responsible for

14. So called from the journals in which they were first published, the *Lyceum der schönen Künste* and the *Athenaeum*.

most of the fragments, and for the most important ones, with his brother, August Wilhelm, a very distant second, and Schleiermacher and Novalis bringing up the rear with only a very few contributions.[15] Still, though the work is largely Friedrich's, the very notion of a shared creation, of a collaborated work of art, gives us an idea of how fresh (in a double sense) the fragments were, how much against the usual conceptions of what a literary work should be like; and in this the fragments of course resemble *Lucinde*. No wonder then that at least one reader thought they had been written by a madman.

The choice of the word "fragments" to describe his new work indicates that Schlegel was attempting to differentiate his kind of aphorism from those of his predecessors, notably Chamfort. And in fact he saw himself quite consciously as the "restorer of the epigrammatic genre." This boast holds less true of the *Lyceum Fragments* in which the fragments, like Chamfort's, tend to be brief and self-contained, very much in the manner of traditional aphorisms. The *Athenaeum Fragments*, however, as Hans Eichner has suggested,[16] is unusual in that it forms a unit in a way most collections of aphorisms do not; and in that a number of the fragments refer back and forth to each other, and indeed often become comprehensible only when seen in their mutual relations. Also, it seems clear that although the *Athenaeum Fragments* does cover a great deal of rather variegated territory (moral, political, philosophical, historical), it is nonetheless primarily literary. And it is in this last respect that it is possibly most unusual, for never before had there been such a curious form of criticism. Indeed, one of Schlegel's own definitions for his fragments was "condensed essays and reviews," and certainly a large number of the fragments are just that. And even more certainly the impression they made at the time and

15. According to Hans Eichner, the fragments may be assigned as follows: to Friedrich 216 certain, and 97 probable or possible; to August Wilhelm 85 certain and 4 possible; to Schleiermacher 29; to Novalis 13; and to mixed authorship 4. See the introduction to *Kritische Friedrich-Schlegel-Ausgabe*, vol. 2, p. cxiii.

16. Ibid., p. xl.

have left behind is very definitely literary. (For Schlegel and his friends, we should remember, the distinction between works of literature and works of philosophy was by no means as strict as it is today.) More specifically, it was Schlegel's proclamation here of the doctrine of Romanticism that gave the fragments and himself immortality.

But before we turn to the ticklish problem of Romanticism, a few more words on the fragments are in order. One of these should probably be a word of warning: the fragments are often extremely difficult — not merely to translate, but simply to understand. It should be remembered that even his own brother objected to the difficult terminology of the *Athenaeum Fragments*, and that one of his best friends and closest intellectual associates, Schleiermacher, complained to him about the incomprehensibility of the *Ideas*. It should also be recalled that Schlegel replied to these charges in his essay "On Incomprehensibility," where he rests his defense largely on the contention that the fragments are incomprehensible because they are ironic. In any case, the passage of time, the acceptance of "Romantic" or nonrational modes of thought, the labors of critics and intellectual historians, have rendered the obstacles somewhat less formidable, but Schlegel nonetheless was probably right when he predicted in one of his fragments (*Ideas*, 135) that no one would ever "probe entirely" the intention of his work, or when he proclaimed in another fragment which appears in the manuscript but which he apparently lacked the courage to print (*Ideas*, 129a): "You are not really supposed to understand me, but I want very much for you to listen to me." It is possible that part of this attitude may simply be the result of putting a good (or bad) face on a bad (or good) show, but certainly that is not the whole explanation. That is, this "sublime impudence," as he called it, does not mean that Schlegel is merely mocking his readers in the manner of Dada or Pop-Camp; not at all. It means rather, that Schlegel was here relying to some extent at least on inspiration rather than rhetoric; and he probably would have been among the first to agree that he too was incapable of fully probing his own intention.

It is possible that something like this perception may lurk behind the name Schlegel chose for his petite and plentiful progeny. For surely one of the reasons why the fragments are fragmentary, ruins and not complete edifices, is that Schlegel wants us to intuit what might have been but never was, wants us to take the fragment and make of it a whole, take the ruin and reconstruct the edifice. Another reason they are fragments clearly derives from the fact that they are literally fragments, or at least that a good many of them are. That is, they are bits and pieces which Schlegel extracted from his notebooks, from the jottings of years, from his grand attempt to build a system of literature which would put order into the criticism and understanding of the classics. This great work was, as we have seen, never completed; only the blueprint of the vast system and a great many abandoned building materials and some unfinished structures remain, and from these Schlegel decided to salvage the fragments. So we can see that the fragments, despite their form and, to use Goethe's image for them, despite their waspishness, are not in revolt against the idea of systems; Schlegel was too much of a disciple of Kant to do that. No, the fragments are not against systems, they are a substitute for one, a brilliant substitute, for unlike a fully formulated system they need exclude nothing because it is contradictory, or even self-contradictory; they can and do bring the entire noisy federation of literary and philosophical quarrels under one roof.

It was the *Athenaeum Fragments* and the new, revolutionary doctrine it unsystematically but powerfully proclaimed that provided the critical base for the creative activity of the writers who now began to gather around Schlegel and his brother. This group, formed early in 1798, included besides the Schlegel brothers, Tieck,[17] Schleiermacher, and, somewhat later, Novalis. They were

17. Johann Ludwig Tieck (1773–1853), German poet, novelist, and critic. Perhaps best known for his fairy-tale-like stories, such as "Der blonde Eckbert," and his humorous drama, *Der gestiefelte Kater* (*Puss 'n Boots*).

Introduction

the nucleus of what in the nineteenth century came to be known as the early Romantic movement (*Frühromantik*), a nucleus which, through the pages of its "official" journal, the *Athenaeum* (edited and largely written by the two Schlegels), exploded over Germany, destroying as best it could the old neoclassical precepts.

This new doctrine, Romanticism, was Schlegel's answer to the question of what was essentially or ideally modern, the question which had occupied him since the last of his classicist essays. It was an answer that derived ultimately from a new emphasis on and understanding of the function of the novel. In fact, it was the novel, that distinctively modern genre, which gave the name to the new movement. Out of the German (originally French) word for novel, *Roman*, Schlegel constructed his all-important adjective, *romantisch*.

The most concise, and for that reason probably most enigmatic, statement of Schlegel's new doctrine is contained in the famous *Athenaeum* fragment 116, but Schlegel also elaborated it more fully elsewhere, particularly in his review of Goethe's *Wilhelm Meister* (1798) and in the section entitled "Letter on the Novel" in his *Dialogue on Poetry* (1799). These three works form the basic texts, the manifestos of the Romantic movement in Germany. In brief, they advocate what Schlegel termed a "progressive, universal poetry." The novel is progressive, as we have seen, because it belongs to a civilization which is progressive, but it is also universal because it contains within itself all things. The perfect novel is a perfect mixture of all previous genres, a fusion and confusion of epic, dramatic, lyric, critical, and philosophic elements. Since, however, such a perfect union is humanly impossible, the perfect novel is unattainable, is something which one can only approximate, never achieve. Romantic poetry is therefore inherently progressive, or in the words of fragment 116, "the romantic kind of poetry is still in the state of becoming; that, in fact, is its real essence: that it should forever be becoming and never be finished."

The novel, though the most perfect expression of romantic art, was not its only manifestation. Although Schlegel had based his concept on the word novel (*Roman*), he also made use of other existing connotations of *romantisch*, connotations referring back to the medieval romances and to the literature of the Middle Ages as a whole. Indeed, Schlegel saw the novel as a return to and a development of this medieval tradition. It was this sense of the word *romantic* that enabled Schlegel, for example, to consider Shakespeare as a romantic writer par excellence, though, to be sure, Shakespeare also qualified by virtue of his anti-classic mixture of tragedy and comedy, as well as by his irony.

But once Schlegel broadened the application of his term *romantic* in this way, it was inevitable that he should lose control over it. Soon he began to discover all sorts of "romantic" traits in even the most classical writers, and in the end only the Greek tragedians were excluded. So, by a curious process of irony, his earlier attempt to make modern literature classic had ended by making almost all literature romantic.[18]

Schlegel's intense preoccupation with literary theory, particularly with the theory of the novel, quite naturally led him to the idea of putting his new doctrine into practice. As early as 1794, Schlegel had toyed with the idea of writing a novel and it is even possible that he may have written portions of one. When, in the late fall of 1798, Schlegel began seriously to work on *Lucinde* he may have made use of some of the materials for this earlier novel, but whether or not he did so does not really matter. For the plot of *Lucinde* is the least important thing about it, since it has practically no plot; and whatever shape the earlier novel may have had, it did not resemble *Lucinde*'s. The classicist Schlegel of 1794 would hardly have been capable of producing the kind of "formless" novel that *Lucinde* is. Only Schlegel's new Romantic doctrine can account for it.

The impetus to write *Lucinde* was, however, not wholly theo-

18. For a broader discussion of Romanticism and its place in European intellectual history, see René Wellek, "The Concept of Romanticism in Literary History," *Comparative Literature*, 1 (1949), 1–23, 147–172. Reprinted in *Concepts of Criticism*, ed. Stephen G. Nichols, Jr. (New Haven, 1963).

Introduction

retical. The very fact that the title character is a woman who bears a striking resemblance to Schlegel's then mistress, Dorothea Veit, shows that the novel is an expression not merely of Schlegel's theory, but also of his life. Schlegel had met Dorothea at Henriette Herz's salon soon after his arrival in July 1797.[19] Dorothea was not a particularly attractive woman, and she was almost eight years older than Schlegel, but she more than made up for these defects by her charm, vivacity, and intelligence. The daughter of a well-known philosopher and friend of Lessing's, Moses Mendelssohn, she had been given what for a woman of her time was an extraordinarily good education. At the age of eighteen, however, her parents arranged a marriage for her to the banker Simon Veit, a man considerably older than herself and hardly the sort either to understand or to share her intellectual and artistic interests. By the time she met Schlegel, she had borne Veit four sons (only two of whom survived infancy), but even these were not sufficient to reconcile her to her unhappy marriage.

A physical and spiritual love at first sight seems to have seized both Schlegel and Dorothea. Except for Caroline (his brother's wife from 1796 to 1803), Schlegel had never met a woman of such brilliance and charm: Dorothea was completely overwhelmed by Schlegel's intellectual superiority, which she was to acknowledge for the rest of his life, and which she was to venerate for the rest of her own. In 1798 Dorothea separated from her husband and after her divorce lived with Schlegel. Though Schlegel and Dorothea did not marry until 1804, the main reason for the delay does not seem to have been a desire to shock the bourgeoisie. Rather, it seems to have been Dorothea's wish to retain some legal influence on the lives of her children, which she could not have done had she married Schlegel at once.

From the very beginning of their relationship, Schlegel assumed the role of the enthusiastic spiritual and intellectual leader, and Dorothea that of the equally enthusiastic follower. Under his in-

19. For a brief account of Dorothea's life, see Josef Körner, "Mendelssohns Töchter," *Preussische Jahrbücher*, 214 (November 1928), 167–182.

ducement and supervision, Dorothea undertook a whole series of translations and adaptations, and even wrote a novel of her own, *Florentin* (1801). Just before their marriage, Dorothea left Judaism to become a Protestant and when, in 1808, Schlegel converted to Catholicism, Dorothea did likewise. For the rest of her life, Dorothea remained a sincere and dedicated Catholic, determined and successful in converting members of her family to her new religion.

———◇———

The further details of Schlegel's and Dorothea's life need not be given here, since they do not contribute to any fuller understanding of *Lucinde*. It is enough to know that the later Schlegel, after converting to Catholicism, was quite a different man from the earlier one. To be sure, he was still interested in literature and philosophy, but as he became Catholic, he also became conservative, and his thinking and criticism reflected that change. The radical younger Schlegel gradually merged and disappeared into the middle-aged propagandist and *Hofsekretär* in Metternich's conservative Austrian empire. As with so many other Romantics, Schlegel's Romanticism led to the Church and to an uncritical self-immolation at its altars.[20]

III

As might be expected from the outline of Schlegel's critical theories on the novel given in the preceding section, *Lucinde* is a mixture of many things. This mixture may, on a first and even second reading, seem confusing, and there is perhaps no real consolation in knowing that it was meant to be so. But disappointing as *Lucinde* may be initially, it will repay close reading and study, for the novel illustrates, perhaps better than any other work of fiction to come out of the German Romantic movement, the relation between Romantic theory and practice. It belongs, after all, to that

20. For a brief survey of Schlegel's later life, see Hans Eichner's *Friedrich Schlegel*, especially chapters 6 and 7.

Introduction

highly unusual category of literature: a work of art of major importance by a critic of major importance.

The master key to the mystery of *Lucinde* is the recognition that it is first and foremost a religious book. At the time Schlegel was writing this novel, he became convinced of the necessity of a new religion and of his fitness to be its prophet. This "religion" was, of course, not to be a rigidly structured one; that would have gone too much against the grain of his critical thinking, as well as his personality. It was to be, rather, more in the nature of a new mythology, a new morality, and a new philosophy. *Lucinde* represents the first installment (the "erster Teil," as the original title page has it) of this new vision; it is not so much a novel in the conventional, traditional sense as it is a fusing together of fictionalized philosophy, figurative morality, and allegorical religion.

There are numerous and continual references in *Lucinde* to support the contention that this is a religious book: references to Julius as a priest, Lucinde as a priestess, to both being purified, to his being anointed, to her being, at least in a vision, beatified. Indeed, the "Apprenticeship for Manhood," the longest single block of the novel, is concerned with the delineation of an increasingly intense spiritual crisis from which Julius is finally saved by Lucinde and by what Lucinde represents. The question which this whole section of the novel faces and attempts to resolve is the question of what and why one should believe, and how, in consequence, one is to act.

The religion of which Julius and Lucinde are priest and priestess is the religion of love. Though in the abstract this may seem rather trite, in practice it is not so. For from this religion there follow certain rules of behavior which attack not merely the usual conceptions of morality, but also the customary sentimentalities of love. There are two main dogmas in this religion — at least as it is fragmentarily presented here — which, in turn, form the two main themes of the novel: the love of man for man, or friendship; and the love of man for woman, or passionate love. Friendship, it is made amply clear in the course of the novel, is possible only among men, for in Schlegel's conception, women are wholly passionate and consequently incapable of Platonic disinterestedness. But if woman's passionate nature is her weakness, it is also her strength, for unquestionably the love of woman is more significant and important for Schlegel than the love of man. It is not by accident that the title of the novel is identical with the name of its female rather than its male protagonist; at the center of Schlegel's new religion stands, quite unmistakably, the feminine ideal. Lucinde — a name derived from the Latin *lux*, meaning light — is Julius's illumination.[21] Ironically, however, her light is not the light of day; it is, instead, as we can see from the section entitled "Yearning and Peace," the light of night, the light of the pale moon and stars. Lucinde, like Diana, is a priestess of the night, and, like Diana's symbol, the moon, her illumination is indirect and by reflection, as the moon reflects the light of the sun. The moon and the woman are mirrors, are passive, and the man who loves a woman truly sees his own light and his own image reflected in her; he loves himself, Narcissus-like, in her. The love of woman leads, consequently, to a fuller awareness of the self.

It is in this sense that *Lucinde* is what H. A. Korff calls it: the most complete formulation of the Romantic ideal of marriage, and hence a most revolutionary work. Unquestionably, one of Schlegel's most important objectives in this novel is to define man's relation to woman, and, in doing so, implicitly to contrast it with the attitude of the Enlightenment. This attitude — which Schlegel had attacked explicitly in his extended review of F. H. Jacobi's *Woldemar* — was that sexual love and intellectual love do not mix, that, as in Jacobi's novel, a man must not sleep with the woman he loves, that he must not defile "true" love by carnal lust. It is this ridiculous attitude that Schlegel attempts to explode in this fragmentary anti-*Woldemar*, though, to be sure, his zeal sometimes carries him too far in the other direction, as for example in Julius's assertion that disinterested love between man and woman is quite impossible.

21. Schlegel probably also intended an allusion to Lucina, Roman goddess of childbirth. For it is by meeting Lucinde that Julius is reborn.

Introduction

Essentially, however, Schlegel's attitude toward love anticipates that of D. H. Lawrence: it is both — and must be both — a spiritual and a sexual union, but not a narrow, exclusive one, not a perverse institution designed to restrict experience, but an organic means for exploring it more broadly and deeply.

Still, for Schlegel, as for most of his contemporaries, woman is the symbol of passivity, a symbol which is obviously derived from woman's sexual role. But unlike his contemporaries, or, for that matter, traditional Western attitudes, Schlegel does not find this passivity inferior to the male's activity. Quite the reverse: Schlegel turns upside down the usual concept which makes passivity weakness and activity strength; for him, it is passivity which is to be idealized, not activity.

For Schlegel passivity is, however, not merely sexual, or more accurately, not exclusively sexual. Indeed, in the second section of the novel, entitled "A Dithyrambic Fantasy on the Loveliest Situation in the World," it is precisely the reversal of roles in sexual intercourse which Schlegel sees as the "loveliest situation." Passivity is for Schlegel not merely a feminine but a universal attitude; it is the preference of the unconscious to the conscious, of the imagination to the rational faculty. It is only through man's submission to nature that man can fulfill himself most completely. Carlyle was later to make much of this idea.

Though woman is for Julius (and Schlegel) the most obvious and most important symbol and manifestation of nature's principle of passivity, she is not the only one. The plant and the night also occupy places of considerable importance in Schlegel's symbology. The plant represents passivity and unconsciousness par excellence, since it instinctually obeys the mandates of nature and does not need to discover rules by which to develop itself. Nature has taken care of all that already. The plant grows, blossoms, and withers in harmony with the seasons and the course of nature; it does not rebel against dying because it cannot be conscious of rebellion. It exists for nothing but itself; it is its own achievement and purpose. Mankind, on the other hand — at least perverted, conventional

25

mankind — rebels against nature and makes its own rules. Man attempts to live according to ideals and purposes outside himself and outside of nature. He seeks to impose his own consciousness upon nature. According to Schlegel, this is man's perversion. Man must be dis-educated from such falseness, and brought back to an awareness that he can achieve perfection only in passivity, or, as Julius remarks, in a state of *"pure vegetating."* Man must live like a plant; he must be passive and purposeless.

Though the identification of man with plant occurs sporadically throughout the novel, it is made most emphatic in the section entitled "Idyll of Idleness." Toward the end of this section, Schlegel also extends this identification and the active-passive distinction on which it is based into a further distinction which in its phrasing is evocative of Nietzsche's later dichotomy of Dionysian and Apollonian. This distinction is introduced by a vision in which Julius imagines himself in a theater. On the stage, there is a figure of a bound Prometheus in the act of creating men, while in the background are seen the shapes of Hercules, Hebe, Venus, and Cupid. Prometheus is helped as well as controlled in his task by a number of creatures who resemble little devils. The audience is made up of the men Prometheus has created and continues to create. They display no individual traits whatsoever; they are like the products of an assembly line.

This vision is intelligible only in terms of Schlegel's principle of passivity. Here Schlegel is making a distinction between two types of creation: the Promethean and the Herculean. Prometheus rebelled against the gods (against nature) in bringing fire to mankind and in creating mankind unnaturally, that is, mechanically and not organically. Prometheus's perversion of nature makes him a prisoner of the Satanic creatures — and Satan, of course, was also a rebel against God — a prisoner, in other words, of a rebellious, perverted morality; and he is forced to create man, whether he wants to or not, in accordance with the stultifying demands of this morality. Hercules, on the other hand, does not create mankind in this mechanical and immoral fashion. His creation is organic; he could keep "fifty girls busy during a night." Hercules creates through love and passion – he is accompanied by the stimuli of Hebe, Venus, and Cupid. And, as a consequence, their fates differ: Prometheus is bound, Hercules free; Prometheus was brought down from the divine to the human, whereas Hercules was deified. Consequently, if man is to become god he must work through nature, not against it.

A further symbol of passivity in the novel is the night. Lucinde is called the "priestess of the night," and it is apparent that she holds her office because it is the night which – at least in relation to the day – is passive. The night is the time of rest, of dreams rather than thought, but also of love and passion. For true passivity, according to Schlegel, does not mean inactivity, boredom, or laziness; it means, rather, a passivity in relation to nature, a passivity which in turn makes man really and naturally creative. The word passion, in German ("Leidenschaft," from "leiden," to suffer) as in English (from the Latin "pati," to suffer), is derived from the same concept, that of suffering, of passivity, of being done to rather than doing; but, again both in English and German, the word passion denotes an emotional force of great power. Stated differently, passion is something which cannot be consciously willed, but only triggered by nature; and once released, it possesses enormous energy. Consequently, the truly creative and energetic man is one who is passive and in accordance with nature; he does not obey the arbitrary rules of reason or man, but succumbs instead to divine inspiration. The true artist lets his work of art grow as a plant grows, naturally and for itself alone.

It is this perception which explains a good deal of the curious and otherwise inexplicable form of *Lucinde*. As Julius remarks in speaking of this "poem of truth," this is the reason why he resolves never "to prune its living fullness of superfluous leaves and branches"; he wants to let it grow naturally and unhindered. It is for the same reason that he asserts at the beginning of the novel his "incontestable right to confusion" in matters of form. He will not be bound by man-made rules; he will only be bound by the rules of nature and by the impulse of his inspiration. The much criticized formlessness of *Lucinde* is therefore not a blunder on Schlegel's part: it is an integral and necessary element of the principle which infuses the work as a whole.

This does not mean, however, that *Lucinde* has no form or shape. It means only that it has its own shape, just as every flower and fruit has a shape, but not the same shape every other flower or fruit does. *Lucinde* is formless only when the concept of form is considered in a neoclassic, Aristotelian sense. Looked at for itself, it reveals its own form.

Lucinde is a novel which is very much aware of itself, so much so in fact that at times it makes criticisms of itself and its structure. Indeed, at the end of one of the first sections of the novel, the "Allegory of Impudence," the author speculates upon the reception which this "mad little book" would enjoy "should it ever be found, perhaps printed, and even read." The interruptions, the lack of artful transitions, the chaotic confusion of proper time sequence, all these are not the result of inartistic insensitivity, but carefully planned occurrences. For example, in the first part of the novel, the letter from Julius to Lucinde is interrupted just when Julius wants to begin relating the history of his life, something which he is therefore able to do only later in the novel. This interruption is blamed on an "unkind chance" which, since it is not further explained at this point, could mean virtually anything. But this supposedly unkind chance is really not so unkind after all, for it allows Schlegel to draw the reader's attention to the connection between the novel's formal construction and its theme, and to warn him that, though chance has interrupted him, chance has also provided him with further opportunities, particularly the opportunity to mold chance, and let it carry him beyond the limitations of any kind of orderly, rational plan. Thus chance, which at first seems merely arbitrary, becomes the ordering principle of nature, becomes the inspiration which will convey to the work a wholeness more real and organic than any man-made principles could impose.

This self-consciousness, and the formal peculiarities which accompany it, must also be seen, if they are to be properly understood, in relation to the persona of the novel. For, despite the fact that this is demonstrably in part an autobiographical novel, it is not irrelevant to introduce the concept of the persona, that is, of a speaker in the novel who is distinct from its real author. After all the subtitle of *Lucinde* is "Confessions of a Blunderer," and on at least one occasion an explicit reference is made to the fact that the novel is being written in the mask of a blunderer (see page 52). Consequently, at least some of the apparent "blunders" of the novel are to be seen not as the faults of Schlegel, but as those of his mask, Julius.

The concept of the persona is one which interested Schlegel a great deal. It was this concept, in fact, that shaped his ideas of irony and wit, ideas of paramount importance for *Lucinde*. Schlegel traced the technique of the persona to what he believed were its origins in ancient Greek comedy, specifically to the device of the "parabasis," that is, a speech in the name of the poet delivered to the audience in the middle of the play. Schlegel perceived that this technique of interruption — or what Brecht was later to call the alienation effect — was essentially the same method practiced by the personae or narrators of Cervantes, Diderot, Sterne, and Jean Paul,[22] all novelists whom Schlegel admired. The interruptive method of *Lucinde* seems clearly modeled on the novels of particularly the last two of these authors.

In Schlegel's mind, the idea of interruption or parabasis was intimately connected with the idea of irony. Indeed, in one of his fragments he states that "irony is a permanent parabasis." In other words, irony consists of a continual self-consciousness of the work itself, of an awareness of the work of art as a fiction and as an imitation of reality at one and the same time. In this respect, the irony of a work of art corresponds to the ironic attitude which Schlegel

22. Johann Paul Friedrich Richter (1763–1825), German comic novelist, who wrote eccentric novels in the manner of Laurence Sterne, among the best known of which are *Leben des Quintus Fixlein* (1796), *Siebenkäs* (1796–1797), and *Flegeljahre* (1804–1805).

saw as mandatory in actual life. Only through irony could man achieve simultaneously a closeness to reality and a distance from it. Only the ironic attitude enabled man to commit himself wholly to finite reality and at the same time made him realize that the finite is trivial when viewed from the perspective of eternity.

Schlegel's conception of wit is related to his understanding of irony. When he uses the word "wit" he is not using it primarily in the present-day sense of joking or punning; for him wit is rather — as it was for most of the eighteenth century — the capacity to discover similarities and to form ideas: wit in the sense of intelligence rather than of simple humor. Perhaps the closest modern synonym for wit in this older sense is "serendipity." It is through wit that truth is divined, not rationally understood. Wit is not reason: reason comprehends mechanically and laboriously, wit perceives immediately and through inspiration.

From this idea of wit or serendipity, it follows that a work of art should not be ordered by reason but by wit. It should not possess a rational, conventional form, but a natural and, as Schlegel calls it, "witty form." In one of his fragments, Schlegel states that every novel must have "chaos and eros" and that it must combine a "fantastic form" with a "sentimental plot." But this idea of a "fantastic" form does not mean that the author is to follow any and every whim which happens to strike him; rather, he is, according to the "Dialogue on Poetry," to follow a "cultivated arbitrariness" and construct his work according to an "artistically ordered confusion." Schlegel — despite his occasionally striking similarities to the surrealists — is not an advocate of automatic writing. Again and again he refers to the right and duty of the author to select and order his materials. For example, after the first interruption in the opening section of *Lucinde*, the narrator, Julius, explains to us why he has *chosen* to insert the "Dithyrambic Fantasy" in this particular place. Sterne's Tristram and Fielding's narrators in *Joseph Andrews* and *Tom Jones* had earlier done much the same thing.

As might be expected, in *Lucinde* Schlegel does not adhere to the usual practice of parceling his materials into chapters of roughly equal length. Rather, the novel is divided into thirteen sections (each prefaced by some kind of descriptive title) of greatly varying length. The longest of these, the "Apprenticeship for Manhood," is almost wholly narrative and occupies virtually the entire middle third of the novel. Its length and central placement fairly clearly indicate that it is to represent the focal core of the novel. Though the relatively formal conventionality of this section presents few structural problems, the remaining twelve non-narrative sections pose questions which are at times hard to explain — for example, what is the point of their order of sequence, how do they relate to the central section and to each other? In theory, at least, an answer to these questions should not be difficult, since, if *Lucinde* does indeed possess its vaunted natural or "organic" form, it ought to be possible to show how all the separate parts form a unified whole.

It is easy enough to demonstrate that *Lucinde* displays a kind of formal symmetry: the central section, the "Apprenticeship," is preceded and followed by six short sections. But the fact of this symmetry is certainly not sufficient to allow us to claim unity for the novel as a whole; unity does not consist of such a strictly external ordering. Still, the fact that there is symmetry does give us an indication that there is some kind of ordering sense present in *Lucinde*; if nothing more, it suggests that the first six sections are a preparation for the central section, and that the last six represent either some sort of further growth of the ideas contained in the central section or a denouement of the action of that section.

One way of getting at the function of the opening six parts of the novel is to investigate the function of the central part. On the most obvious level, it is a story, narrating, as the title suggests, the growth of the protagonist's mind. But the presentation of this process of maturation is curious. Though obviously a story, it does not, for example, really focus on character analysis or plot development. The characters, including even Julius, are only rudimentarily described and the narrative line is virtually without suspense. The focus throughout this section seems to be elsewhere: not on analysis, but on a simple description of Julius's life and the events which lead him first into and then out of his spiritual crisis. It seems to follow necessarily, therefore, that if this section is to achieve full meaning and impact, it must be placed within a context which will give it such significance. That is precisely what the preceding and following short sections do.

In a very rough way, the structure of *Lucinde* works as follows. The first six parts of the novel provide us with a picture of what Julius is, the central part shows us how he came to be what he is, and the last six parts adumbrate the further directions of his growth. This ordering corresponds more or less to the way we would normally approach any object in nature: first we observe what it is; then we inquire how it came to be what it is; and, lastly, we speculate upon what it will become. Seen from this point of view, the form of *Lucinde* is definitely natural and organic.

The first sections serve not only to give us some notion of the character of the persona, Julius, but also to prepare us for the unorthodox formal and thematic qualities of the novel. The first part, the letter from Julius to Lucinde, symbolically suggests several of the themes which will occupy the novel: its setting in a garden indicates the importance of nature; its expression of passionate love for Lucinde (as girl, woman, and mother) strikes a note which will be picked up repeatedly later on; its dichotomy of illusion and reality prepares us for subsequent fantasies and allegories — all of them, significantly, products of the imagination; and, finally, its emphasis upon confusion in nature and art warns us to expect further innovations in the structure of the novel.

The next three sections explore some of the thematic implications of the first part, particularly those relating to love and sexual passion. Almost necessarily — considering the time when this novel was published — they are also concerned with conventional attitudes and reactions toward sex and the literary expression of sexual matters. "A Dithyrambic Fantasy on the Loveliest Situation in the World" is, like some of the later sections, a veiled and semihumorous description of sexual intercourse, which begins to suggest the extremely important place of woman in this novel. "A Description of Little Wilhelmine" continues this focus upon women, and begins, by means of a rather playful allegory, to make a distinction between conventional morality and the morality of nature. This distinction is developed more fully in the following section, the "Allegory of Impudence." Indeed, here Schlegel describes figuratively and in brief the process which Julius is to undergo explicitly and directly in the main section of the novel. This process is one in which Julius learns to reject the old, conventional moral code and to accept the new, unconventional one. The religious framework within which this spiritual transformation is cast indicates further that this is not an ordinary process, but one of great significance: it is not merely a change of moral systems, but a religious conversion.

"An Idyll of Idleness" defines in greater detail the nature and principles of this new religion, emphasizing particularly the importance of the principle of passivity. Next to the gods Wit, Impudence, and Fantasy, it now admits into the Schlegelian pantheon the god Hercules as a deity subsidiary to the demiurge Nature. And it further establishes Julius as a prophet worthy — or one who has now become worthy — of proclaiming the new religion.

The following section, "Fidelity and Playfulness," consisting entirely of dialogue between Julius and Lucinde, demonstrates the practice of this new religion. Its rituals, we now see, are few and simple. Essentially there appear to be two which are important: the first a purification/confession, the removal of all misunderstandings between the lovers; and the second a consummation, sexual intercourse — or, to use Julius's phrase, "appeasing the offended gods." To a lesser extent, this section also serves as an occasion to discuss other implications of the new religion, particularly those having to do with social behavior. These implications are also, as might be expected, sexual.

It is at this point that Schlegel inserts the main segment of the novel, "Apprenticeship for Manhood," and it is an apt point, because now that we have been properly instructed in the nature and practice of the new religion, it should be made apparent to us as well how this religion came to be, and how Julius was converted to it. This is in essence what this section does. We see Julius at the beginning moving into a mood of spiritual despair in which everything loses meaning for him; then we watch him move gradually out of this despair as a result of his encounters with and loves for various women. And we see him, finally, gain peace spiritually and physically in his love for Lucinde, a love which releases within him his latent creative energies. Julius has rejected the values of conventional society, those unnatural and destructive values, and accepted in their place the values of nature, which are creative and constructive, and which convey to him for the first time a sense of the organic wholeness of his being. In discovering his love for Lucinde, Julius has discovered, as Schlegel says at the end of the third-person narrative, "the most beautiful religion."

The last two or three pages of this section form a transition from the "Apprenticeship" proper to the shorter sections which follow. These pages are narrated in the first person and apparently represent the viewpoint of an older Julius looking back upon the experiences which he has recorded. Julius here observes that there is something in these experiences which can be communicated not by means of a story but only through symbols. It is this attempt at symbolic communciation which shapes much of the following sections. And, further, these later sections concern themselves with a Julius who is moving into and speculating about his future.

The section which immediately follows the main one corresponds in function roughly to the earlier "Allegory of Impudence." Its title, "Metamorphoses," explicitly reveals that it is concerned with change, specifically a change in Julius's character and outlook. It sums up, symbolically, the transformation that Julius has undergone in the "Apprenticeship": one here described as a metamorphosis from the egoism of Narcissus to the duality of Pygmalion, from the self-sufficiency of one life to the self-sufficiency of two lives. The point which this section makes is the same as that of the preceding one: man can realize the wholeness of his own being only through the love of another, not by himself alone.

Introduction

The first of the following "Two Letters" reveals Julius moving to a point beyond the one reached at the end of the "Apprenticeship for Manhood." The fact that Lucinde is about to have a baby forces Julius to new realizations about the nature of human existence. He reaches a new stage of awareness: he now knows the metamorphosis described in the preceding section is not final, but only one in a progressive (perhaps infinite) series. Faced with the prospect of fatherhood, Julius discovers within himself not only a new esteem for parental responsibility and useful, domestic objects, but also the knowledge that the union of two bodies and spirits is not final and complete. A more complete union, a greater wholeness, can only be achieved through the creation of new life. And in creating new life, Julius and Lucinde act in accordance with the dictates of nature. For nature demands that every plant bear fruit. Now it becomes clear to Julius that his love for Lucinde and her love for him is something which exists not simply for itself alone: it leads, rather, to a fuller love of all things. What illuminates them, illuminates the world as well.

The second letter consists almost wholly of a vision induced by a report of Lucinde's severe and, as Julius thinks, fatal illness. In this vision, he imagines what the course of his future life would be if he were compelled to live it without Lucinde. This produces two new realizations: the first that, though it is possible for him to exist without Lucinde, a meaningful and satisfying life would be impossible without her. Though his love for Lucinde may, as the first letter showed, lead to further loves, without Lucinde there can be no love at all — except the love of death. This forms the basis for his second realization: that in certain circumstances, death can be meaningful and beautiful, that it can be a transformation devoutly to be wished, for it re-establishes the possibility of union.

The next section, "A Reflection," [23] is an elaborate pun based on a confusion of philosophical and sexual imagery and terminology.

23. For a discussion of Fichte's influence upon this section, see Jean-Jacques Anstett, "*Lucinde: Eine Reflexion*, Essai d'Interprétation," *Études Germaniques*, 3 (April–Sept. 1948), 241–250.

Schlegel's *Lucinde* and the Fragments

The "reflection" in other words, is not merely a mental but also a sexual action. But Schlegel's intention here is not merely humorous. For him, the sexual act is symbolic of the action of nature and the universe. Sexual union is, after all, the union of opposites, just as in certain philosophical systems, particularly those of Hegel, Fichte, and Schelling,[24] the motive principle of the universe is a fusion of opposites. Beneath the humor, there is definitely a level at which Schlegel is attempting to demonstrate symbolically that man and woman cannot exist for themselves alone, but can find wholeness as well as individuality only in each other. "A Reflection" serves, then, the function of generalizing upon Julius's experiences and his new awareness: out of these he has constructed a philosophy and religion which are valid not merely for himself but for all mankind.

The following section reverts once more to the form of letters, though this time they are directed not at Lucinde, but at a friend, Antonio. Both letters are concerned with the question of friendship and serve as a kind of definition of what friendship among men should be. This is a problem which had earlier concerned Julius in the "Apprenticeship for Manhood," but here it is elaborated not only more fully but also from a somewhat different point of view. It is appropriate that a discussion of friendship should be inserted at this point because it represents a different manifestation, or new transformation, of love. It is a further means of achieving the unity of one's being.

Julius's treatment of the idea of friendship seems at times to suggest that this word is being used as a synonym for homosexuality, but it would be unwise to make such an identification too hastily. In "Fidelity and Playfulness" as well as elsewhere in the novel, Julius had already observed that friendship was impossible among women because women, passionate by nature, were incapable of a

24. Friedrich von Schelling (1775–1854), German philosopher, professor of philosophy at the University of Jena from 1798 to 1805. His philosophy, which bases itself largely on Fichte's, had a considerable influence on the Romantic movement. In 1803 he married Caroline Böhmer, who in the same year had divorced August Wilhelm Schlegel.

purely intellectual relationship. This disqualification of women is based upon a dichotomy of the intellect and passion. For a woman, love must be a mixture of intellect and passion; for a man it may be either. Friendship, therefore, it would appear, is not a bodily, but a spiritual thing.[25] What seems quite clear, however, is that for Julius friendship functions as a further fulfillment of his being; it represents another stage of growth. Friendship — at least true friendship — is a different kind of union, a different kind of transformation from that which he experienced in his love for Lucinde. It is one more way of penetrating into the heart of nature.

"Yearning and Peace," which follows, not merely acts as a kind of balance to the earlier "Fidelity and Playfulness" (both consist almost wholly of dialogue), but also furthers the idea of the growth or expansion of love. The underlying notion of this section, that peace can only be found in yearning and yearning only in peace, echoes the earlier idea proposed in "Reflection," the idea of a union of opposites. And, in both instances, this union of opposites is indicative of a process, a series of transformations, a state of becoming, not of being. Furthermore, here the growth or transformation of love is not merely suggested in general philosophic and symbolic terms but concretely realized. Julius and Lucinde are no longer the only members of the new religion: Julius dreams of his Juliane (probably Caroline), and Lucinde of her Guido. The union which originally comprised only Julius and Lucinde is expanding into a far more comprehensive one.

The final section of the novel, "Dalliance of the Imagination," represents both a summation of Julius's growth and an indication of further transformations. It also, as the title indicates, reasserts the importance of the imagination — the imagination which has created this novel — as a kind of ultimate weapon for achieving union with nature and the infinite. It is through the imagination that man transforms himself most fully and can see himself finally achieve the fullest awareness of his being and the most complete

25. See also *Athenaeum* fragment 342.

closeness to nature. In the end, it is the imagination which perceives, unifies, creates, and, through its anointed priest, reveals.

———— ◇ ————

Lucinde is a fragment. The novel, as it was first published in 1799, represents only a part of the whole novel Schlegel intended to write, and indeed only a part of what Schlegel did write. The continuation, as he planned it, was to be primarily in the form of poems with relatively brief connecting prose passages. For various reasons which need not concern us here, Schlegel never brought himself to putting all the pieces of this second part together and publishing it, though he did publish separately many of the poems which he had written for the continuation. The prose passages, however, were not published during his lifetime; more than a century was to pass before Josef Körner brought them once again to light.[26]

Lucinde, as is apparent from Schlegel's notebooks and from the novel itself, was intended, even in its projected complete form, to be only a part of a more grandiose plan. This larger plan envisioned the writing of four novels (the immortal Four Novels of the "Allegory of Impudence"), which would incorporate the whole of Schlegel's new religion and philosophy.[27] But, as with almost all of Schlegel's grandiose plans, this one was doomed never to come to fruition. With Schlegel, as with Julius, it seems that the greater his plans, the smaller were the chances of their ever being realized.

Still, the form of the projected continuation of the novel and the place the completed *Lucinde* was to occupy in Schlegel's tetralogy do permit us to see the fragmentary novel in proper perspective. *Lucinde*, we can reasonably surmise, was planned as one of the four gospels in Schlegel's new religion; each further gospel was to present another aspect of this religion until, with the last, St. Fried-

26. For further information on Schlegel's continuation of *Lucinde*, see Körner, "Neues," and Eichner's introduction to *Dichtungen*.
27. An extensive discussion of Schlegel's plans for the "immortal four Novels" is contained in Hans Eichner, "Neues aus Friedrich Schlegels Nachlass," *Jahrbuch der deutschen Schillergesellschaft*, 3 (1959), 218–243.

rich's evangelical work would have been accomplished. It is this idea of a progressively more complete revelation which also accounts for the mixture of formal techniques in *Lucinde*: letters, allegories, puns, symbols, fantasies, visions, dialogues, autobiography, prose poetry, and — in the unpublished continuation — rhymed poems. This mixture of forms represents an attempt to reflect formally the profusion and confusion of nature, the wealth of different forms which inhabit the universe. *Lucinde*, in other words, represents an attempt to portray not only thematically but also formally a spiritual and intellectual growth and union. The intellectual and spiritual transformations are accompanied by formal ones. This structural and thematic pattern, of course, matches exactly the one proposed by Schlegel in his fragment 116 with its doctrine of a progressive and universal poetry. And, ironically, in its incompleteness, *Lucinde* matches another part of this doctrine as well: for since it is incomplete, *Lucinde* can never *be* a novel, but must forever be attempting to *become* one.

LUCINDE, *a Novel*

PETRARCH smiles with emotion as he surveys and introduces the collection of his immortal romances. Subtle Boccaccio speaks politely and flatteringly to the ladies at the beginning and at the close of his opulent book. And even the sublime Cervantes — still amiable and full of delicate wit, though old and wracked by pain — clothes the colorful spectacle of his vibrant works in the costly tapestry of a preface that is in itself already a beautiful romantic painting.

Lift a magnificent plant out of the fertile maternal earth, and much will cling to it lovingly that only a miser would think superfluous.

But what should my spirit give its son, who, like it, is as poor in poetry as rich in love?

Only a word, an image as a farewell — not only the royal eagle can despise the croaking of the ravens; the swan too is proud and does not hear it. Nothing concerns him but to keep the brilliance of his white feathers pure. His only thought is to nestle in the lap of Leda without hurting her; and then to breathe out in song every shadow of mortality.

Confessions of a Blunderer

Julius to Lucinde

MEN and their doings and desires seemed to me, when I recollected them at all, like ash-gray figures without movement. But in the holy solitude around me everything was light and color, and a fresh warm breath of life and love touched me, and stirred and murmured in all the branches of the luxuriant grove. I looked, and I delighted in everything at the same time: the vigorous green, the white blossom, and the golden fruit. And so too with the eye of my spirit I saw the one and only and forever beloved in many forms: sometimes as a childlike girl, sometimes as a woman in the full bloom and strength of love and femininity, and sometimes as a worthy mother with her earnest little boy in her arms. I breathed the spring, saw clearly the eternal youthfulness around me, and I said with a smile: "Even if this world isn't the best or the most useful, still I know that it's the most beautiful." Nothing could have shaken me in this feeling or conviction, neither general doubt nor my own fear. For I believed I was looking deeply into the secrets of nature; I felt that everything lived eternally and that even death was only an amiable deception. But, actually, I didn't think about this very much — at least I wasn't particularly disposed to classify

43

and analyze abstract concepts. Instead I lost myself gladly and deeply in all the comminglings and intertwinings of joy and pain from which come the savor of life and the bloom of feeling, spiritual voluptuousness as well as sensual beatitude. A subtle fire flowed in my veins; what I dreamed of wasn't just a kiss or the embrace of your arms; it wasn't just a wish to break the tormenting thorn of yearning and cool the sweet flames in surrender; I didn't yearn only for your lips or your eyes or your body. It was, rather, a romantic confusion of all these things, a wonderful mixture of the most various memories and yearnings. All the mysteries of male and female frivolity seemed to hover about me as suddenly your real presence and the gleam of blooming happiness on your face inflamed my lonely self. Wit and rapture alternated between us and became the common pulse of our united life and we embraced each other with as much wantonness as religion. I begged you that for once you might give yourself completely over to frenzy, and I implored you to be insatiable. Still, I listened with cool composure for every faint sign of bliss, so that not a single trace might escape me and leave a gap in our harmony. I didn't simply enjoy but felt and enjoyed the enjoyment itself.

You're so extraordinarily clever, my dearest Lucinde, that you'll doubtless already have suspected that all this is nothing but a beautiful dream. So it is, alas, and I would be inconsolable if I couldn't hope that soon we'll be able to realize at least a part of it. The truth of the matter is that just now I was standing by the window — how long I don't quite know, for, together with the other dictates of reason and morality, I had lost all sense of time. And so I was standing by the open window, looking out into the open. The morning certainly deserves to be called beautiful: the air is still and quite warm, the grass before me brilliantly green and the silvery stream, broad and quiet, winds its way — like the gentle rise and fall of the open plains — in great swinging arcs into the distance, bearing with it, as it slowly disappears into infinity, the imagination of the lover that rocks itself like a swan on its waters. The visionary grove and its southerly coloration were probably induced by the sizable heap of flowers and oranges lying next to me. All the rest is easily explained by psychology. It was an illusion, my dear friend; everything was an illusion except that a moment ago I stood by the window and did nothing, and that now I am sitting here and doing something, a something which is perhaps only a little more, or even a little less than doing nothing.

———— ◇ ————

I had written this much to you about my communion with myself when I was interrupted in the middle of my profound feelings and tender ideas about the wonderful and wonderfully complicated dramatic interrelation of our embraces by a rude and unkind chance. I was just in the process of unrolling before you in limpid, true periods the precise and untarnished history of our imprudence and my ineptitude, and was about to relate the gradual, step-by-step, naturally progressive clarification of those misunderstandings which had attacked the hidden center of our most exquisite life. I was interrupted when I was about to describe the manifold results of my clumsiness as well as the apprenticeship of my manhood, a time I can never review in whole or in part without a good many smiles, a little melancholy, and considerable self-satisfaction. But, as an educated lover and writer, I want to attempt to shape raw chance and mold it to the purpose. No purpose, however, is more purposeful for myself and for this work, for my love for it and for its own structure, than to destroy at the very outset all that part we call "order," remove it, and claim explicitly and affirm actually the right to a charming confusion. This is all the more necessary since writing about our life and love in the same systematic and progressive way we experienced them would make this unique letter of mine insufferably unified and monotonous, so that it would no longer be able to achieve what it should and must achieve: namely the re-creation and integration of the most beautiful chaos of sublime harmonies and fascinating pleasures. I'm making use, therefore, of my incontestable right to confusion and am inserting

45

here — in quite the wrong place — one of the many scattered pages I wrote or scribbled on when I longed for you impatiently and couldn't find you where I thought you must be, in your room, on our sofa — these pages I wrote with a pen you'd just used, and filled with the first words that came to mind and which you kindly and without my knowing it carefully preserved.

It's not hard for me to make a selection. For of all the dreams that are entrusted here to you and the immortal written page, the memory of the most beautiful of worlds is still the most substantial, and bears, more than any other, a certain kind of resemblance to what people call thoughts. That's why I choose before any other the dithyrambic fantasy about the loveliest situation in the world. For once we're sure we inhabit the most beautiful of worlds, then our next duty is unquestionably to get detailed knowledge from others or ourselves about the loveliest situation in this most beautiful world.

A Dithyrambic Fantasy
on the Loveliest Situation in the World

A large tear falls on this sacred page that I've found here in place of you. How honestly and simply you've expressed the old, daring thought of my most cherished and secret intention. In you it's come to fruition and I'm not afraid to admire and love myself in such a mirror. Only here do I see myself complete and harmonious, or rather, see all of humanity in me and in you. For your spirit, too, stands well defined and perfected before me; no longer does it consist of features that appear and melt away. No: like one of those beings that live forever, your spirit looks at me joyfully through noble eyes and opens its arms to embrace me. The slightest and holiest of those fragile features and expressions of the soul that seem like bliss to those who don't know the greatest joy are merely the everyday atmosphere of our spiritual breath and life.

These words are dull and turbid. Still, amid this throng of impressions I can do no more than repeat and repeat forevermore the single inexhaustible feeling of our pristine harmony. A great future

A Novel

beckons me to rush deeper into infinity: every idea opens its womb and brings forth innumerable new births. The farthest reaches of unbridled lust and silent intimation exist simultaneously in me. I remember everything, even my sufferings, and all my former and future thoughts bestir themselves and arise against my will. Wild blood rages in my swollen arteries, my mouth thirsts for union, and my imagination, alternately choosing and rejecting among the many forms of joy, finds none in which desire can finally fulfill itself and be at peace at last. And then I think suddenly and movingly again of that dark time when I was always waiting without hope, when I loved intensely without knowing it, when my inmost being was completely filled with an indeterminate yearning that was only seldom expressed in half-suppressed sighs.

Yes: I would have thought it a fairy tale that there could be such happiness and such love as I feel now — and such a woman, at once the most delicate lover, the most wonderful companion, and the most perfect friend. For in friendship particularly I sought for all that I lacked and didn't expect to find in any woman. In you I've found everything and even more than I could have hoped for; but, then, you're not like the others. You're untouched by the faults that custom and caprice call female. Aside from your little idiosyncrasies, the femininity of your soul consists simply in your making life and love synonymous. You feel completely and infinitely; you know of no separations; your being is one and indivisible. That is why you are so serious and so joyful. That is why you take everything so solemnly and so negligently, and also why you love me completely and don't relinquish any part of me to the state, to posterity, or to my friends. Everything belongs to you, and we are in every respect closest to each other and understand each other best. You're at my side at every stage of human experience, from the most passionate sensuality to the most spiritual spirituality; and only in you have I seen true pride and true womanly modesty.

The most extreme sorrows, if they merely enveloped us and didn't separate us, would seem to me nothing more than a refreshing contrast to the sublime frivolity of our marriage. Why

47

shouldn't we interpret the bitterest whim of chance as a lovely witticism and an exuberant caprice, since we, like love, are immortal? I can no longer say *my* love or *your* love: both are identical and perfectly united, as much love on one side as on the other. This is marriage, the timeless union and conjunction of our spirits, not simply for what we call this world or the world beyond death, but for the one, true, indivisible, nameless, unending world, for our whole eternal life and being. Therefore, if I thought the time had come, I'd drink a cup of poison with you just as gladly and easily as the last glass of champagne we drank together when I said: "This is how we should drain the rest of our life to the dregs." Having uttered these words, I drank hurriedly before the noblest spirit of the wine could vanish; and so — I repeat once again — so let us live and love. I know that you wouldn't want to outlive me either. You too would follow your rash husband into the grave, and willingly and lovingly descend into the flaming abyss into which an insane law forces Indian women and, by its rude intention and command, desecrates and destroys freedom's most delicate shrines.

Perhaps yearning will be satisfied more fully there. I often marvel at that: every idea and whatever else is formed within us seems perfect in itself, as unique and indivisible as a person. One idea supplants the other and what just now seemed near and immediate soon vanishes again into obscurity. And yet then again, there are moments of sudden, universal clarity, when, through some miraculous marriage, several such spirits of the inner world fuse completely into one, when many a forgotten fragment of our Ego shines with a new light, illuminating with its bright radiance even the night of the future. The same is true, I think, on both small and large scales. What we call a life is for the complete, timeless, inner human being only a single idea, an indivisible feeling. For him too there are such moments of the deepest and most complete consciousness when all lives occur to him, combine in various ways, and then separate again. There will come a time when the two of us will perceive in a single spirit that we are blossoms of a single plant or petals of a single flower, and then we will know with a smile that what we now call merely hope is really remembrance.

Do you still remember how the first seed of this idea grew in my soul, and how it immediately took root in yours as well? So is it that the religion of love weaves our love ever more closely and tightly together, just as the child, echolike, redoubles the happiness of its tender parents.

Nothing can separate us and certainly every absence would only draw me more powerfully to you. I imagine how, in our final embrace, torn violently by conflicting emotions, I would break out simultaneously in tears and laughter. Then I would grow quiet and, in a kind of stupor, absolutely refuse to believe that I was away from you until my new surroundings would convince me against my will. But then irresistibly my yearning would also grow until, brought to you on its wings, I would sink into your arms. Let men or words try to bring misunderstanding between us! That deep pain would quickly ebb and soon resolve itself into a more perfect harmony. I'd pay as little attention to it as a woman in love does to the slight hurt she suffers in the heat of pleasure.

How could distance make us more distant, since for us the present is, as it were, too present? We have to lessen and cool the consuming fire with playful good humor, and therefore the wittiest of all the shapes and situations of happiness is for us also the loveliest. One above all is wittiest and most beautiful: when we exchange roles and in childish high spirits compete to see who can mimic the other more convincingly, whether you are better at imitating the protective intensity of the man, or I the appealing devotion of the woman. But are you aware that this sweet game still has quite other attractions for me than its own — and not simply the voluptuousness of exhaustion or the anticipation of revenge? I see here a wonderful, deeply meaningful allegory of the development of man and woman to full and complete humanity. There is much in it — and what is in it certainly doesn't rise up as quickly as I do when I am overcome by you.

———— ◇ ————

That was my dithyrambic fantasy on the loveliest situation in the most beautiful world! I remember well how you received it at the time and what you thought of it. But I think I know just as well what your opinion of it will be when you run across it here in this little book in which you expected to find more faithful history, plain truth, calm reason, and, yes, even morality, the charming morality of love. "How can you want to write what you should hardly talk about, what you only should feel?" My answer: if you feel something, then you should want to tell it too, and what you want to tell, you should also be allowed to write.

First I wanted to demonstrate and prove to you that there is essentially and congenitally in the nature of the male a certain doltish enthusiasm that readily blurts out all sorts of delicate and holy things. It often stumbles over its own guileless zeal, and in a word, is godlike almost to grossness.

To be sure, I should be safe because of this apology, but perhaps only at the expense of my reputation for masculinity, for as highly as you women think of men in individual cases, you still hold a great many grudges against the species as a whole. And so I want to have absolutely nothing to do with this kind of race and would rather excuse my freedom and impertinence simply by citing the example of little innocent Wilhelmine, particularly since she is also a lady whom I love most dearly. For this reason, I'd like to draw a little sketch of her at this point.

A Character Sketch of Little Wilhelmine

If you look at this unusual child not from the point of view of any one-sided theory, but rather, as one ought to do, from all possible points of view, then one might easily say (and it's perhaps the very best that one could possibly say of her) that she's the cleverest person for her age — or of her time. And that's saying a great deal, for how often do we find a two-year-old with a well-rounded education? The strongest of the many convincing proofs of her inner perfection is that she's so pleased with herself. After eating, she usually spreads out both of her arms on the table and with a kind of impish seriousness leans her little head on them. Then she opens her eyes wide, looks slyly at the whole family, straightens herself up with the most vivid expression of irony on her face, and smiles at her own cleverness and our inferiority. She really has a great deal of the buffoon in her and a great feeling for buffoonery. If I imitate her gestures, she immediately copies my imitations of her, and in this way we've invented for ourselves a language of mimicry and communicate with each other by means of the hieroglyphics of the theater. I think she has much more of a liking for poetry than philosophy, and so prefers to be driven about and walks only when she has to. The harsh discordant sounds of our Nordic mother tongue blend on her lips into the soft sweet harmony of the Italian and Indian languages. She's particularly fond of rhymes, as she is of everything beautiful, and never tires of repeating and singing to herself all of her favorite verses — a kind of classic anthology of her little pleasures. Poetry braids the blossoms of all things into an airy wreath, and so too Wilhelmine names and rhymes together places, times, events, people, playthings, and foods, with everything mixed up in a Romantic confusion — an image for every word. And that without any of those digressions and artificial transitions which after all only serve the purposes of reason and impede the bolder flights of the imagination. In her imagination all of nature is endowed with life and soul; and I often recall with pleasure how, hardly more than a year old, she looked at and touched her first doll. A heavenly smile lit up her little face and immediately she pressed an affectionate kiss on the painted, wooden lips. Unquestionably there lies deeply rooted in the nature of man a desire to eat everything he loves and put every new object he encounters immediately into his mouth in order to break it down, if possible, into its primal constituents. A healthy hunger for knowledge makes him want to apprehend the object completely, to penetrate and bite through to its inmost center. Touching it, on the other hand, stops at the surface and every touch confers only an indirect and imperfect knowledge. But for all that, it is interesting to see a clever child looking at an image of herself, trying to understand it with her hands and orienting herself with those first and last feelers of reason. The little stranger shyly crawls into himself and hides, while the baby philosopher remains diligently at his heels, pursuing the object of her investigation.

But, of course, intelligence, wit, and originality are as rare among children as they are among adults. But all of this and much more doesn't belong here, and to continue in this vein would lead me beyond the limits of my intention! For this character sketch is supposed to portray nothing more than an ideal that I want to keep before me always, so as never to stray from the fine line of propriety in this little work of art, this work of lovely and elegant worldly wisdom; and to make you forgive me in advance for all the liberties and indelicacies I propose to take and commit; or at least to have you judge and appreciate them from a more elevated point of view.

Am I wrong when I look for morality primarily in children, and for delicacy and elegance in word and thought primarily in women?

And now look! This adorable little Wilhelmine quite often takes an inexpressible pleasure in lying on her back and kicking her legs up in the air, careless of her dress and the world's opinion. If Wilhelmine does that, what may I not do, since I am after all, by God, a man, and do not need to be more modest than the most modest of women!

Oh enviable freedom from prejudice! You too, my dear friend, should cast off all remnants of false shame, just as I've often torn off your hateful clothes and strewn them all over in a lovely chaos. And if this brief story of my life seems too wild, remember it's only a child and tolerate its innocent playfulness with motherly forbearance, and let it caress you.

If you aren't too particular about the plausibility and consistency of an allegory, and are ready to accept as much narrative clumsiness as one has to expect in the Confessions of a Blunderer — provided one doesn't want to betray the disguise — then I'd like to recount for you here one of my most recent waking dreams, since it

makes much the same point as the character sketch of little Wilhelmine.

Allegory of Impudence

Without a care in the world, I stood in a sumptuous garden near
a round flower bed that blazed with a chaos of the loveliest exotic
and native flowers. I inhaled the fragrant aroma and delighted in
the many colors. But suddenly an ugly monster leaped out of the
middle of the flowers. It seemed to be swollen with poison, its transparent skin like a rainbow of colors, and one could see its entrails
coil themselves like snakes. It was large enough to make one feel
afraid and it had crablike claws opening up on all sides of its body.
At times it would jump like a frog, and then again it would crawl
with disgusting agility on innumerable little feet. I turned away in
horror, but since it tried to pursue me, I summoned up my courage
and, with a powerful blow, cast it on its back. Immediately it appeared to be nothing more than a common frog. I was rather
amazed at this, and even more astonished when suddenly a voice
spoke from behind me: "That was Public Opinion, and I am Wit.
Those false friends of yours, the Flowers, have already wilted entirely." I turned around and I saw a man of medium size. The features of his noble face were exaggerated and elaborate in the way
Roman busts often are. A friendly fire shone from his clear, open
eyes, and two long locks of hair fell and massed themselves
strangely on his bold forehead. "I'm going to renew an old spectacle for you," he said: "some youths at the crossroads. I myself
have thought it worthwhile to beget them with divine Fantasy in
my leisure time. They're the genuine Novels, four in number and
immortal like ourselves." I looked in the direction he nodded, and
saw a beautiful, almost naked youth running across the green plain.
He was already far away and I could barely see him swing himself
onto a horse and gallop away as if trying to overtake the mild evening breeze and mock its slowness. On the hill there appeared a
knight in full armor, tall and noble, almost a giant. But the precise
proportions of his body and form, along with the open friendliness

of his expressive eyes and ceremonious movements, lent him a kind of antiquated elegance. He inclined himself toward the setting sun, dropped slowly to one knee and seemed to be praying with great fervor, his right hand on his heart, his left on his forehead. The boy who'd been so quick before was now lying quietly on the slope and bathing himself in the last rays of the sun. Then he jumped up, undressed, plunged into the river and played with the waves, dived under the water, came up again, and again plunged into the river. Far below in the darkness of the grove, there hovered something like a shape clothed in a Greek robe. But if it does have substance, I thought, then it can hardly belong to this earth. So lusterless were the colors, and so much was everything enveloped in a holy mist. But after I'd looked at it longer and more carefully, it too turned out to be a youth, though of a completely different sort. This tall form was leaning its head on an urn. The grave eyes seemed first to examine the ground for something they had lost, then to ask something of the pale stars that had already begun to shine. His lips parted in a sigh, and a gentle smile hovered about them.

Meanwhile the first youth — the sensuous one — had grown tired of his solitary gymnastics, and was hurrying with easy steps straight toward us. Now he was completely clothed, almost like a shepherd, but very colorfully and strangely. He could have gone to a masquerade like that, and in fact his fingers were playing with the laces of a mask. This fantastic boy could just as well have been mistaken for a spirited girl who had disguised herself on a whim. Up to this point he'd been coming straight toward us, but suddenly his steps became uncertain. First he went to one side, then rushed back to the other, all the time laughing to himself. "This young man doesn't know whether he ought to give his allegiance to Impudence or Delicacy," said my companion. To the left I saw a group of beautiful women and girls, to the right a single imposing woman standing alone, but as I tried to look at that mighty shape her eyes met mine so sharply and fearlessly that I looked away. In the center of these ladies was a young man in whom I immediately recognized a brother of the other Novels. He was a man of the kind you see nowadays, but much more cultivated; his form and face weren't handsome, but fine, very intelligent, and extremely attractive. He could have been taken for a Frenchman just as well as a German. His clothing and his whole manner were simple, but meticulous and completely modern. He was talking with the group and seemed to be showing a lively interest in all its members. The girls were quite active in the vicinity of the most distinguished lady of the group and were chattering a great deal among themselves. "I *do* have more feeling than you do, my dear Morality!" said one. "But then my name happens to be Soul — in fact, Beautiful Soul." Morality grew rather pale at this and seemed ready to break into tears. "But I was so virtuous yesterday," she said, "and I'm always making progress in my efforts to be more so. I get enough reproaches from myself. Why do I have to listen to more from you?" Another girl, Modesty, was jealous of the girl who called herself Beautiful Soul and said, "I'm mad at you; you just want to use me." Decency, when she saw poor Public Opinion lying so helplessly on his back, shed two and a half tears, and then in an interesting way made as if to dry her eyes. But by then her eyes weren't wet anymore. "Don't be amazed at this frankness," said Wit. "It's neither ordinary nor accidental. Almighty Fantasy has touched these incorporeal shadows with her magic wand so that they might reveal their inmost natures. You'll hear more shortly. Impudence, however, speaks as she does of her own free will."

"That young dreamer there," said Delicacy, "is going to be a real source of amusement to me; he'll always be composing beautiful verses about me. I'll keep him at a distance like the knight. Of course, the knight is handsome, if only he wouldn't look so serious and formal. But probably the cleverest one of the lot is that dandy who's now talking with Modesty. I think he's making fun of her. At any rate, he said a great many nice things about Morality and her insipid face. Still, he's spoken mostly to me and perhaps he might even seduce me sometime, if I don't change my mind, or if no one else appears who's even more fashionable." By now the knight had also approached the group. His left hand rested on the hilt of his huge sword, and with his right hand he was offering a polite greeting. "Really, you're all ordinary and I'm bored," said the modern man, yawned and left. Now I noticed that these women who at first had seemed beautiful were really only young and well behaved, but otherwise unremarkable. If one looked closely, one could even discern certain vulgar features and signs of depravity. Now Impudence seemed less harsh to me. I could look at her boldly, and with astonishment had to admit to myself that her figure was tall and noble. She went rapidly toward the Beautiful Soul and seized her by the face. "That's only a mask," she said; "you're not the Beautiful Soul, but at best Daintiness, and sometimes Coquetry as well." Then she turned to Wit with these words: "If you're the maker of those who are now called Novels, then you might have spent your time more profitably. In the best of them I can hardly find any trace of the inspired poetry of fleeting life. But where has the daring Music of hearts maddened with Love fled to — she who moves everything along with her, so that even the most savage barbarian sheds gentle tears and the eternal rocks themselves dance? No one is so foolish and so prosaic that he doesn't babble about Love; but whoever still knows her doesn't have enough heart and faith to speak her name." Wit laughed, the heavenly boy signaled his approval from a distance, and she continued: "If those who are spiritually impotent want to beget children with Spirit, and if those dare to live who don't understand what living means, then I call that highly indecent, because that is the greatest perversion and indecency. But for wine to flow over and for lightning to flash is absolutely right and proper." The giddy-headed Novel had now made his decision. While Impudence was speaking he had come to her side and seemed to be completely devoted to her. Arm in arm she hurried off with him, and only in passing said to the knight: "We'll meet again." "Those were only external appearances," said my protector, "and you'll soon see the inner part of yourself. And, by the way, I'm a real person and real Wit; I swear that to you on my own being, without extending my arm infinitely." Everything vanished then, and Wit too grew and expanded until he was no longer there. But though he was no longer before me and outside me, I thought I found him again inside me, a piece of myself and yet distinct, alive in himself and independent. A new sense seemed to have opened up in me: I discovered in myself a pure mass of gentle light. I turned back into myself and into the new sense upon whose wonders I gazed. This new sense perceived so clearly and precisely, like a spiritual eye directed inwards; yet at the same time its perceptions were as deep and silent as those of the sense of hearing, and as immediate as the sense of touch. Soon I recognized the surroundings of the external world again, but transfigured and purer: above me the blue canopy of the sky, below me the green carpet of the rich earth, soon teeming with happy shapes. For I had only to make a wish, and whatever I wished for would come alive immediately, and crowd out in front of me, even before I had clearly thought of it. And so I soon saw the shapes of people I knew and didn't know, hidden by strange masks, like a big carnival of pleasure and love: inner saturnalia not unworthy of noble antiquity in their strange variety and licentiousness. But these spiritual Bacchanalia hadn't spent themselves long in reveling when my whole inner world was torn apart as if by a lightning bolt, and I heard — I don't know how or from where — the familiar words: "Destruction and creation; one and all; and so may the eternal spirit hover forever over the eternal stream of time and life, and observe each bold wave before it ebbs away." The voice of Fantasy sounded terribly beautiful and very remote, but the words that followed were gentler and more as if directed to me: "The time has come. The inner being of God may be revealed and described. All mysteries may be uncovered and fear shall cease. Consecrate thyself and proclaim to the world that nature alone is worthy of being honored, and health alone of being loved." At the mysterious words, *the time has come*, a spark of heavenly fire fell into my soul. It burned and consumed my inmost being; it strove and stormed to express itself. I reached for weapons in order to leap into the warring tumult of the passions, who use prejudices as weapons. I wanted to fight for love and truth: but there were no weapons to be had. I opened my mouth in order to proclaim love and truth in song, and I thought that all creatures must hear my song and the whole world resound in harmony. But I remembered that my lips hadn't learned how to re-create the songs of the spirit. "You mustn't try to communicate the immortal fire in its pure and raw form," said the familiar voice of my friendly companion. "Create, discover, transform, and retain the world and its eternal forms in the perpetual variation of new marriages and divorces. Veil and bind the spirit in the letter. The real letter is all-powerful; it's the true magic wand. It is the letter with which the irresistible will of that great magician, Fantasy, touches the sublime chaos of all-encompassing nature, touches it and calls the infinite word to light, the word that is an image and a mirror of the divine spirit, and that mortals call the universe."

The female spirit has an advantage over the male spirit, just as women's clothing has an advantage over men's clothing, because with a single daring stroke one can set oneself above all cultural prejudice and bourgeois convention and in a moment find oneself at the heart of innocence and in the womb of nature.

To whom, then, should the rhetoric of love direct its apology for nature and innocence if not to all women? In their gentle hearts lies deeply enclosed the holy fire of divine voluptuousness — a fire that can never be wholly extinguished no matter how much it is neglected and contaminated. And after women, of course, it should be directed at young men, as well as at those men who have remained youthful. But with these one already has to make an important distinction. One could divide all young men into those who have what Diderot calls the sensitivity of the flesh, and those who don't. A rare gift! Many talented and perceptive painters strive in vain for it all their lives, and many virtuosi of masculinity end their careers without ever having had the faintest idea of it. One doesn't gain it in the ordinary way. A libertine may know how to undress a girl with a kind of good taste. But only love teaches the youth the higher art of voluptuousness by which alone masculine strength is transformed into beauty. It is an electricity of feeling and yet at the same time a still, secret listening inside, and a certain clear transparency outside, as in those luminous places in paintings that a sensitive eye feels so distinctly. It is a wonderful mixture and harmony of all the senses: thus, there are in music, too, completely artless, pure, and profound tones that the ear doesn't seem just to hear but actually to drink, when feeling thirsts for love. But beyond this, the sensitivity of the flesh can't be defined. To do so would be unnecessary in any case. It is enough to say that it is the first grade young men attain in the art of love while it is an innate gift with women, by whose grace and favor alone men can discover and acquire it. One must not speak of love to those unlucky ones who don't know this gift; for by nature man feels a need for love, but has no notion what it is like. The second level in the art of love already has something mystical about it and might easily appear to be irrational like every ideal. A man who can't completely fulfill and satisfy the inner longing of his beloved doesn't really know how to be what he really is and ought to be. He's actually impotent and can't contract a valid marriage. To be sure, even the highest finite greatness disappears in face of the infinite, and consequently even with the best intentions the problem can't be resolved by brute force. But whoever has imagination can also communicate imagination, and where imagination is, lovers will gladly go hungry in order to be extravagant. Their way leads inward, their goal is intensive infinity, inseparability without number and measure; and actually they need never want because their magic can replace everything. But no more of these secrets! The third and highest level is the abiding feeling of harmonious warmth. Any young man who possesses it no longer loves only like a man, but at the same time like a woman too. In him humanity has reached perfection, and he has climbed the summit of life. For it is a fact that men are by nature only hot or cold: they have to be educated first to warmth. But women are by nature sensually and spiritually warm, and have a feeling for warmth of every sort.

If this mad little book should ever be found, perhaps printed and even read, then it will certainly make more or less the same impression on all happy young men: only differently according to the different levels of their development. In those of the first level it will arouse carnal sensibility; in those of the second complete satisfaction; and in those of the third only warmth.

It will be wholly different with women. There are none among them who are uninitiated; for every one of them already contains love completely within herself, a love of whose inexhaustible essence we youths are forever learning and understanding only a little more. A love already developed or still in embryo; it doesn't make any difference. A girl in her naive ignorance already knows everything, even before the lightning bolt of love has struck into her gentle womb and before the closed bud has opened into the full flower of sensuality. And if a bud could feel, wouldn't the presentiment of the flower be more distinct in it than the consciousness of itself?

Therefore in feminine love there are no levels and stages of development; nothing general at all, but only so many individuals, so many particular types. No Linnaeus can classify and spoil for us all these beautiful growths and plants in the great garden of life; and only the initiated darling of the gods understands their wonderful botany. Only he understands the divine art of finding out and recognizing their hidden strengths and beauties, of knowing in what season they bloom and what kind of earth they need. At the point where the world begins or at least where humanity begins, there too is the true center of originality, and no wise man has ever plumbed the depths of femininity.

One thing, however, seems to divide women into two large classes. Namely, whether they respect and honor the senses, nature, themselves, and masculinity; or have lost this real inner innocence, and so purchase every pleasure with remorse, even to the point of being bitterly insensitive to their inner disapproval. This is of course what happens to so many women. First, they shy away from men, then they're sacrificed to unworthy men whom they soon hate or deceive until they despise themselves and their womanly destiny. They consider their own limited experience to be the experience of all women and think of everything else as ludicrous. That narrow circle of vulgarity and meanness in which they always move becomes their whole world and it doesn't occur to them that there might be other worlds. For women like this, men aren't human beings, but just men, a species unto themselves who are dangerous but unfortunately indispensable for avoiding boredom. They then become simply types themselves: one like the other, without originality and without love.

But are they incurable because they have not been cured? It's so perfectly obvious to me that there's nothing more unnatural for a woman than prudery (a vice I can never think of without a kind of inner rage), and nothing more wearisome than unnaturalness; and so I wouldn't draw the line anywhere and think of any woman as incurable. I think their unnaturalness can never take firm root in them no matter how expert and cool they are at it, even to the point of putting an air of consistency and credibility into the role. It still remains mere semblance. The fire of love is absolutely inextinguishable, and even under the deepest heap of ashes there are still some sparks aglow.

To awaken these sparks, to purify them of the ashes of prejudice, and, where the flames already burn brightly, to feed them with a modest sacrifice — that would be the highest goal of my manly ambition. Let me confess it: I don't love you only, I love womanhood itself. And I don't merely love it, I worship it; because I worship humanity, and because the flower is the apex of the plant, the apex of its natural beauty and form.

The religion I have returned to is the oldest, the most childlike and simple. I worship fire as being the best symbol of the Godhead. And where is there a lovelier fire than the one nature has locked deeply into the soft breast of woman? Ordain me priest, not so that I may idly gaze at the fire, but so that I may liberate it, awaken it,

and purify it: wherever it is pure, it sustains itself, without sur-
veillance and without vestals.

I write and enthuse, as you see, not without unction; but, then,
that doesn't happen without having been called, called, in fact, by
the gods. What may *he* not venture to whom Wit himself has
spoken with a voice coming down from the open heavens: "You
are my beloved son in whom I find favor." And why shouldn't I
say of myself out of my own absolute power and choosing: "I am
Wit's beloved son," just as many a noble soul, wandering through
life in search of adventure, has said of himself: "I am Good Fortune's beloved son."

Anyway, I really wanted to talk about the impression this fantastic novel would make on women, if chance or fate were ever to
find it and bring it before the public. And in fact, it would be quite
improper if I weren't able to give you — quite briefly — some small
proof of prophecies and divinations so that I might substantiate my
right to the priesthood.

Every woman would understand me, and no one misunderstand
and misuse me more than uninitiated young men. Many would understand me better than I do myself, but one only would understand me completely: namely you. I hope alternately to attract and
to repulse all the others, hurt them often and just as often conciliate
them. With every refined woman the impression would be completely different and completely unique; as unique and as different
as their own particular manner of being and loving. Clementine
would find the whole work interesting only as an oddity in which
there might after all be some kind of meaning; but still a part of it
would seem true to her. People call her harsh and temperamental,
but nevertheless I believe in the warmth of her heart. Her temper
reconciles me to her harshness, even though outwardly both seem
to be getting worse. If there were only harshness in her, then it
would seem coldness and lack of heart; but her temper shows that
the holy fire is in her and trying to break out. You can easily imagine what she would be like with someone she loved in earnest.
Gentle and vulnerable Rosamunde will always be turning toward

and away from love until "shy tenderness becomes bolder and sees only innocence in love's intimate affairs." Juliane has as much poetry in her as she does love, as much enthusiasm as wit; but each quality is too isolated in her and so she will sometimes react with feminine terror to the daring chaos of this work and wish on the whole for somewhat more poetry and somewhat less love.

I could go on in this way for much longer, for I'm trying with all my power to understand human nature and often I know of no better way to use my solitude than to think about how this or that interesting woman would behave in this or that interesting situation. But enough for now; otherwise it might be too much for you and this many-sidedness might get your prophet into trouble.

Don't think so badly of me, and believe that I'm not just writing for you but for my contemporaries as well. Believe me: I'm only concerned with the objectivity of my love. For this objectivity and everything connected with it really confirms and creates the magic of writing; and since it's not given to me to breathe out my flame in song, I have to trust the beautiful mystery to these silent strokes of the pen. But in doing so I'm as little concerned with any of my contemporaries as I am with posterity. Still, if there must be an age which I ought to keep in mind, then let it be the past. Let love itself be eternally new and eternally young but its language free and daring in the manner of the classics, not more chaste than the Roman elegy and the greatest men of that greatest nation, and not more rational than great Plato and holy Sappho.

An Idyll of Idleness

"Behold, I've taught myself, and a god has implanted many melodies in my soul." I can say this unabashedly now that I'm not talking of the joyful science of poetry but of the godlike art of idleness. And with whom should I rather think and talk about idleness than myself? And so this is what I said to myself in that immortal hour when my guardian genius inspired me to proclaim the noble gospel of true pleasure and love: "Oh Idleness, Idleness! You are

the life breath of innocence and inspiration. The blessed breathe
you, and blessed is he who has you and cherishes you, you holy
jewel, you sole fragment of godlikeness come down to us from
Paradise!" When I spoke to myself like this I was sitting like a pen-
sive maiden in a thoughtless romance by the brook, watching the
waves as they passed by. But the waves fled and flowed by as
calmly, quietly, and sentimentally as if Narcissus were about to
mirror himself in its clear surface and intoxicate himself with beautiful egoism. It might also have tempted me to lose myself more
and more deeply in the inner perspective of my spirit if my personality weren't so unselfish and practical that even my specula-
tions are always and exclusively concerned with the general good.
And so I got to thinking seriously, though my mind was so comfortably relaxed and my body done in by the great heat, about the
possibility of a lasting embrace. I thought about ways of prolong-
ing our time together, and in future doing away with all those
childishly pathetic elegies about sudden parting, rather than taking
delight as we did before in the comic aspects of this kind of act of
fate, simply because it had happened and couldn't be changed. Only
after the power of my concentrated reason broke at the unattain-
ability of this ideal and slackened off, did I give myself over to the
stream of my thoughts and listen eagerly to all those colorful fairy
tales with which desire and invention, irresistible sirens in my own
breast, bewitched my senses. It didn't occur to me to stoop to criticize this seductive delusion, though I knew quite well that most
of it was just a lovely lie. The delicate music of the imagination
seemed to fill all the gaps of my yearning. Gratefully did I observe
this and decide in future to reproduce for both of us with my own
powers of invention what good fortune had given me this time. I
resolved to begin for you this poem of truth. That is how the first
germ of that wonderful plant of love and caprice was conceived.
And as freely as it sprouted, I thought, should it also grow and run
wild; and never, from a base love of order and frugality, will I
prune its living fullness of superfluous leaves and branches.

Like a wise man of the East, I was completely sunk in a holy brooding and silent scrutiny of the eternal substances, particularly of yours and mine. Greatness in repose, the masters say, is the noblest subject of the fine arts; and without clearly wanting to or basely working at it I shaped and composed our eternal substances in this noble style. I looked back in memory, and I saw us at the moment when a gentle sleep overtook us, locked in each other's arms. Now and then one of us opened his eyes, smiled at the sweet sleep of the other, and awoke just enough to begin a playful phrase or a caress. But even before the playfulness had ended, both of us fell, tightly embraced, back into the sacred womb of half-conscious self-forgetfulness.

Then, with the greatest indignation, I thought of those evil people who want to subtract sleep from life. Probably they've never slept as well as never lived. Why are the gods the gods, if not because they consciously and intentionally do nothing, because they understand this art and are masters of it? And how hard the poets, the wise men, and the saints strive to resemble the gods in this way too! How they vie with each other for the fame of solitude and leisure, of tolerant recklessness and inactivity! And quite rightly so: for everything good and beautiful already exists and can support itself. What's the point, then, of this unremitting aspiration and progress without rest and purpose? Can this storm and stress provide nourishing sap or beautiful form to the infinite plant of humanity, growing unnoticed by itself and cultivating itself? This empty, restless activity is nothing but a Nordic barbarity and so leads to nothing but boredom — our own and others! And what does it begin and end with but the antipathy toward the world that's now so common? Inexperienced self-conceit doesn't even guess that this antipathy is mere lack of sense and understanding, and so it considers it high-minded displeasure at the general ugliness of the world and life. But self-conceit doesn't even have the slightest notion of what the world and life really are. It can't conceive of them because industry and utility are the angels of death who, with fiery swords, prevent man's return to Paradise. Only calmly and gently, in the sacred tranquillity of true passivity, can one remember one's whole ego and contemplate the world and life. How does any thinking and writing of poetry take place, if not by complete dedication and submission to some guardian genius? And yet talking and ordering are only secondary matters in all the arts and sciences: the essence is thinking and imagining, and these are possible only in passivity. To be sure, it's an intentional, arbitrary, and one-sided passivity, but it's still passivity. The more beautiful the climate, the more passive one is. Only Italians know how to walk and only Orientals how to repose. And where has the spirit taken a more delicate and a sweeter form than in India? And in all parts of the earth it is the right to idleness that distinguishes the superior from the inferior classes. It is the intrinsic principle of aristocracy.

Finally, where is there greater pleasure, greater endurance, intensity, and spirit of enjoyment? In women, whose role we term passive? Or, in men, in whom the transition from impatient fury to boredom is more rapid than the transition from good to evil?

Really, we shouldn't neglect the study of idleness so criminally, but make it into an art and a science, even into a religion! In a word: the more divine a man or a work of man is, the more it resembles a plant; of all the forms of nature, this form is the most moral and the most beautiful. And so the highest, most perfect mode of life would actually be nothing more than *pure vegetating.*

I resolved, satisfied with the enjoyment of my existence, to raise myself above all finite and therefore contemptible ends and means. Nature herself seemed to support me in this undertaking and at the same time exhort me with polyphonic hymns to further idleness, when suddenly something new was revealed to me. I imagined myself invisible and inside a theater: on the one side there were the familiar boards, lamps, and painted pasteboards; on the other a vast mass of spectators, a real sea of inquisitive faces and interested eyes. In the foreground, on the right-hand side, there was, instead of decoration, the figure of Prometheus in the act of creating men. He was tied down by a long chain and was working with great haste and strain; and standing next to him were several monstrous creatures who were continually driving him on and whipping him. A great amount of glue and other material was lying about and he was taking fire out of a large coal-pan. Facing him on the other side was the similarly mute figure of the deified Hercules, with Hebe on his lap. Running about and talking at the front of the stage were a great many youthful figures who were very happy and who didn't merely appear to be alive. The younger resembled cupids; the older ones the images of satyrs, but every one of them had his own peculiar manner, a striking originality of facial expression. And all of them had some similarity with the devil of the Christian painters or poets — one could have called them little devils. One of the smallest said: "A man who can't despise, can't admire. You can only do either one infinitely, and proper form consists in toying with humanity. Isn't a certain kind of aesthetic malice, then, an essential part of a well-rounded education?" "Nothing could be more insane," said another, "than the moralists reproaching you with being egotistic. They're completely wrong: for what god can possibly deserve man's respect who isn't his own god? All of you are, of course, wrong in thinking you have an ego. But if in the meantime you identify the ego with your body, your name, and your property, then at least you're making room for one if it should ever happen to come." "And you should honor Prometheus properly," said one of the biggest ones. "He made all of you and is always making more like you." In fact, the companions of Prometheus were throwing every new human being, as soon as he was finished, down into the audience, where he immediately became indistinguishable from the others; they were all so much alike. "He's wrong only in the way he does it!" continued the little devil. "How can anyone want to create human beings all by himself? Those aren't the proper tools at all." And, while talking, he nodded at the rough figure of the God of the Gardens who was standing at quite some distance in the background of the stage between a Cupid and a very lovely, naked Venus. "In that respect our friend Hercules was much more sensible — he could keep fifty girls busy during a night for the good of humanity, and heroic girls to boot.

He labored too, and strangled many fierce monsters, but the goal of his career was really always a sublime leisure, and for that reason he became one of the Olympians. Not so this Prometheus, the inventor of education and enlightenment. It's from him you inherited your inability to stay put and your need to be constantly striving. It's also for this reason that, when you have absolutely nothing else to do, you foolishly feel compelled to aspire to having a personality, or else you're eager to observe and plumb each other's depths. That's a bad beginning. But Prometheus, because he seduced mankind into working, now has to work himself, whether he wants to or not. He'll have plenty of opportunity to be bored, and will never be free of his chains." When the spectators heard this, they broke into tears and jumped on the stage in order to assure their father of their heartfelt sympathy. And so this allegorical comedy vanished.

Fidelity and Playfulness

"You're alone, aren't you, Lucinde?"

"I don't know . . . perhaps . . . I think so."

"Please, please, my dear Lucinde. You know that when little Wilhelmine says 'please, please,' and one doesn't obey her immediately, then she screams louder and louder until she gets her way."

"You wanted to tell me that, and just because of that you ran into the room so breathlessly and frightened me?"

"Don't be angry, you sweet woman! O let me, my child, my beauty! Don't reproach me, my dear girl!"

"Well, aren't you going to tell me pretty soon that I ought to lock the door?"

"So? . . . I'll answer you right away. Only first a good, long kiss, then another one, then some more and then many many more."

"Oh, you shouldn't kiss me like that if I'm going to keep my wits. That makes one think wicked thoughts."

"You deserve them. Can you really laugh, my ill-tempered lady?

Who would have thought it! But I know very well that you're only laughing because you're mocking me. You're not doing it out of pleasure. For who looked as serious as a Roman senator just a moment ago? You could have looked really charming, my dear child, with your dark, holy eyes and your long black hair brilliantly reflecting the setting sun — if you hadn't sat there as if you were sitting in judgment. By God, the way you looked at me really startled me. I almost forgot the most important thing and got quite confused. But why aren't you saying anything? Am I repulsive to you?"

"Well, that's funny! You crazy Julius! Do you ever let anyone put a word in edgewise? Your tenderness is really pouring out of you today like a spring shower."

"Like your talk at night."

"Oh, leave my scarf alone, sir."

"Leave it alone? Not at all. What's the point of this miserable stupid scarf? A prejudice. Away with it."

"If someone should come in now!"

"There she goes again, looking as if she wanted to cry! You are feeling well, aren't you? Why is your heart beating so? Come, let me kiss it. Yes, you were speaking a moment ago about closing doors. Fine, but not like this, not here. Quickly down through the garden, to the pavilion where the flowers are. Come! Oh, don't make me wait so long!"

"Sir, as you command!"

"I don't understand. You're so strange today."

"If you're going to start moralizing, dear friend, then we might as well go back again. It's better if I give you another kiss, and then run on ahead."

"Oh, don't run so quickly, Lucinde, morality isn't going to overtake you. You'll fall, my love!"

"I didn't want to make you wait any longer. But now we're here. And you were in quite a hurry too."

"And you are very obedient. But this isn't the time to quarrel."

"Calm down, calm down."

"See, here you can rest comfortably and properly. Now, if this time you don't . . . then you'll have no excuse at all."

"Aren't you going to let the curtain down first?"

"You're right. The light is so much more enticing that way. How beautifully this white hip gleams in the red light! . . . Why so cold, Lucinde?"

"Darling, put the hyacinths further away; the aroma is stifling me."

"How firm and solid, how smooth and fine! *This* is a well-rounded education."

"Oh no, Julius! Don't, I beg you; I don't want to."

"Can't I feel if you're as passionate as I am? Oh, at least let me listen to the beating of your heart, and cool my lips in the snow of your breast! . . . Don't push me away. I'll get my revenge! Hold me tighter, kiss against kiss; no, not many: one eternal one. Take my soul completely, and give me yours! . . . Oh, beautiful, magnificent — at the same time! Aren't we children? Say something! How could you have been so indifferent and cold before, and afterwards, when at last you drew me closer to you, you made a face at the same moment as if something were hurting you, as if you were sorry to respond completely to my passion. What's the matter with you? You're crying? Don't hide your face! Look at me, my love!"

"Oh, let me lie here next to you; I can't look you in the eyes. It was bad of me, Julius! Can you forgive me, my love? Will you leave me? Can you still love me?"

"Come to me, my sweet wife! Here to my heart. Do you still remember how nice it was when, not long ago, you cried in my arms? And how it relieved you? But tell me now what's the matter with you, my love. Are you angry with me?"

"I'm angry with myself. I could hit myself. . . . Of course, it would have served you right. And if, in the future, you should ever again exercise your husbandly prerogative, then I shall take greater care that you shall also find me a true wife. You can depend on that. I have to laugh at how it surprised me. But don't imagine, my

dear sir, that you are so terribly lovable. This time I broke my resolution of my own free will."

"The first and last impulses of the will are always the best. In exchange for usually saying less than they mean, women sometimes
do more than they intend. That's no more than fair; good will leads
you astray. Good will is something very good, but the bad thing
about it is that it's always there, even when you don't want it."

"That's a beautiful fault. But you men are full of ill will and you
persist in it."

"Oh no! If we seem to persist, then it's only because we can't
really will; therefore it isn't ill will, actually, but a lack of will.
And whose fault is it, if not yours, since you don't want to share
any of your superabundance of good will but try to keep it all to
yourselves? Besides, it's happened quite against my will that we've
gotten into this discussion about will, and I don't know myself
what to make of it. In any case it's always better that I should vent
my feelings in words, rather than break the beautiful china. This
has given me a chance to recover a little from my surprise at my
lady's unexpected pathos, her splendid discourse and laudable resolution. Indeed, this is one of the strangest of those tricks which my
lady has done me the honor of making me acquainted with; and as
far as I am able to remember, my lady has not spoken for some
weeks in such stately and full periods as in today's sermon. Might
it be my lady's pleasure to translate her meaning into prose?"

"You've really forgotten already about last evening and all those
interesting people? Of course, I didn't know that."

"So — that's why you're angry; because I talked too much with
Amalie?"

"Talk as much as you like, sir, and with whomever you please.
But you must be polite to me: I insist on that."

"You were talking very loudly. That stranger was standing
right next to us, and I was afraid and didn't know what else to do."

"Except to be rude in your clumsiness."

"Forgive me! I confess my guilt; you know how self-conscious

I am with you in society. It hurts me to talk to you in the presence of others."

"How nicely he knows how to talk himself out of it!"

"Don't ever overlook something like that in me again; from now on be really attentive and strict with me. But look what you've done now! Isn't this a desecration? Oh no! It isn't possible; it's more than that. Admit it, it was jealousy."

"You'd forgotten me all evening long. I wanted to write you about it this morning, but I tore up what I'd written."

"And then when I came in?"

"Your being in such a hurry annoyed me."

"Could you love me if I weren't so easily aroused and so electric? Aren't you that way yourself? Have you forgotten our first embrace? Love comes in one moment wholly and forever, or not at all. Everything divine and everything beautiful is sudden and easy. Or do you think you can accumulate happiness like money or other material possessions just by being consistent? Great happiness surprises us like a melody out of the air; it appears and then vanishes."

"That's how you appeared to me, my dear! But you won't vanish, will you? You won't, I won't let you."

"I don't want to. I want to stay with you, now and forever. . . . Listen, I'd like very much to have a long conversation with you on the subject of jealousy, but actually we should first placate the offended gods."

"I'd prefer the conversation first and then the gods."

"You're right. We're not yet worthy, and it takes you a long time to get over something once you've been disturbed and annoyed. How good it is that you're so sensitive!"

"I'm not more sensitive than you are, only in a different way."

"Well, then, tell me how it is that, though I'm not jealous, you are?"

"Am I jealous without reason? Answer me, sir!"

"I don't know what you mean."

"Well, actually, I'm not really jealous. But tell me, what were you two talking about all evening?"

"Jealous of Amalie then? Is it possible? Such childishness! I said nothing to her and that's why it was so amusing. And didn't I talk just as long with Antonio, whom just a short while ago I used to see almost every day?"

"You're asking me to believe, then, that you talk in the same way with that coquettish Amalie as with quiet and serious Antonio? It's nothing but a simple, pure friendship, is it?"

"Oh no, you shouldn't and mustn't believe that; it's not that way at all. How can you think me so stupid? Because it really is something stupid if two people of opposite sexes try to form a relationship which they imagine to be one of pure friendship. With Amalie it's nothing more than my playing at loving her. I wouldn't like her at all if she weren't a little bit coquettish. If only there were more people like that in our circle! Actually, one ought to play at loving all women."

"Julius! I believe you're going completely insane."

"Now, listen carefully to what I'm saying; not actually all of them, but only those who are lovable and whom one happens to run across."

"That's nothing more than what the French call *galanterie* and *coquetterie*."

"Nothing more, except that I think of it as something beautiful and amusing. And then people have to be aware of what they're doing and what they want, and that's rarely the case. In their hands the subtly amusing is immediately transformed into the vulgarly serious."

"Only this playing at love isn't at all amusing to watch."

"That's not the fault of the game; that's nothing but confounded jealousy. Forgive me, love! I don't want to be angry but I simply can't understand how it's possible to be jealous, for between lovers it's not possible to just give offense, just as it's not possible to be merely generous. So it must come from insecurity, lack of love,

73

and infidelity to oneself. For me happiness is a certainty and love is identical with fidelity. To be sure, the way people usually love is quite another thing. With them, the man loves only the species in the woman, and the woman only the degree of the man's natural gifts and his social position, and they love their children only for being their own bungling creations and their property. With them being faithful is a merit and a virtue; and there too jealousy has its proper place. Because they're quite right in tacitly assuming that there are lots of people just like them, that as human beings one of them is worth just about as much as another, and that all of them put together aren't worth particularly much."

"So you consider jealousy nothing more than empty vulgarity and lack of culture."

"Yes. Or false culture and perversity, which is just as bad or even worse. According to the usual system, actually the best thing for one to do is to marry purposely out of sheer complacency and politeness; and, indeed, for these types it must be quite convenient and amusing to live away their lives together in a state of mutual contempt. Women especially can develop quite a passion for marriage; and when one of them has really found a taste for it, it's not uncommon for her to marry half a dozen men one after the other, spiritually or physically. And then there's never a lack of opportunity to be 'delicate' amid such variety, and to talk a great deal about friendship."

"You talked a moment ago as if you thought us incapable of friendship. Do you really think so?"

"Yes, but the incapacity, I believe, is to be found more in the nature of friendship itself than in women. Everything you love, you love completely, like your lover or your child. With you even the love for a sister would take on such a hue."

"You're right about that."

"For you friendship is too many-sided and too one-sided. Friendships have to be completely spiritual, and must have absolutely fixed limits. Your womanly nature would be destroyed by this kind of division: more subtly perhaps, but just as completely as it would in a purely sensual, loveless relationship. But for society friendship is too serious, too profound, and too sacred."

"Can't people even talk to each other without first thinking about whether they're men or women?"

"That could easily turn out rather badly. At best you would have an interesting club. You know what I mean. It would already be quite an achievement if people could speak easily and wittily and not be either too wild or too stiff. But the finest and the best part would always be lacking — what's always the spirit and soul of good society — namely, the playing at love and the love of playfulness, which without a feeling for love would degenerate into mere boorishness. On the same grounds, I would also defend the use of double entendres."

"Are you teasing me or just making a joke?"

"No, no! I'm completely serious."

"But not so serious and solemn as Pauline and her lover?"

"Good God, no. Those two would have the church bells rung every time they embrace each other, if it were only proper to do so. Oh, it's true, my dear — man is inherently a serious beast. But one should fight against this shameful and abominable inclination with all one's might and in every way. To that end, double entendres also do good service, except that they are so rarely ambiguous. When they're not and allow of only one interpretation, then they're not immoral but simply obvious and stupid. Frivolous conversations must have as much spirit, delicacy, and modesty as possible. For the rest, they can be as outspoken as you like."

"That's all very well, but precisely what place does that kind of conversation have in society?"

"To keep it fresh, like salt with food. It's not at all a matter of why one should have such a conversation, but only of how one should conduct it. For one can't and shouldn't do without it. It would be really boorish to speak with a charming girl as if she were some sexless amphibian. It's one's duty and obligation to allude to what she is and what she's going to be. And with society as indelicate, stiff, and guilty as it is, being an innocent girl really puts one in a funny situation."

"That reminds me of that famous clown who, while making everyone else laugh, was often very sad himself."

"Society is a chaos that only wit can organize and bring into harmony. And if one doesn't trifle and amuse oneself with the elements of passion, then passion gathers itself into thick masses and makes everything grow dark."

"Then there must be passion in the air here, since it's almost dark."

"Surely the lady of my heart must have closed her eyes! Otherwise a universal brightness would certainly illuminate the room."

"I wonder which one of us is more passionate, Julius? You or I?"

"Both of us are quite passionate enough. If that weren't the case, I wouldn't want to live. And, look, that's why I could reconcile myself to jealousy. There is everything in love: friendship, pleasant society, sensuality, and passion too; and all these must be present in love, and the one must strengthen and soften the other, animate and ennoble it."

"Let me embrace you, my faithful one!"

"But I can allow you to be jealous on only one condition. I've often felt that a little dose of cultivated, refined anger suited a man not at all badly. Perhaps it's the same way with you when you're jealous."

"Touché! And so I don't need to abjure it completely."

"If only jealousy would always show itself as beautifully and as amusingly as it did in you today!"

"Do you think so? Well, the next time when you get magnificently and amusingly angry, I'll tell you the same thing and praise you too."

"Aren't we worthy now of appeasing the offended gods?"

"Yes, if you've finished your speech; otherwise, say the rest."

Apprenticeship for Manhood

Playing cards with the appearance of being passionately involved and yet detached and inattentive; in one moment of fever-
ish excitement wagering everything, and having lost that, turning
away indifferently: this was only one of the bad habits in which
Julius spent his wild and stormy youth. This single example is
enough to describe the quality of a life that in the fullness of rebellious powers contained in itself the inescapable germ of early
ruin. There burned in him a love without object that shattered his
inner being. At the slightest inducement, the flames of passion
would break out; but soon, from pride or willfulness, this passion
seemed to scorn its object and would turn back, doubly enraged,
on itself and him, in order to feed on the core of his heart. His
spirit was in a state of continual turmoil. At any moment he expected something extraordinary to happen to him. Nothing would
have surprised him, his own destruction least of all. Without aim
and without occupation he moved among things and people like a
man who frantically looks for something on which his whole happiness depends. Everything could fascinate, nothing satisfy him.
It was for this reason that any new form of dissipation could interest him only until he had tried it and knew it better. But nothing of
this kind could become a real habit with him, for he had as much
contempt in him as he did frivolity. He could join in some revelry
with complete presence of mind and in the same breath abandon
himself to its enjoyment. But neither here nor in the various amusements and studies which he would attack with a youthful enthusiasm and voracious hunger for knowledge did he find the great
happiness that his heart passionately demanded. Traces of this frustration were everywhere visible in him and baffled and embittered
his violent temperament. He was most attracted by social life of
every kind, and though even this would often tire him, it was still
to these social amusements that, in the end, he would always go
back. Women he actually didn't understand at all, though he had
been accustomed to being with them since he was a boy. They
seemed wonderfully strange to him, often absolutely incompre-

hensible and hardly like creatures of the same species. But he reacted to young men who were more or less like him with passionate warm love and a real rage for friendship. But that alone wasn't enough to satisfy him. He felt as if he wanted to embrace a world and yet couldn't grasp anything. And so, because of his unsatisfied yearning he degenerated more and more. He became sensual from spiritual despair, committed imprudent acts out of spite against fate, and was genuinely immoral in an almost innocent way. He could see the abyss before him but didn't think it worth his while to slow his step. Like some savage hunter, he preferred to run madly down the steep slope of life rather than subject himself to the slow torture of caution.

With this kind of personality, it was inevitable that he should often feel lonely in even the friendliest and liveliest society; and actually he felt least lonely when no one was with him. At such times he would intoxicate himself with the images of his hopes and memories and intentionally let himself be seduced by his own imagination. Every one of his wishes grew almost instantaneously from an initial slight impulse into a boundless passion. All his thoughts took on visible form and motion and reacted in him and toward each other with almost physical clarity and force. His mind didn't try to keep the reins of self-control close, but heedlessly threw them off in order to plunge greedily and wantonly into this chaos of inner life. He hadn't lived through much and yet was full of all kinds of memories, including memories of his early youth. A strange moment of passionate feeling, a conversation, idle babbling that came from the depths of the heart would remain forever clear and distinct to him, and even after the passage of years he still knew them as exactly as if they were taking place in the present. But everything that he loved and thought of with love was isolated and disconnected. In his imagination his whole existence was a mass of unrelated fragments. Each fragment was single and complete, and whatever else stood next to it in reality and was joined to it was a matter of indifference to him and might just as well not have existed at all.

A Novel

He still hadn't become completely corrupted when his wistful solitude was shattered by a sacred picture of innocence which struck his soul like a bolt of lightning. A ray of longing and memory lit up his soul and fired it, and this dangerous dream was decisive for his whole life. He remembered a lovely girl with whom he had flirted happily and innocently in the happy times of his early youth. Since he was the first one who had ever attracted her by his interest in her, the sweet child turned her soul toward him like a flower inclining itself toward the light of the sun. The fact that she was scarcely grown-up, that she was hardly more than a child, only served to excite his desire more irresistibly. To possess her seemed to him the greatest possible happiness. He was resolved to risk everything and thought he couldn't live without her. Yet at the same time he loathed the faintest taint of bourgeois morality, just as he loathed every sort of compulsion.

He hurried back to her and found her more polished, but still just as noble and unique, as thoughtful and proud as before. What charmed him even more than her sweetness were the signs of deep feeling in her. She seemed to flutter happily and thoughtlessly through life as if it were a meadow full of flowers, and yet to his discerning eye she betrayed a very definite tendency toward unbounded passion. Her liking for him, her innocence, her discreet and reserved nature gave him plenty of opportunities to see her alone; and the danger of the undertaking made it even more exciting. But he had to admit to himself with vexation that he wasn't any nearer his goal, and he reproached himself for being too clumsy even to seduce a child. She gave herself willingly over to a few caresses and responded to them with bashful sensuality. But as soon as he attempted to go beyond these limits, she resisted him with unyielding stubbornness, though without seeming to be offended; doing so perhaps more out of a belief in some impersonal law than out of a feeling on her own part about what might be permissible and what was absolutely forbidden.

Nevertheless, he didn't grow tired of hoping and watching. One day he surprised her when she least expected it. She had already been alone for quite some time and had perhaps given herself up more than usually to her imagination and to an indefinable longing. When he became aware of this, he didn't want to forfeit this possibly unique opportunity foolishly, and because of this sudden hope he fell into a frenzy of rapture. A stream of entreaties, flatteries, and sophisms flew from his lips. He covered her with caresses and went mad with ecstasy when the lovable little head finally fell on his breast like an overly full flower sinking on its stem. Without reserve her slender figure pressed itself close to him, the silky locks of her golden hair flowed over his hand, the bud of her beautiful mouth opened in delicate desire, and an unaccustomed fire shone and languished in her devout, dark blue eyes. Now she resisted only weakly his boldest caresses. Soon even this resistance ceased, she suddenly let her arms fall, and everything was surrendered to him, the tender virginal body and the fruits of her young breasts. But in the same moment a stream of tears broke from her eyes and the most bitter despair disfigured her face. Julius was violently startled, not so much because of the tears, but because with a jolt he had returned to full awareness. He thought of all that had gone before and would follow; he thought of the victim before him and of the wretched destiny of man. Then a cold shudder ran down his spine, and a subdued sigh rose from the depths of his breast and escaped his lips. He despised himself from the height of his own feeling and forgot the present and his intentions in thoughts of universal sympathy.

The moment of opportunity had passed. He tried to console and soothe the good child, and with revulsion hurried from the place where he had rashly intended to rip the garland of innocence to shreds. He knew quite well that many of his friends who believed even less than he did in feminine virtue would consider his behavior bumbling and ridiculous. He almost came to believe that himself when once more he began to reflect soberly on his actions. Still he concluded that his stupidity was in its own way magnificent and interesting. He thought it necessary for noble minds to seem foolish or mad in the eyes of the masses. The next time he met the girl she seemed, as he cleverly observed or thought he did, rather dissatisfied at not having been completely seduced so that he grew more set in his distrustfulness and became extremely bitter. A feeling almost of contempt came over him, something he actually had no right to. He fled the place, withdrew once more into his old loneliness, and ate his heart out again with his own yearning.

And so he went back to living in his former ways, fluctuating between depression and elation. The only friend who had enough strength and seriousness to be able to console and occupy him, to check his ruinous downward course, was far away, and so his yearning was frustrated here as well. Passionately he stretched out his arms toward him, feeling as if he would have to come to him at last, and disconsolately he let them fall again after having waited long in vain. He shed no tears, but his spirit fell into an agony of hopeless sadness from which he roused himself only to commit further stupidities.

He laughed out loud when in the magnificent morning sun he looked back at the city he had loved since childhood and where only minutes ago his whole life had been concentrated and which now he hoped to leave forever. Already he inhaled the fresh life of the new homeland that awaited him in foreign parts and whose image he was already passionately in love with.

Soon he found another charming place to live which, though it didn't fascinate him, still attracted him in many ways. All his powers and interests were stimulated by the new objects around him, and without any aim or standard in his heart, he went everywhere and became involved in every superficial affair that promised to be in any way remarkable.

Since he was quickly bored and disgusted by this kind of bustle as well, he often returned to his solitary dreams and to poring over the fabric of his unsatisfied desires. He shed a tear of sorrow over himself when once he looked into a mirror and saw how pale he was, how gloomily and piercingly the fire of his suppressed love burned in his dark eyes and how beneath the wild, black locks of his hair faint furrows were being dug into his brow. He sighed over his misspent youth. His spirit rebelled, and he chose among the beautiful women of his acquaintance the one who lived most freely and who distinguished herself most in good society. He made up his mind to try to gain her love and allowed this object to fill up his heart completely. What had begun so wildly and arbitrarily couldn't end well, and the lady, as vain as she was beautiful, could only find it odd and more than odd how Julius would begin almost to surround her and besiege her with his earnest attentions, and, while doing so, be at one moment as impudent and confident as an old husband, and at the next as bashful and formal as a complete stranger. Since he behaved so strangely, he would have needed to be far more wealthy than he was in order to exercise these pretensions.

She was of an easy, cheerful disposition and her conversation seemed charming to him. But what he took for divine frivolity on her part was nothing more than thoughtless enthusiasm without any real joy or cheerfulness, or even spirit, except for just enough intelligence and wit to mix everything up intentionally and pointlessly, attract and manipulate men, and intoxicate herself with flattery. Unfortunately, he received some signs of her favor, of a sort that don't commit the giver because she can't admit she has given them, but which bind the ensnared novice even more inextricably because of the magic with which this secrecy endows them. A furtive glance or a squeeze of the hand was enough to bewitch him, or a word spoken in front of everyone but understood only by himself in its real context — all he needed was to have this cheap and simple gift made piquant by the illusion of some unique and special significance. She gave him, or so he thought, an even more unmistakable sign, and he was deeply offended that she should show so little understanding by anticipating him in this way. He was rather proud that this did offend him, and yet he was irresistibly aroused when he thought he had only to be quick about it and seize the favorable opportunity in order to arrive unhindered at his goal. He was already reproaching himself bitterly about his delay when he suddenly began to suspect that her forwardness was merely a deception and that she wasn't being honest with him. And when a friend explained the whole affair to him, he could doubt it no longer. He realized that people found him ridiculous, and he had to admit to himself that they were quite right in doing so. Realizing this enraged him and he might very well have done something regrettable if he hadn't already observed very closely and therefore absolutely despised these empty people, their petty affairs and quarrels, the whole spectacle of their secret motives and concerns. Once again he became unsure, and since his mistrust now no longer knew any bounds, he even grew mistrustful of that. At one moment he would see the cause of his trouble only in his own willfulness and exaggerated sensitivity, and then he would be filled with new hope and new faith. At another moment he would see in all those misfortunes, which really seemed to hound him intentionally, only the evil machinations of their vengefulness. Everything lost its fixity, and the only thing that became increasingly clearer and more certain to him was the fact that great and perfect folly and stupidity were intrinsic prerogatives of men, and wanton malice, combined with naive coldness and laughing insensitivity, the congenital art of women. That was all he learned from his painful attempt to gain an understanding of human nature. In any given particular case he would always ingeniously fail to grasp the truth of the matter because he would forever presuppose subtle motives and deep plots, and because he had no feeling whatsoever for insignificance. At the same time he developed a passion for gambling. He was interested in its random complications, peculiarities, and strokes of luck, just as if on a higher plane he were wagering, or thought he was wagering, his passions and their objects in a completely arbitrary way.

And so he became more and more entangled in the intrigues of a corrupt society and spent whatever time and energy he had left after this whirl of dissipations with a girl whom he tried as hard as possible to possess for himself alone, even though he had met her among women who were practically prostitutes. What made her so interesting to him was not merely the quality that had made her popular and, as it were, famous everywhere: namely, the rare skill and inexhaustible variety of her sensuality. Her naive wit, as well as the bright sparks of her untrained but capable intelligence, surprised him more and attracted him most. But he was most intrigued by her decisive air and her consistent behavior. In surroundings of the greatest depravity, she displayed a kind of character; she was full of idiosyncrasies and her egoism was not of the common sort. Next to independence she loved nothing so passionately as money; but she knew how to make use of it. Still, she was moderate to anyone who wasn't very wealthy and even to the rich she was candid in her greed and devoid of tricks. She seemed to live heedlessly and for the present alone, and yet she was always mindful of the future. She saved money on small things in order to squander it in her own way on big ones — in order to have the greatest luxuries. Her boudoir was simple and without the usual items of furniture; only on all sides of the room there were large, expensive mirrors, and, where there was any space left, some good copies of the most voluptuous paintings of Correggio and Titian, as well as a few beautiful original still lifes of flowers and fruit. Instead of paneling, there were some extremely lively and delightful figures done in bas-relief in plaster of paris, in the classical style. Instead of chairs, there were genuine Persian rugs and a few groups of marble statues reduced to half life-size: a lustful satyr about to overcome a nymph already fallen in flight; a Venus raising her gown and looking across her voluptuous back at her hips; and more statues of the same kind. In this room she often remained alone for days on end, sitting in the Turkish way with her hands resting idly in her lap, because she hated any kind of womanly work. She only refreshed herself from time to time by inhaling perfumes and by having, at the same time, her servant — a lovely boy whom she had seduced when he was fourteen — read stories, travel accounts, and fairy tales to her. She paid little attention to them except when she heard something ridiculous, or some general observation she felt was true. For she had no respect for anything and a sense only for what was real, and so found all poetry ridiculous. She had once been an actress, but only for a short time; she would willingly laugh at her own clumsiness in acting and at the boredom she had endured while doing it. It was one of her many peculiarities that on such occasions she would speak of herself in the third person. When she talked about her life, too, she would simply call herself Lisette, and would often say that if she could write, she would very much like to write the story of her life, but write it as if it were someone else's. She had no feeling whatsoever for music, but so much for the plastic arts that Julius would often talk to her about his work and his ideas, and would consider those sketches best that he had made while with her and talking to her. Still she valued only the living force in sculpture and drawing, and in painting only the magic of color, the reality of the flesh, and perhaps, too, the illusion of light. If anyone spoke to her of rules, of the ideal, and of so-called draftsmanship, she either laughed or didn't listen. She was too lazy and too spoiled and too satisfied with her own way of life to try her hand at anything herself, no matter how many eager teachers offered their services.

Nor would she put any faith in flattery, but remained quite convinced that, try as she might, as an artist she would never achieve anything significant. If someone praised her taste and her room — into which she would only bring a rare, selected favorite — then she would answer by praising in a mocking way first good old Providence, then clever Lisette, and finally the English and the Dutch as the best nations of all that she knew. For it was the full pocketbooks of some neophytes of this type that had provided the first solid foundation for the luxurious decor of the room. Altogether, she was very happy when she had managed to put something over on someone stupid; but she did it in a droll, witty, almost childlike manner, and more out of high spirits than grossness. She devoted all of her ingenuity to protecting herself against the importunity and rudeness of men. She was so successful in this that these coarse and dissolute people would speak of her with a sincere respect that seemed very odd to someone who didn't know Lisette personally but only her profession. And it was this fact that first induced Julius to make so strange an acquaintance, but he soon found even more reason to be amazed. With ordinary men Lisette did and endured whatever she thought she owed them: she was precise, skillful, and artistic, but completely cold. But if a man pleased her, then she led him into her inner sanctum and there seemed to become a completely new person. Then she would fall into a beautiful, bacchantic fury; wild, extravagant, and insatiable, she almost forgot all artistry and sank into a ravishing adoration of the male. For that reason Julius loved her, and also because she seemed so completely attached to him, although she didn't say so openly. She was quick at perceiving if someone was intelligent, and when she thought she had found such a person she was open and warm, and would gladly listen to what her friend had to tell of his experiences in the world. Many men had taught her in this way, but no one had understood her inner self so well, had been so considerate of her, and had respected her real worth so much as Julius. Therefore she was more devoted to him than may be said. For perhaps the first time she felt moved to recall the days of her early youth and innocence, and became dissatisfied with the surroundings that at other times had satisfied her so fully. Julius felt this and was glad of it, but he never could master the feeling of disdain which her position and her depravity produced in him, and he thought that his inextinguishable distrust was quite justifiable in this case. How indignant he was, therefore, when she announced to him unexpectedly that he was to become a father. Didn't he know very well that, despite her promise, she had only recently accepted a visit from another man? She hadn't been able to refuse making the promise to Julius. Probably she would have kept it gladly, but she needed more money than he could give her. She knew only one way to earn it, and from a sense of delicacy she had for him alone, she took only the smallest fraction of what Julius wanted to give her. Furious, he gave no consideration to any part of this; he thought he had been deceived. He said so to her harshly, and left her in this passionate frame of mind, forever as he thought. Not long afterwards her little servant-boy came looking for him in tears and wouldn't leave off until he had gone with him. He discovered her in the already darkened room, almost completely undressed; he sank into those beloved arms and she embraced him as passionately as ever, but then her arms immediately slid down his side. He heard a deep, moaning sigh, her last; and when he looked at himself, he was covered with blood. He jumped up full of horror and wanted to make his escape. He stopped only to pick up a long lock of hair lying on the floor next to a bloodied knife. She had cut off this lock in an attack of frenzied despair shortly before stabbing herself repeatedly and fatally. She had probably done so with the thought of yielding herself up as a sacrifice to death and destruction. For, according to the boy, while doing so she had spoken out loud the following words: "Lisette must perish, perish now: that is the will of an iron fate."

The impression this surprising tragedy made on the young man was ineradicable, and, by means of his own goading, was branded ever more deeply into him. The first consequence of Lisette's ruin was that he worshipped her memory with fanatical respect. He compared her noble energy to the contemptible intrigues of the lady who had ensnared him, and his feelings forced him to decide clearly that Lisette had been more womanly and moral; for the coquette had never done a small or a great kindness without an ulterior motive, and yet she was respected and admired by the whole world, as were so many others who were like her. Because of this, his mind passionately opposed all those false and true opinions that people have of female virtue. Though before he had only disregarded the prejudices of society, he now made it a principle to despise them openly. He thought of gentle Louise who had nearly become a victim of his desires, and he was alarmed. For Lisette, too, had been of good family, had fallen early, had been seduced and abandoned far from home, had been too proud to return, and had learned from her first experience more than most women learn from their last. With painful pleasure he collected many interesting details about her early youth. As a little girl she had been more given to melancholy than frivolity, though in the depth of her being she had been completely passionate; and one could have observed her looking at pictures of nude figures, or have seen in her on other occasions the most remarkable expressions of passionate sensuality.

Lisette was too unique an exception to Julius's usual ideas of the female sex, and the surroundings in which he had met her were too unclean for him to have been able to arrive at a true understanding of women by this experience. On the contrary, his feelings drove him to break off his contact with women almost completely, as well as with those social groups where women set the tone. He was afraid of his passionate nature, and consequently devoted himself exclusively to friendships with other young men who, like him, were capable of being enthusiastic. To these he gave his heart; they alone were truly real to him. As for the rest — that crowd of phantasmagoric wretches — he was pleased to despise them. He would brood and quarrel within himself, passionately and speciously, about his friends, about their good qualities, and their relationship to him. He would grow heated by his own thoughts and inner dialogues and become intoxicated with pride and masculinity. Indeed, the whole group of his friends glowed with noble love, and many a great talent slumbered undeveloped in them. They would often utter — crudely but effectively — sublime things about the wonders of art, the value of life, and the essence of virtue and independence, but particularly about the divine quality of male friendship, which Julius intended to make the true business of his life. He had many friends, and was insatiable in making new ones. He sought out every man who seemed interesting to him, and didn't rest until he had won him, had conquered the other's reserve through his youthful forwardness and confidence. It is obvious that Julius, who felt that practically anything was permitted to him and was able to put himself above ridicule, had a different sort of propriety in mind than the commonly accepted one.

In the company and conversation of one friend he would find a more than feminine consideration and delicacy of feeling combined with a sublime intelligence and a firm, cultivated character.

A Novel

Another friend shared his noble and burning dislike of this evil age, and wanted to accomplish something great. The amiable personality of a third was still a chaos of intimations, but he had a tender feeling for everything and perceived the world intuitively. One friend Julius worshipped as his master in the art of living life worthily. Another he thought of as his disciple, and only for the moment did he plan to let himself go down to the level of his excesses in order to get to know him completely and win him over, and then rescue his great talent, hovering as close to the abyss as his own.

They had great aims and strove earnestly to achieve them. But for all that, they didn't get beyond high-sounding phrases and splendid hopes. Julius didn't progress or arrive at a clearer understanding; he didn't act and didn't create. Indeed, he had hardly ever neglected his art more than when he deluged himself and his friends with projects for all the works of art he wanted to finish and which in the first moments of enthusiasm already seemed complete. He would stifle in music the few sober impulses that still remained in him. And music became for him a dangerous and bottomless abyss of longing and melancholy in which he would gladly and willingly immerse himself.

This inner ferment could have been healthy for him. Through despair he might finally have achieved peace, stability, and a clearer understanding of himself. But the fury of his frustration lacerated his memory: never had he had less of a conception of the whole of his ego. He lived only in the present, hung upon it with thirsty lips, and unceasingly engrossed himself in every infinitesimally small and yet unfathomable part of enormous time, as if at last he might find in this particular moment what he had sought for all this long while. Inevitably this fury of frustration made him fall out and quarrel with his friends, who for the most part, though extremely talented, were just as inactive and at odds with themselves as he was. One friend seemed not to understand him, another admired only his mind but expressed a distrust of his feelings, and was really unfair to him. That made him think that his honor was deeply hurt, and he felt torn by secret hate. He gave himself up entirely to this emotion, because he believed that it was possible to hate only those whom one should respect, and that only friends could hurt each other's tenderest feelings so deeply. One of the youths was ruined through his own fault; and another actually began to turn ordinary. With a third, friendship had become strained and almost coarse. It had been completely spiritual at first and should have remained so. But precisely because it had been so delicate, when the first bloom went, everything was gone. They fell to competing against each other in point of generosity and gratitude and actually in the end began in the depths of their souls to make material claims against each other and draw comparisons.

Soon chance mercilessly loosened all the bonds that only the will had passionately held together. Julius fell more and more into a state distinguishable from madness only by the fact that to a greater or lesser degree he could control when and to what extent he would give himself over to its power. His outward behavior conformed to all the bourgeois social norms; and precisely at a time when a confusion of pains was tearing his inner being apart, and when the disease of the spirit gnawed ever more deeply and furtively at his heart, did people begin to call him sensible. It was more an emotional disturbance than a mental insanity, but the malady was all the more dangerous because he seemed outwardly happy and cheerful. This had become his habitual disposition and people actually found him agreeable company. Only when he had drunk more wine than usual did he become extremely depressed and inclined to tears and lamentations. But even then, when others were present he bubbled over with bitter witticisms and would mock at everything; or else he made sport of eccentric and stupid people. Their company he now loved more than anything, and he knew how to put them in the best of moods so that they spoke to him from their hearts and uncovered their real natures to him. He was attracted and amused by this vulgarity not because of any kindhearted condescension on his part, but because he thought them foolish and mad.

He didn't think about himself. Only now and then did the distinct feeling that he would suddenly be destroyed overcome him. Proudly he repressed his remorse: thoughts and visions of suicide had been such familiar companions to him since his earliest youthful moods of depression that they had lost all the charm of novelty for him. He would have been quite capable of carrying out a decision of this kind if he had been at all capable of arriving at *any* decision. It seemed to him scarcely worth the trouble since he really didn't hope to escape the boredom of existence and his revulsion against fate in this way. He despised the world and everything in it — and he was proud of it.

This malady, like all the others before it, was cured the moment he caught sight of a woman, a unique woman who moved him to the very depths of his heart for the first time. His previous passions had been merely superficial, or had been passing things without any relevance to the rest of his life. Now he was seized by a new and unknown feeling that this woman was the only right one and that this impression of his would be eternal. The first glance decided it, and with the second he already knew and told himself that now it had come, that what he had waited for unconsciously for so long had really come. He was amazed and horrified, for though he believed it would be the greatest possible happiness to be loved by her and to possess her eternally, he felt at the same time that he would never be able to fulfill this wish, his greatest and only one. She had chosen and had given herself: her choice was his friend, too, and was deserving of her love. Julius was their confidant, and so he knew the source of his unhappiness intimately, passed strict sentence on his own unworthiness, and turned the whole force of his passion against it. He renounced all expectation of happiness, but resolved to be worthy of it and become master of himself. He abhorred nothing more than the thought of revealing his true feelings by some careless word or surreptitious sigh. And certainly any kind of declaration would have been absurd. Since he was so impulsive and she so refined, and their relationship so delicate, a single hint of the sort that seems to be involuntary but really wants to be observed would have inevitably complicated matters further and put everything into confusion. For this reason he forced all of his love back into himself and let his passion rage, burn, and consume him from within. But his external appearance was completely transformed; he assumed a mask of childlike candor and inexperience, and a kind of brotherly harshness, which he put on so that he shouldn't lapse from flattery into lovemaking. He succeeded so well in this disguise that she never suspected him in the least. She was cheerful and easy in her happiness, had no misgivings and therefore shrank from nothing, but gave free rein to her wit and her temperament whenever she found him in a bad mood. She possessed, indeed, every sublime and delicate quality characteristic of women, as well as all their divineness and mischief; but everything was refined, well-bred, and feminine. Every single characteristic was freely and strongly developed and expressed, as if it existed for him alone; and yet this rich, daring mixture of such disparate elements formed a whole that was not chaotic because it was animated by a single spirit, a living breath of harmony and love. In one and the same hour she could mimic some comic nonsense with all the playfulness and subtlety of a trained actress, and could read a sublime poem with the ravishing nobility of an artless song. At one moment she would want to flirt and shine in society, at another she would be completely inspired, and at still another she would be helpful both in word and deed, as serious, modest, and friendly as a tender mother. She could transform some trivial event into a beautiful story by her charming way of telling it. She enveloped everything in tenderness and wit; she had a feeling for everything, and everything emerged transfigured out of her shaping hand or her sweetly speaking lips. Nothing good and great was too sacred or too common for her to take part in passionately. She understood every allusion and answered those questions, too, which had not been asked. It wasn't possible to lecture to her; by themselves those lectures turned into conversations and, as they became more and more interesting, a continually renewed music of spirited looks and lovable expressions played upon her face.

When one read her letters — which she conceived as if she were carrying on a conversation — one could almost see those changes of expression, so clearly and soulfully did she write. Whoever knew only this side of her might have thought that she was merely a pleasant person, that she would have been a superb actress, and that her sayings lacked only meter and rhyme to be changed into tender poetry. And yet, this same woman showed amazing courage and strength on every important occasion, and that, too, was the lofty perspective from which she formulated her judgment of men.

This greatness of soul was the side of her nature that so captivated Julius at the beginning of his passion because this was the side that fitted in best with his own seriousness. His whole being had, as it were, drawn back from the surface into his inner self. He became quite reserved and avoided the society of men. His favorite companions were the rough, rocky crags; he would muse at the shore of the solitary sea and consult his own thoughts there; and when the noise of the wind roared in the lofty pines, he thought the mighty waves far below wanted to draw near him out of compassion and sympathy; and he would follow mournfully with his eyes the distant ships and the sinking sun. This was his favorite place; in his memory it became for him the sacred home of all his sorrows and resolutions.

The worship of his sublime friend became for him the spiritual foundation and fixed center of a new world. Here all his doubts disappeared; in this genuine possession he felt the value of life and intuited the omnipotence of will. Truly he stood on the fresh green ground of a mighty maternal earth, and a new sky shaped itself in an infinite vault above him in the blue ether. He recognized in himself a high calling to divine art, berated his laziness for having put him so far behind in his development and for making him too weak to meet any great challenge. He didn't let himself sink into idle despair, but followed the heralding call of this sacred duty. Now he exerted all those powers which his dissipations had still left him. He broke all his former ties and with one stroke made himself completely independent. He dedicated his strength and his youth to sublime artistic inspiration and achievement. He forgot his own times and modeled himself on the heroes of those former ages whose ruins he loved to adoration. And for himself the present didn't exist either, since he lived only in the future and in the hope of someday completing an immortal work as a monument to his virtue and honor.

He lived and suffered in this way for many years, and whoever saw him thought him older than he was. Whatever he created was conceived on a grand scale and in a classical style, but his seriousness was intimidating, the forms were almost monstrous, his classicism became a fixed mannerism, and, despite all their precision and insight, his paintings were stiff and rigid. There was much to praise in them, but there was no grace; and in this he himself resembled his creations. His character had been tempered in the fiery sorrows of godlike love and it shone in its bright power; but it was inflexible and hard like real steel. He was tranquil in his coldness, and would only become excited when he was more than usually enchanted by some high and lonely landscape in the wilderness of nature; or when he was giving his distant friend a faithful report of the struggle of his self-education and the aim of all his work; or when his enthusiasm for art overcame him in the presence of others, so that after long silence a few sayings would break forth from his inmost being. But that happened rarely, for he took as little interest in other people as he did in himself. He could only smile in a friendly way at their happiness and their endeavors, and he took them at their word when he noticed how unloving and unlovable they found him. Still one noble woman seemed to give him a little notice and prefer him to others. Her subtle mind and delicate feeling attracted him greatly, all the more because she had eyes filled with silent melancholy, and a charming figure which, at one and the same time, was both lovable and extraordinary. But as soon as he tried to become more intimate with her, his old distrust and habitual coldness overcame him. He saw her often and could never express his feelings to her, so that in the end this stream of feeling also flowed back into the inner sea of his general enthusiasm. Even the mistress of his heart stepped back into a sacred obscurity, and would have seemed remote to him even if he had seen her again.

The only thing which put him in a milder and warmer mood was his association with another woman, whom he respected and loved as a sister, and whom he considered only as such. He had already known her socially for quite some time. She was sickly and a little older than he was, but at the same time she possessed a clear, mature mind and was straightforward and commonsensical, and even with strangers she was fair to the point of kindness. Whatever she did was informed with a spirit of friendly order, and, as if by themselves, her present activities would develop out of her former ones and just as peacefully merge with those of the future. Observing her, Julius realized clearly that consistency was the only real virtue. But her consistency was not a cold and stiff agreement of calculated principles or prejudices, but the persevering faithfulness of a motherly heart which humbly enlarges the sphere of its activity and love, finds its perfection in itself, and shapes the raw materials of the surrounding world into friendly possessions and instruments of social life. At the same time she had none of the limitations of the ordinary housewife; she spoke with profound consideration and true gentleness about the prevalent opinions of mankind, and the excesses and anomalies of those who lived counter to the general stream of things. Her mind was as incorruptible as her heart was pure and unadulterated. She talked with great pleasure, usually on moral subjects, would carry the arguments into the realm of generalities, and would betray a liking for subtleties if there seemed to be something in them, or if they sounded significant. She did not stint her words nor was her conversation governed by any timid rules. It was a charming confusion of individual ideas and general sympathy of continual attentiveness and sudden distraction.

At last nature rewarded the motherly virtue of this wonderful woman, and when she had almost given up hope, a new life was conceived beneath her faithful heart. This filled the young man with happiness, for he was very much attached to her and took the warmest interest in her domestic happiness. But it also roused much in him that had long lain dormant.

At this time a few of his artistic attempts gave him new confidence, and his first taste of praise from great masters encouraged him. His art took him to new and remarkable places, and brought him together with new and happy people. For this reason, his feelings began to grow gentler and flow powerfully, like a great river when the ice melts and breaks and the waves rip through their old channel with renewed power.

He wondered at seeing himself once again relaxed and happy in the company of other people. In his solitude, his manner of thinking had become masculine and rough, but his heart childlike and shy. He longed for a home, and thought of a happy marriage which wouldn't interfere with the demands of his art. When he found himself in the company of young, blooming girls, he had no difficulty in finding one or more of them delightful. He thought he ought to marry immediately, even if he wasn't yet able to love his wife. For the concept and even the name of love were supremely sacred to him and remained quite remote. At such times he would smile at the apparent limitation of his momentary desires and would realize how infinitely much he would still be missing if they were suddenly to be fulfilled by some stroke of magic. At another time he laughed loudly at the impulsiveness that came from such long self-restraint, doing so after a chance opportunity had given him a fresh pleasure by putting a novel in his way which he'd read through in the span of a few minutes, thereby relieving his temper of at least some of its volatility.

One very cultivated girl was attracted to him because he had shown warm and obvious admiration for her deeply felt conversation and fine spirit, and because he revealed his devotion to her, not by means of any overt flattery, but by the way he behaved when in her company. This pleased her so much that eventually she granted him all her favors except the last. And she didn't even set this limit out of any coldness, prudence, or principle, for she was certainly passionate, had a real liking for everything frivolous, and lived in the most unrestrained surroundings. Her reluctance was due to womanly pride and to a distaste for something she considered crude and bestial. As little as this kind of affair — without chance of being consummated — was to Julius's taste, and though he had to smile at the girl's little idiosyncrasy, still when in his mind he compared this unnatural and overly refined woman with the creation and working of almighty nature, her eternal laws, and the nobility and grandeur of motherhood, and when he thought of the beauty of the male who is seized by the fervor of life in the prime of health and love, or of the woman yielding herself up to it, even then he was still glad to see that he hadn't lost his taste for subtle and refined sensuality.

But soon he forgot these and similar trivia, for he met a girl who, like himself, was an artist, and passionately worshipped beauty, and seemed to love solitude and nature as much as he did. One could see and feel the living breath of real air in her landscapes, and they always presented a complete view. The outlines were too vague in a way that revealed a lack of fundamental training, but the proportions harmonized in a unified emotional whole which was so clear and distinct that it seemed impossible to have any other reaction to it. Painting was not a profession or an art for her, but simply a pleasure and a labor of love. When, on her wanderings, she found some pleasing or striking view, she would make either a pen and ink drawing or a watercolor of it, depending on what her mood was and how much time she had. She didn't have enough patience or diligence to paint in oils; she seldom made a portrait, and then only when she thought the face extremely fine and deserving. But then she worked with the most conscientious fidelity and care and knew how to handle the pastel colors with an enchantingly soft touch. Even if these attempts were of limited value as works of art, still Julius was not a little pleased by the lovely wildness of her landscapes and the spirit with which she conceived the unfathomable variety and wonderful harmony of human faces. And as simple as the features of her own face were, still they weren't unremarkable, and Julius found in them a great expressiveness that remained forever new.

Lucinde had a decided bent for the romantic. He was struck by this further similarity to himself and was always discovering new ones. She also belonged to that part of mankind that doesn't inhabit the ordinary world but rather a world that it conceives and creates for itself. Only whatever she loved and respected in her heart had any true reality for her; everything else was spurious: and she knew what was valuable. Also she had renounced all ties and social rules daringly and decisively and lived a completely free and independent life.

This wonderful similarity soon attracted the young man to her. He noticed that she felt their kinship too, and both became aware that they weren't indifferent to each other. They hadn't known each other for very long and Julius only dared to speak single, disconnected words to her, words full of meaning but not very clear. He longed to know more about her fate and former life, something she had been extremely secretive about to others. She confessed to him — but not without severe emotional agony — that she had been the mother of a lovely boy who had died soon after birth. He, too, recalled his past, and by telling her about it saw his life for the first time as a connected whole. How happy Julius was when he talked with her about music and heard from her mouth his own inmost thoughts about the sacred enchantment of this romantic art! How happy he was when he heard her singing and listened to that pure and powerfully formed voice softly rising from the depths of her soul! How happy when he accompanied her, and their voices merged into one, and when they exchanged unspoken questions and answers in the language of the tenderest feelings. He couldn't resist the temptation and pressed a bashful kiss on her fresh lips and fiery eyes. With eternal rapture he felt the divine head of this noble creature sink upon his shoulder, and saw the black hair flow over the snow of her full breasts. Softly he said "magnificent woman!" — and just then some accursed guests came into the room.

According to his principles, she had now actually granted him everything. It wasn't possible for him to begin quibbling in a relationship which had been so purely and nobly conceived, and yet every delay was intolerable. It seemed to him that one shouldn't ask a goddess to grant something that one conceives of only as a means to an end, a transition to something else, but admit openly and confidently just what it is one wants. And so he asked her with unaffected innocence for everything a lover can grant, and described to her with flowing eloquence how his passion would destroy him if she was going to be too feminine. She was quite surprised but foresaw that he would be more loving and faithful to her after her surrender than before. She was unable to arrive at a decision and so left the matter to arrange itself by chance. They had been alone only a few days when she gave herself to him forever and opened up to him the depths of her soul and all the power, nature, and holiness that was in her. She had also lived long in enforced seclusion, and now all at once from the depths of their hearts their suppressed faith and sympathy broke out in streams of words that were interrupted only by embraces. In a single night they alternated more than once between passionate tears and loud laughter. They were completely devoted and joined to each other, and yet each was wholly himself, more than he had ever been before, and every expression was full of the deepest feeling and the most unique individuality. At one moment an everlasting rapture would seize them, at another they would flirt and tease each other, and Cupid was here truly what he is so seldom — a happy child.

It became clear to Julius from what was revealed to him that only a woman could be truly unhappy and truly happy, and that, having remained the creatures of nature in the midst of human society, women alone possessed that childlike consciousness with which one has to accept the favors and gifts of the gods. He learned to value the beautiful happiness he had found, and when he compared it with that ugly, false happiness that he had earlier tried to extort artfully from stubborn chance, then his happiness seemed to him like a natural rose on a living branch compared to an artificial one. But neither in the ecstasy of night nor in the bliss of day did he want to call it love. So profoundly had he convinced himself that love was not for him and he not for love! It wasn't difficult to concoct a rationalization to justify this self-deception. He decided that he was harboring a violent passion for her and that he would be her friend eternally. What she gave to him and felt for him he called tenderness, remembrance, devotion, and hope.

Meanwhile time passed and their happiness grew. Julius rediscovered his youth in the arms of Lucinde. The voluptuous fullness of her beautiful body was more exciting to the fury of his love and senses than the fresh charm of the breasts and mirrorlike bodily smoothness of a virgin. The ravishing power and warmth of her embraces were more than girlish; she was inspired by an ardor and a profundity which only a mother can possess. When he saw her form poured out in the magical soft glow of twilight, he could not stop touching and caressing its swelling outlines, and feeling the warm streams of its remarkable life beneath the gentle covering of its even skin. At the same time his eyes would feast themselves on the colors which, in the play of shadow, seemed to change continually and yet remain the same. It was a pure mixture where neither white, brown, nor red contrasted or predominated. Everything was veiled and fused into a single harmonious sheen of gentle life. Julius, too, was beautiful in a manly way, but the masculinity of his body did not show itself in pronounced muscular strength. On the contrary, the outlines of his body were soft and his limbs full and round, though he was not in the least fat. Under a bright light the surface of his body revealed broad masses, and his smooth skin seemed as solid and firm as marble. And in their amatory battles the whole richness of his powerful figure would suddenly be revealed.

They delighted in their young life; the months went by like days and more than two years passed. Now Julius began to realize for the first time the extent of his clumsiness and stupidity. He had looked for love and happiness in all the places where they weren't to be found; and now that he possessed the greatest good he hadn't even known it or dared to give it its right name. Now he recognized that love — a completely simple and indivisible emotion for a woman — can be for a man only an alternation and mixture of passion, friendship, and sensuality; and with happy astonishment he saw that not only did he love infinitely, but that he was the object of an infinite love.

It seemed to be predestined that every event in his life should surprise him by its peculiar conclusion. At the beginning, nothing had attracted him so much and struck him so powerfully as the realization that Lucinde was of a similar, or even of the same mind and spirit as he was; and now he was forced to discover new differences every day. To be sure, even these differences were based on a fundamental similarity, and the more richly her character revealed itself, the more various and intimate did their communion become. He had not suspected before that her originality would be as inexhaustible as her love. Even her outward appearance seemed to be younger and more glowing when she was with him; and in this way too her spirit was illuminated through contact with his spirit and shaped itself into new forms and new worlds. He believed that now he possessed united in one person all those things which before he had loved separately and disjointedly: the beautiful newness of the senses, the ravishing passion, the modest activity, the docility, and the noble character. Every new relationship, every new opinion was for them a new organ of sympathy and harmony. Their belief in each other grew with their feeling for each other; and with their belief, their courage and their strength.

They shared an inclination for the arts. Julius finished some paintings: now they came to life, a stream of inspiring light seemed to spill over them, and the real flesh glowed in living colors. His favorite subjects were girls bathing, a young man looking with furtive pleasure at his own image in the water, or a fond, smiling mother with her darling child in her arms. The shapes themselves perhaps did not always conform to the conventional rules of artistic beauty, but they appealed to the eye because of a certain quiet grace, the deep expression of calm and happy life and the enjoyment of that life. They seemed to be animated plants created in the godlike forms of men. His pictures of embraces also had the same quality of warmth and he was prolific in producing variations on this theme. Painting them was his greatest pleasure because there he was able to show the charm of his art to its best advantage. There it really seemed that he had surprised the fleeting and mysterious moment of the most intense being with a silent magic and seized it for all eternity. The more his treatment of the subject was remote from bacchantic frenzy and the more modestly and lovingly he shaped it, the more seductive was its effect, and looking at it, women and young men would be flooded by sweet fire.

Just as his artistic ability developed and he was able to achieve with ease what he had been unable to accomplish with all his powers of exertion and hard work before, so too his life now came to be a work of art for him, imperceptibly, without his knowing how it happened. A light entered his soul: he saw and surveyed all the parts of his life and the structure of the whole clearly and truly because he stood at its center. He felt that he would never lose this unity; the mystery of his life had been resolved and he had found the Word. It seemed to him that everything in his life had been predestined and created since the beginning of time so that he would find the answer in love, in the love for which with youthful incomprehension he had considered himself too clumsy.

The years flowed by easily and melodiously like a lovely song. They lived a cultured life; their surroundings also assumed a harmony, and their simple happiness seemed more the result of a rare talent than a singular gift of chance. Julius had also changed his outward mode of behavior; he had become more sociable and though he had stopped seeing many people completely so as to tie himself more closely to a few, still he was no longer so strict and one-sided in his friendships but had learned to discover the noble in the ordinary. Gradually he attracted many excellent people to his side, and Lucinde united them and kept them going and in this way a free society came into being — or rather, a big family, which because of its high cultural niveau never grew stale. Deserving foreigners also had access to the circle — Julius didn't speak to them often but Lucinde knew how to entertain them. She did it with an air of grotesque universality and cultivated vulgarity so that there was never a pause or dissonance in the spiritual music whose beauty consisted precisely in its harmonious variety and change. In the social arts, besides the grand, ceremonious style, there should be a place too for merely charming mannerisms or passing fancies.

Julius seemed to be inspired with a feeling of universal tenderness, not just some pragmatic or pitying sympathy for the masses, but the joy of watching the beauty of mankind — mankind which lives forever while individuals vanish.

And he was moved also by a lively, open sensitivity to his own inmost self and that of others. He was almost always just as ready to take part in some very childlike sport as in the most sacred solemnity. No longer did he love the idea of friendship in his friends but loved them for themselves. When he talked to people who felt as he did, he tried to bring out every beautiful intuition and intimation that dwells in the soul. So his spirit was made whole and enriched in a variety of ways and circumstances. But here too he found full harmony only in Lucinde's soul — the soul in which the germs of everything magnificent and everything holy awaited only the sunlight of his spirit in order to unfold themselves into the most beautiful religion.

———— ◇ ————

Gladly do I return to the springtime of our love. I see all the changes and the transformations, relive them once more and would like to seize at least a few of the hazy outlines of our fleeting life, shape them into a permanent image, and do so now while the full, warm summer is still in me, now before it leaves me as well, before it is too late. While we live, we mortals are only the greatest creations of this beautiful earth. Man forgets that so easily: he disapproves highly of the eternal laws of the world and wants to find his beloved surface once again placed squarely in the center. Not so you and I. We are thankful for and satisfied with what the gods want and what they've written out so clearly in the holy scripture of nature's beauty. The humble mind recognizes that its natural destiny, like that of all things, is to blossom, to ripen, and to wilt away. But it knows that there is still something in it that will never die — namely, the eternal longing for eternal youth, which always exists and is always elusive. Even now in every beautiful soul gentle Venus still laments the death of her graceful Adonis. Sweetly desirous she awaits and looks for the youth; tenderly sad she remembers the heavenly eyes of her beloved, remembers his delicate features and childlike chatter and jokes, and then she smiles a tear, blushing sweetly to see herself now too among the flowers of the motley earth.

I want at least to suggest to you in divine symbols what I can't tell you in words. For as much as I think about the past and try to penetrate into my ego to examine my memories in the clarity of the present — and let you examine them as well — still something is always left that can't be described outwardly because it is wholly inward. Man's spirit is his own Proteus: it transforms itself and won't account for itself when it tries to come to grips with itself. In that deepest center of life, the creative will produces its magic. There are the beginnings and the ends where all the threads of the fabric of spiritual culture disappear. Only whatever advances gradually in time and extends in space, only what happens is the subject of history. But the mystery of a momentary beginning or transformation can only be divined and it can only be divined in allegory.

It's not without a reason that the fantastical boy whom I liked best of the four immortal Novels who appeared to me in the dream was playing with a mask. Allegory has crept even into what seems pure description and fact, and has mixed meaningful lies with beautiful truths. But only as a spiritual breath does allegory hover over the whole mass of things, like Wit who plays invisibly with his creation, only a trace of a smile playing on his lips.

There are poems in the old religion which even there seem

uniquely beautiful, delicate, and holy. Poetry has shaped and transformed these poems so finely and richly that their beautiful mean-
ingfulness has stayed ambiguous, and so permitted ever new interpretations and re-creations. In order to indicate to you something
of what I divine about the metamorphoses of the loving heart,
I've chosen among these poems those I believed the God of Harmony might have recounted to the Muses or heard from them after
Love had led him from the heavens to the earth and made him a
shepherd. At that time too, I believe, by the banks of the Amphry-
sos did he invent the Idyll and the Elegy.

Metamorphoses

Sweetly reposing the childlike spirit slumbers and the kiss of the
loving goddess stirs only happy dreams in him. The rose of shame
colors his cheek; he smiles and seems to open his lips, but does not
awaken and does not know what is happening to him. Only after
the stimulus of the outer world, multiplied and intensified by an
inner echo, has penetrated into every corner of his being, does he
open his eyes, rejoicing at the sun, and remembering the magic
world he saw in the glimmering light of the pale moon. The wonderful voice which woke him is still with him, but now, instead of
answering him, it re-echoes from the external objects; and when
with childlike timidity he tries to escape from the mystery of his
existence and, sweetly curious, seeks the unknown he hears everywhere only the resonance of his own yearning.

So the eye sees in the mirror of the river only the reflection of
the blue sky, the green banks, the swaying trees, and the form of
the gazer lost in contemplation of himself. When a heart full of
unconscious love finds itself where it hoped to find another's love,
then it is struck with amazement. But soon man lets himself be
tempted again, and deceived by the magic of self-observation into
loving his own shadow. Then the moment of graciousness has
come, then the soul once more constructs its shell, and blows the
last breath of perfection through its form. The spirit loses itself in

its translucent depths and, like Narcissus, rediscovers itself as a flower.

Love is greater than such graciousness, and how soon would the bloom of beauty wilt away fruitlessly without the complementary creation of shared love!

This moment, the kiss of Cupid and Psyche, is the rose of life. Inspired Diotima revealed to Socrates only the moiety of love. Love is not merely the quiet longing for eternity: it is also the holy enjoyment of a lovely presence. It is not merely a mixture, a transition from mortal to immortal: rather it is the total union of both. There exists a pure love, an indivisible and simple feeling without the slightest taint of restless striving. Each person gives exactly what he takes, each like the other; everything is equal and whole and complete in itself, like the eternal kiss of the divine children.

Through the magic of joy the great chaos of conflicting forms dissolves into a harmonious sea of forgetfulness. When the sunlight of happiness is refracted by the last tear of yearning, Iris is already painting the eternal brow of heaven with the delicate colors of her rainbow. The happy dreams come true, and the pure outlines of a new world arise from Lethe's waves, beautiful as Anadyomene, and unfold their shapes in place of the vanished darkness. In golden youth and innocence, time and man wander amid the godlike peace of nature; and ever Aurora returns, ever more beautiful.

Not hate, as the wise men say, but love, separates living creatures, and shapes the world; and only in love's light can you find this and observe it. Only in the answer of its "you" can every "I" wholly feel its boundless unity. Then the mind tries to unfold the inner bud of godlikeness, comes ever closer to succeeding, and is determined to shape the soul as the artist shapes the one work he loves most. In the mysteries of creation the spirit sees the operation and laws of destiny and life. Pygmalion's statue moves, and the astonished artist is seized by a tremor of happiness in the awareness of his immortality. And like the eagle with Ganymede, a divine hope bears him on mighty wings to Olympus.

Two Letters

I

It's really true then? What I've so often wished in secret and haven't dared to express? — I see the light of a sacred joy smiling on your face; and modestly you make the beautiful annunciation to me.

You're going to be a mother!

Adieu to yearning and to my gentle reproaches; the world is beautiful again. Now I love the earth, and the rosy dawn of a new spring raises its radiant head over my immortal existence. If I had laurel, I'd bind it around your brow to consecrate you to a new seriousness and a new activity: because a new life is now beginning for you too. But to me you should give the myrtle wreath. It's right that I should be adorned with the symbol of young innocence, since now I dwell in nature's paradise. What existed between us before was only love and passion. Now nature has tied us more closely together, more completely and inextricably. Nature alone is the true priestess of joy; only she knows how to tie the knot of marriage: not by means of empty words that have no blessing, but by fresh blossoms and living fruits from the fullness of her power. In the endless succession of new forms, creative time weaves the wreath of eternity, and the man who is touched by the joy of fruitfulness and health is blessed. We're not just sterile blossoms in the order of nature; the gods don't want to exclude us from the great chain of productive things; and they give us unmistakable signs of their will. And so let us earn our place in this lovely world, let us bear also the immortal fruits which the spirit and the will create, and let us enter into the dance of humanity. I want to plant myself in the earth, I want to sow and reap for the future and the present, I want to use all my powers as long as it is day, and then in the evening refresh myself in the arms of the mother who will forever be my bride. Our son, the little earnest imp, will play at our feet and connive with me to play mischievous tricks on you.

———◇———

Lucinde

You're right: we definitely have to buy that little estate in the country. I'm glad you took care of all the details at once without waiting for my decision. Arrange everything according to your taste: only, please don't make it too beautiful, or too functional, and, above all, don't make it too elaborate.

If you arrange everything entirely according to your own taste and don't let yourself be persuaded by anyone about what is "usual" and proper, then everything will be quite right, just as it should be and as I want it to be. Then I'll be tremendously happy with our beautiful property. Up to now whatever I've used, I've used thoughtlessly and without any feeling of ownership. I lived on this earth, but I was not at home on it. Now the sanctity of marriage has given me citizenship in the state of nature. I'm no longer suspended in the vacuum of a universal enthusiasm: now I'm happy in my gentle bondage, I understand the idea of utility in a new way, and find everything truly useful that joins an eternal love with its object — in short, anything that serves a real marriage. External objects themselves fill me with respect if they're good for something in their own way, and the time will come when you'll hear me sing rapturous praises about how good it is to have one's own home and how honorable domesticity is.

Now I understand your preference for living in the country: I share your preference and feel as you do. I can't bear anymore looking at those ungainly lumps of everything that's rotten and sick in mankind; and when I think of men in general terms they seem to me like wild animals on a chain who can't even rage in freedom. In the country, people can still be with each other without crowding themselves so vilely. In the country — if everything were as it ought to be — lovely houses and charming cottages could adorn the green earth like fresh plants and flowers, and make it a garden worthy of God.

To be sure, we'll find in the country the same meanness that still reigns everywhere else. All mankind should really be divided into only two separate classes: the creative and the created, the male and the female; and in place of all this artificial society there should

be a great marriage between these two classes and a universal brotherhood of all individuals. But instead there is only an infinity of
barbarity and, as insignificant exceptions, a few who are prevented
by virtue of their false education! But in the open air, the individ-
ually good and beautful can't be crushed by the evil mass and the
illusion of its omnipotence.

Do you know what period of our love glows particularly brilliantly in my memory? Of course, I remember everything as beautiful and pure, and I even think back to our first days with wistful
delight. But best of all these happy memories are still those last days
we spent together on the estate. One more reason for living again
in the country!

Another thing. Don't let them prune the vines too much. I'm
writing this only because you thought them simply too wild and
luxuriant, and because it might occur to you to try to make the
little house absolutely neat inside and out. The green lawn is also
to stay the way it is. There the baby shall romp, play, crawl, and
roll about.

———◇———

I've really made up for the pain which my sad letter caused you,
haven't I? Amid all these magnificent joys and in an ecstasy of
hope, I can no longer torment myself with worry. You weren't
hurt any more by it than I was. But what does it matter if you love
me, really love me deeply inside without holding anything back?
What pain would be worth talking about if we gain a warmer and
more profound consciousness of our love by means of it? You feel
that too. Everything I say to you, you've known long ago. In fact
there's no rapture or love in me that wasn't already hidden in some
deep recess of your infinite and happy being!

Misunderstandings are good too in that they provide a chance
to put what is holiest into words. The differences that now and
then seem to come between us aren't in us, in either of us. They're
only between us and on the surface, and I hope you'll take advan-

tage of this opportunity to drive them completely away from you and out of you.

And how do these little discords arise if not because of our common insatiability in giving love and being loved? Without this insatiability there is no love. We live and love to destruction. And if it is love that first makes us true and complete human beings and is the essence of life then love also shouldn't avoid conflict — avoid it as little as life and mankind do. And so the peace of love will ensue as well only after a struggle of opposing forces.

I feel myself fortunate that I love a woman who can love as you do. "As you do" is a mightier phrase than all superlatives. How can you possibly praise my words when, without wishing to, I hit on those that hurt you so much? I'd like to say I write too well to be able to tell you how I feel in the depths of my being. Oh my love! Believe me: there is no question in you that doesn't have its answer in me. Your love can't be more eternal than mine. But your being beautifully jealous of my imagination and its wild flights is delightful. That really shows how boundlessly faithful you are, but it also gives me hope that your jealousy is close to destroying itself in its own excesses.

There is no need for this kind of imagination — the written kind. I'll soon be with you. I'm holier and calmer now than before. In my mind I am always looking at you and standing before you. You feel everything without my telling you about it; and smile happily at your beloved husband and at the child beneath your heart.

———— ◇ ————

Do you remember how I wrote you that no memory could profane you for me, that you were eternally pure like the Holy Virgin of the Immaculate Conception, and that you lacked nothing but a child to make you a Madonna?

Now you have the child, now it exists, really exists. Soon I'll be carrying him in my arms, telling him stories, teaching him quite earnestly, and giving him good advice about how a young man should behave in the world.

A Novel

And then in my mind I return to the mother. I give you an unending kiss, see how your bosom rises in longing, and feel the mysterious stirrings beneath your heart.

———— ◇ ————

When we're together again, we'll try to be completely mindful of our youth, and I want to keep the present holy. You're quite right: one hour later is infinitely later.

It's cruel that just at this time I can't be with you! I do all sorts of stupid things out of impatience. I wander about almost from morning to night in this glorious landscape. I rush about as if I had something terribly important to do, and in the end I arrive at the one place I least wanted to get to. I make gestures as if I were delivering passionate speeches. I think I'm alone and suddenly I find myself in a crowd, and then I have to smile when I notice how lost in thought I was. And I can't write for very long; I only want to get outside again to dream away the lovely evening on the banks of the quiet stream.

Among other things I also forgot today that it was time to mail this letter. To make up for it you're getting an even greater dose of confusion and joy from me.

———— ◇ ————

People are really very good to me. Not only do they forgive me that I so often don't take part in their conversation and then interrupt it in some peculiar way, but they seem even to take a secret and heartfelt pleasure in my happiness. Particularly Juliane. I only tell her very little about you, but she has a great deal of intuition for these things and guesses what I don't tell her. There's really nothing more amiable than this kind of pure unselfish delight in love!

Of course I'm sure that I would love my friends here even if they were less admirable than they are. I feel a great change in my being: there is a general softness and sweet warmth in my soul and mind, a feeling like the beautiful fatigue of the senses that follows the moment of the most intense existence.

And yet it's anything but indolence. On the contrary, I know from now on I'll do everything pertaining to my calling with greater love and renewed strength. I have never felt more courageous and more confident of being able to act as a man among men, of beginning and carrying out a heroic life, and of joining with my friends in a brotherly union performing immortal deeds.

That is my virtue; so does it suit me to become like the gods. Yours is to be, like nature, a priestess of joy, gently revealing the mystery of love, and, surrounded by worthy sons and daughters, hallowing this beautiful life into a holy festival.

———— ◇ ————

I often worry about your health. You don't dress warmly enough and have a liking for the evening air! These are dangerous habits and not the only ones you're going to have to get rid of.

Remember that you're now beginning a new order of things. Up to now I always thought your frivolity was beautiful because it was appropriate at the time and in harmony with everything else. I thought it feminine that you could make a game out of happiness and abandon all thought of consequences and annihilate whole portions of your life or of your surroundings.

But now something else exists which you'll always have to take into consideration, around which your whole world will turn. Now you'll gradually have to adapt yourself to housekeeping—in an allegorical sense, of course.

———— ◇ ————

In this letter everything is really mixed up, just as praying and eating, mischief and ecstasy are mixed up in life. And now, good night. Oh why can't I be with you at least in my dreams, really with you and dreaming in you! For when I'm only dreaming of you, I'm still always alone. You want to know why you don't dream of me, though you think of me so much? My love, don't you often and for a long time keep silent about me?

———— ◇ ————

I was very happy to get Amalie's letter. Of course I see from her flattering tone that she doesn't exclude me from that class of men who need flattery. I don't expect her to either. It would be unfair to ask that she should value me at our reckoning. It's enough that *one* woman understands me completely! And in her own way she does appreciate me so perfectly! Does she know what *worship* is? I doubt it, and I pity her if she doesn't. Don't you too?

———— ◇ ————

Today I found in a French book this statement about two lovers: "They were the universe to each other."

It struck me — and I was moved and smiled at the idea — how something that had been set down so thoughtlessly as hyperbole had become literally true with us!

Actually it's also literally true for this kind of French passion. They discover the universe in each other because they've lost their sense for everything else.

We haven't. Everything that we loved before, we love even more warmly now. It's only now that a feeling for the world has really dawned on us. You've come to know the infinity of the human spirit through me, and I've come to understand marriage and life, and the magnificence of all things through you.

For me everything has a soul, speaks to me, and is holy. When one loves as we do, then even human nature returns to its original state of divinity. In the solitary embrace of lovers, sensual pleasure becomes once more what it basically is — the holiest miracle of nature; and what for others is only something about which they're justifiably ashamed becomes for us again what it is in and of itself: the pure flame of the noblest life force.

———— ◇ ————

Lucinde

Our child will certainly have three things: a great deal of wantonness, a serious face, and some kind of artistic talent. I await everything else with calm resignation. Son or daughter — about that I can have no particular preference. But I've already thought very much about the child's education: that is, how we're going to manage carefully to save it from any sort of "education." I've thought more about this problem than, say, three reasonable fathers would think and worry about how they'll be able to tie up their offspring in a morass of morality, starting right from the moment the baby is in the cradle.

I've made some preliminary sketches that you'll like, and I made them with you in mind. Only make sure you don't neglect art! Would you rather have a portrait or a landscape for your daughter, if it should be a daughter?

———— ◇ ————

How foolish you are with your concern for outer appearances! You want to know what my surroundings are, where, when, and how I do everything, how I live and am? — Just look around you, at the chair next to you, in your arms, in your heart: that's where I live and am. Doesn't a ray of longing strike you and steal into your heart with its sweet warmth, to your lips where it almost overflows with kisses?

And now you're even claiming you've always written such heartfelt letters to me, whereas I only write that way sometimes, you little pedant! In the first place, I always think of you just as you tell me you think of me: I think I'm walking beside you, looking at you, hearing you, speaking to you. But then I think of you in other ways too, particularly when I wake up at night.

———— ◇ ————

How can you even doubt the goodness and godlikeness of your letters! The last one glances and shines with bright eyes; it isn't a letter, it's a song.

I think if I were to stay away from you a few months longer, you'd develop your style fully. But in any case, I think it's more advisable for us to abandon these matters of style and writing for now, and no longer postpone the greatest and loveliest of studies. I've more or less decided to begin my return trip in about a week.

SECOND LETTER

It's odd that man is not afraid of himself. Children are quite right to look so curiously and yet so apprehensively into the faces of strangers. Every single atom of eternal time can contain a world of joy but can also reveal a bottomless pit of sorrows and horror. Now I understand the old story of the man whom a magician let live through a period of many years in a few moments; for I've experienced in myself the terrible omnipotence of the imagination.

Since your sister's last letter — three days ago — I've endured the sufferings of a whole lifetime, from the sunlight of fiery youth to the pale moonlight of hoary old age.

Every little detail she wrote me about your illness together with what the doctor told me the last time you were sick, and what I had seen myself, confirmed my suspicions that this disease was much more serious than any of you realized — in fact, no longer dangerous but hopeless.

Sunk in these thoughts, paralyzed by the impossibility of rushing to you from this great distance, I was really in a desperate state. Only now do I actually realize how desperate I was, now that I've been reborn by the joyful news of your recovery. For you're recovered now, as good as completely well again — I gather this from all the reports with the same confidence with which I condemned us both to death a few days ago.

I didn't think of it as something that was going to happen or that was happening now. It was all finished. You'd already been hidden in the womb of the cool earth for a long time; flowers were budding little by little on your beloved grave, and my tears were already flowing more slowly. I stood silent and alone and saw nothing but the features I loved and the sweet look of your expressive eyes. This image stayed with me ineradicably: only now and then did your pale face, smiling its last in a final slumber, quietly take its place. Or suddenly these different memories would become confused. Their outlines changed incredibly quickly, resumed their previous shape, and changed again, until everything vanished from my overwrought imagination. Only your holy eyes remained in the vacant space and hung there motionless like the friendly stars glimmering forever on our misery. I looked fixedly at the black lights beckoning to me with a familiar smile in the night of my sorrow. Now a piercing pain from dark suns burned me with unbearable brilliance, now a beautiful luminosity hovered and flowed as if to lure me on. Then it seemed as if a fresh morning air were breathing on me; I raised my head up high, and a voice called loudly from within me: "Why should you torture yourself? In a few moments you can be with her."

I was already rushing to follow you, but suddenly a new idea stopped me and I said to myself: "You're unworthy; you can't even endure the minor discords of this ordinary life, and you still consider yourself ripe for and deserving of a higher one? Go, suffer and do what you are called upon to do, and come again when your orders have been carried out." Doesn't it strike you too that everything on this earth strives toward the middle, how everything is so orderly, so meaningless and petty? It's always seemed that way to me; and so I suspect — and, if I'm not mistaken, once told you about this suspicion — that our next life will be greater, more strikingly good and evil, wilder, bolder, more terrible.

The duty to live had won, and I was once again in the turmoil of human life, of its and my weak struggles and flawed efforts. Then a feeling of terror overcame me, like that of a man finding himself suddenly alone in the middle of an immeasurable waste of icy mountains. Everything was cold and alien, and even my tears froze.

Strange worlds appeared and disappeared in this terrifying dream. I was ill and suffered a great deal, but I loved my illness and even welcomed pain. I hated everything earthly and was happy to see it punished and destroyed. I felt so very alone and strange; and just as, in the bloom of happiness, a sensitive person often becomes sad at the prospect of his own joy, and just as the feeling of futility overcomes us at the high point of our lives, so did I look with secret pleasure at my own pain. It became the symbol of all life for me; I thought I was feeling and seeing the eternal discord through which all things come into being and exist, and the lovely forms of peaceful creation seemed to me dead and trivial in comparison to this monstrous world of infinite power, of unending struggle and strife down to the furthest depths of existence.

My sickness was transformed by this strange feeling into a world perfect and complete in itself. I felt that its mysterious life was fuller and deeper than the ordinary health of the dreaming sleep-walkers around me. And along with my sickliness — a sickliness not at all unpleasant to me — this feeling stayed with me and cut me off completely from the rest of mankind, just as I was separated from the earth by the idea that your being and my love had been too holy not to escape quickly from its coarse ties. It seemed to me that it was right that everything should be as it was, and that your fated death was nothing more than a gentle awakening from a light slumber.

It seemed to me too that I awakened when I looked at your picture and saw it transfigured more and more into a serene purity and universality. Serious but charming, completely you and yet no longer you, your godlike form transfused with a wonderful glow. One moment it was like the terrifying light of visible omnipotence, the next a friendly gleam of golden childhood. My spirit drank with long, silent draughts from this source of cool, pure fire, secretly intoxicating itself with it, and in this blissful drunkenness I felt a peculiar kind of spiritual worth because in fact all worldly thoughts were completely foreign to me and I never lost the feeling that I was consecrated to death.

The years slowly passed by and one event tiresomely succeeded another; one work and then another achieved its end, an end as little my own as my taking those events and works merely for what they seemed to be. They were only holy symbols for me, all of them referring to the only beloved one, who was the mediator between my dismembered self and indivisible eternal humanity. My whole existence was an uninterrupted divine service of solitary love.

At last I realized that the end had come. My brow was no longer smooth and my hair had grown white. My life was finished but had not been completed. My most productive years were past and yet art and virtue still stood eternally unattainable before me. I would have despaired if I hadn't seen and worshipped both in you, most gracious Madonna! And seen you and your gentle godliness in myself.

Then you appeared beckoning me with the summons of death. A heartfelt longing for you and for freedom seized me; I yearned to be back in my dear old homeland and was just about to shake the dust of the journey from me when I was recalled again to life by the promise and reassurance of your recovery.

Now I became aware of my waking dream, was alarmed at all its meaningful connections and resemblances, and stood fearful at the edge of the invisible abyss of this inner truth.

Do you know what has become most clear to me because of this? First, that I worship you, and that it's good for me to do so. We two are one, and man only becomes a man and completely himself when he thinks and imagines himself as the center of all things, and the spirit of the world. But why do so when we find the seed of everything in ourselves and yet remain forever only a fragment of ourselves?

And I know now that death can also be a sweet and beautiful thing. I realize how a creature that is free and in the flower of its life can secretly long for its own dissolution and freedom, how it can look on the idea of return as a morning sun of hope.

A Reflection

It has often struck me as strange that sensible and respectable people could repeat this petty game and repeat it again in an eternally recurring cycle, performing it with untiring energy and enormous seriousness. And really the game apparently has no function or purpose, even though it may be the oldest of all games.

A Novel

Then my mind inquired what nature intended — nature that is always so thoughtful, so enormously cunning, and that, instead of merely speaking wittily, *acts* wittily — then I asked myself what nature might mean by those naive allusions that educated people only refer to anonymously.

And this anonymity itself has a double meaning. The more shamefaced and modern one becomes, the more fashionable is it to interpret the anonymity shamelessly. For the gods of antiquity, on the other hand, all life has a certain classical dignity, even the shameless heroic art of begetting life. The number of such productions and the degree of ingenuity determine their rank and nobility in the realm of mythology.

This number and this ingenuity are good, but they are not the best. Then where does the longed-for ideal lie hidden? Or does the searching heart find in the highest of all plastic arts only more mannerisms and never a perfect style?

The mind has this peculiarity, that next to itself it loves to think most about something it can think about forever. Hence, the life of the cultivated and meditative man is a continual cultivation and meditation on the lovely riddle of his destiny. He is continually defining it anew for himself, for that is precisely his whole destiny, to be defined and to define. Only in the search itself does the human mind find the secret that it seeks.*

But what, then, is the definer or the defined itself? For the man it is the anonymous. And what is the anonymous for the woman? The indefinite.

The indefinite is more mysterious, but the definite has greater magical power. The charming confusion of the indefinite is more romantic, but the noble refinement of the definite is more like genius. The beauty of the indefinite is perishable, like the life of flowers and the eternal youth of human feelings; the energy of the definite is fleeting like a genuine thunderstorm and genuine inspiration.

Who can measure and who can compare two things that are in-

* There is a pun throughout this section on *Bestimmung*, which can mean both destiny and definition.

finitely valuable, when both are joined by the real definition that is destined to fill all lacunae and be the mediator between the individual man and woman and eternal mankind?

The definite and the indefinite and the whole wealth of their definite and indefinite relations: that is the one and the all, the strangest and yet the simplest, the simplest and yet the best. The universe itself is only a plaything of the definite and the indefinite; and the real definition of the definable is an allegorical miniature of the warp and woof of everflowing creation.

With eternally immutable symmetry both strive in opposite directions toward the infinite and away from it. In a quiet but sure progression the indefinite expands its innate desire from the beautiful midpoint of the finite into the infinite. The perfectly definite, on the other hand, leaps daringly out of the blessed dream of infinite desire into the limits of finite action, and, refining itself, continually increases in magnanimous self-restraint and beautiful self-sufficiency.

The incredible humor with which nature consistently carries out its simplest and most universal antithesis is revealed here in this symmetry as well. Even in its most ornate and artificial structure these comic barbs of the universe manifest themselves with roguish meaning like a miniature portrait and confer on all individuality — which arises out of and exists only through them and the seriousness of their play — its final shape and perfection.

Through this individuality and that allegory the colorful ideal of witty sensuality blossoms forth out of a striving toward the absolute.

Now everything is clear! Hence the omnipresence of the anonymous unknown Godhead. Nature itself wills the eternal cycle of eternally repeated experiments; and nature also wills that every individual should be perfect in himself, unique and new, a true image of supreme, indivisible individuality.

Plunging deeper into this individuality, my reflection pursued such an individualistic turn that it soon ended and forgot itself.

———— ◇ ————

A Novel

"What's the point of all these allusions that I won't say play but conflict nonsensically, with incomprehensible comprehension, at the heart of sensuality and not just at its borders?"

To be sure, neither you nor Juliane would say something like this, but surely you would ask it.

My dearly beloved! Can a perfect bouquet of flowers only be made up of demure roses, quiet forget-me-nots, modest violets, and any other flower that is virginal and childlike, and not contain whatever else glows with the glory of strange and brilliant colors?

Male clumsiness is full of variety and rich in blossoms and fruits of every kind. Yet even the wonderful plant that I won't name must have its place. At least it serves as a foil for the brightly burning pomegranate and the luminous oranges. Or should there be, perhaps, instead of all this wealth of color, only one perfect flower combining in itself all the beauties of the others and making their existence unnecessary?

I don't excuse myself for something that I'd like to do again immediately, and I have full confidence in your objective feeling for the artistic productions of a clumsiness that often and not unwillingly takes the raw materials of its creations from masculine inspiration.

It consists of a delicate *furioso* and a clever *adagio* of friendship; you'll be able to learn a good deal from it: namely that men know how to hate with extraordinary delicacy, just as you women know how to love; that they transform a quarrel, when it is over, into a distinction; and that you can make as many observations about it as you like.

Julius to Antonio

I

You've changed a great deal of late! Take care, my friend, that you don't lose your feeling for greatness before you're aware of it. And what will be the result of that? You'll finally have acquired so much delicacy and refinement that all your heart and feeling will have disappeared. And where will your manhood and decisiveness be then? The time may yet come when I'll treat you as you treat me, since we're no longer living together but only near each other. I'll have to put limits on you and tell you that even if you do have a sense for everything beautiful, you still lack a sense for friendship. Even so, I'll never set myself up as a moral critic of a friend, of what he does or doesn't do; whoever can bring himself to do that doesn't deserve the rare happiness of having a friend. That you're wronging yourself primarily only makes matters worse. Tell me seriously: do you expect to find virtue in those cool subtleties of feeling, those gymnastics of the spirit that consume the healthy marrow of a man's life and leave him hollow inside?

I've kept quiet and resigned myself to the situation for quite some time now. I didn't have the slightest doubt that you, who know so much, would also know the reasons for the end of our friendship. It seems almost as if I've been wrong in this assumption, since you've shown yourself *so* surprised at my wanting to be intimate with Edward, and since you as it were seemed to ask uncomprehendingly how you had offended me. If it were only that, only some single and definite thing, then it wouldn't be worth asking such a painful question, it would answer and resolve itself. But isn't it more than that, when each time I have to feel it as a fresh desecration to tell you everything about Edward, just as it happened? Of course, you've done nothing against him, or even said anything out loud; but I know and see very well how you do think about him. And if I didn't know and see it, where then would be the invisible communion of our minds and the beautiful magic of this communion? You certainly can't be thinking of holding back any longer and trying to resolve the misunderstanding by sheer finesse, for in that case I'd really have nothing more to say to you.

You two are unquestionably separated by an unbridgeable gulf. The calm, clear depth of your personality and the hot struggle of his fretful activity are at the opposite poles of human existence. He is all action; you have a sensitive and spectatorial personality. For precisely that reason you ought to have a feeling for everything —

and you have it too whenever you don't close yourself off intentionally. And that irks me really. I'd rather you hated this magnificent person than misjudged him! But what will this unnatural habit of yours lead to, this habit of evaluating whatever small portion of greatness and beauty that's still left in the world as cheaply as an intelligent person possibly can without losing all pretense to meaning? In the final analysis you have to become yourself what you want to see in others.

Is this your vaunted tolerance? Of course, you observe the principle of equality: one person doesn't fare much better with you than another — except that each one is misunderstood in his own way. Didn't you also force me never to say anything to you or anyone else about everything Edward holds most sacred? And that's because you couldn't withhold your judgment until the proper time, because your mind is always imagining limitations in others before it has discovered its own. You've almost brought me to the point of having to explain to you how great my own worth actually is, how much better and fairer you would have been if now and then you hadn't judged but believed, if somewhere along the line you had assumed in me the existence of some unknown infinite quality.

Of course, my own negligence is to blame for the whole thing. Perhaps it was also willful of me to want to share all of the present with you and yet not teach you about what the past and the future are. I don't know: my feelings were against it, and I thought it unnecessary, because in fact I had enormous confidence in your intelligence.

Oh Antonio, if I were able to doubt the eternal verities, then you would have brought me to the point of thinking of that calm and beautiful friendship, founded on the simple harmony of being and living together, as something false and perverted!

You still don't understand, then, why it is that I've swung completely over to the other side? I renounce refined pleasures and plunge myself into the wild battle of life. I'm going to Edward. It's all arranged already. We don't plan just to live together but to breathe and act together in a brotherly union. He is rough and un-polished, his virtue is strength rather than sensitivity, but he has a great, manly heart, and in any better age he would have been — I say it unabashedly — a hero.

II

It was good that we finally talked with each other again. I'm glad too of your reluctance to write and your scolding the poor innocent alphabet, because you really do have a much greater gift for talking. But I still have a few things on my mind I couldn't tell you about that I'll try to communicate in writing.

Why in writing? Oh my friend, if I only knew a finer and sub-tler means of communication, some more delicately veiled, more gently detached way than this to tell you what I want to! For me a conversation is too loud, too intimate, too disjointed. The discon-nected words always reflect only a single side, one part of the con-nected whole I want to suggest in its full harmony.

And is it possible for men who want to live together to be too polite to each other? It isn't as if I were afraid of saying something too harsh, and for that reason avoided mentioning certain people and certain matters in our conversation. As far as that's concerned, I think, the dividing line between us has surely been done away with forever!

What I still wanted to tell you is something quite general; and yet I prefer to choose this roundabout way of doing it. I don't know if it's out of a sense of false or true delicacy, but it would be hard for me to say much about friendship face to face with you.

And yet it's about my thoughts on this subject that I must write you. The application — and that's the most important thing — you can easily make for yourself.

To my way of thinking there are two kinds of friendship.

The first is completely external. It rushes insatiably from deed to deed, and accepts every deserving man into the great brother-hood of united heroes; it ties the old knot faster with every virtue and always tries to widen its ranks. The more it has, the more it wants.

Remember the example of former ages and you'll find this sort of friendship everywhere, fighting its just war against everything evil, be it in us or in some object of our love. You'll discover it wherever the noble force influences great masses and creates worlds or rules them.

We live in different times now. But the ideal of this kind of friendship will stay in me for as long as I continue to be myself.

The other kind is completely internal — a wonderful symmetry of the most characteristic qualities, as if it had been predestined that one friend should complement the other in every way. All their thoughts and feelings grow companionable through the mutual stimulation and development of what is holiest in them. And this purely spiritual love, this beautiful mysticism of companionship, doesn't just hover about them distantly like the far-off goal of some possibly futile aspiration. No, it is to be found only as an accomplished fact. And there is no disillusionment in it as in the other, heroic kind of friendship. There, only the result shows if a man is true. But whoever feels and recognizes the world and mankind within himself will not be easily led to look for a universal meaning and a universal spirit where they don't exist.

Only someone who has achieved complete inner composure, and knows how to honor humbly the godlike quality of the other, is capable of this kind of friendship.

When the gods have given such friendship to a man, then he can do nothing more than protect it carefully against any external danger and safeguard its holy essence. For the delicate flower is mortal.

Yearning and Peace

Lightly clad, Lucinde and Julius stood by the window of the pavilion, refreshing themselves in the cool morning air. They were absorbed in contemplating the rising sun that all the birds were greeting with a happy song.

"Julius," Lucinde asked, "why do I feel this deep sense of yearning amid this happy peace?" "Only in yearning do we find peace," replied Julius. "Yes, there is peace only when our spirit remains completely undisturbed in its yearning and seeking after itself, only when it can find nothing higher than its own yearning."

"Only in the peacefulness of night," said Lucinde, "do yearning and love glow and glitter as brightly and fully as this glorious sun." "And during the day," answered Julius, "the happiness of love shines as palely as the moon's chary light." "Or appears and vanishes suddenly into universal darkness," added Lucinde. "Like those flashes of lightning that lit up our room while the moon was hidden."

"Only at night," said Julius, "does the tiny nightingale express its plaints and deep sighs in song. Only at night does the flower shyly spread out its petals and freely exhale its lovely fragrance, making both sense and spirit equally drunk with rapture. Only at night, Lucinde, does the deep fire of love and its daring eloquence flow divinely from lips that in the noise of the day close with tender pride on their own sweet treasure."

Lucinde. I am not, my Julius, the sanctified person you describe, even though I might like to sing laments like the nightingale, and though I am, as I deeply feel, consecrated to the night alone. You are that person. When the turmoil has died down and nothing mean or common distracts your noble soul, then you see reflected in me — in me who am forever yours — the marvelous flower of your imagination.

Julius. Away with such modesty! Don't flatter me. Remember: you are the priestess of the night. Even in the light of the sun, the dark brilliance of your thick hair, the bright blackness of your earnest eyes, and the majesty of your head and body proclaim that fact.

Lucinde. My eyes sink to the ground as you praise them, for now the noisy morning blinds them, and the motley song of happy birds troubles and frightens my soul. At another time, in the still, cool darkness of evening, my ears would wish to drink greedily of my sweet lover's sweet talk.

Julius. It's not simply a product of my imagination. My yearning for you is boundless and always unsatisfied.

Lucinde. Let it be what it may: you are the fixed point where my spirit finds its peace.

Julius. I found holy peace only in that yearning, my love.

Lucinde. And I that holy yearning only in this lovely peace.

Julius. Oh, that the harsh light might be allowed to lift the veil which so concealed these flames, and that the play of the senses might cool and soothe my inflamed soul!

Lucinde. So too shall the eternally cold and earnest day of life in time destroy the warm night, when youth departs and I give you up as you once, in a more noble fashion, sacrificed your great love.

Julius. Oh, that I might show and make my friend known to you; and show *her* the wonder of my wonderful happiness.

Lucinde. You still love her and shall love her as eternally as you shall love me. That is the great wonder of your wonderful heart.

Julius. Not more wonderful than yours. I see you leaning against my breast, playing with the locks of your Guido's hair — the two of us joined in brotherly union, and you girding our honored brows with eternal wreaths of joy.

Lucinde. Let them rest in darkness; don't drag into the light the flowers of the heart's secret depths.

Julius. Where can the wave of life sport with the wild one, whom sensitivity and a harsh destiny dragged brutally into the harsh world?

Lucinde. Uniquely transfigured, the pure image of your noble unknown friend glows in the blue sky of your pure soul.

Julius. Oh eternal yearning! Still at last the fruitless yearning and vain brilliance of the day shall vanish and expire, and a great night of love make itself felt in eternal peace.

Lucinde. So — if I may be what I am — does a woman's heart feel in a breast warmed by love. My heart yearns only for your yearning, finds peace only where you find it.

Dalliance of the Imagination

Life itself, that tender child of the gods, is shunted aside by the difficult and noisy preparations for living, and care, which loves as monkeys do, stifles it miserably in its embraces.

To have intentions, to act according to intentions, to weave one intention artificially into another intention so as to arrive at another: still this perversion is rooted so deeply in godlike man's idiotic nature that if he wants to move freely and for once completely unintentionally on the inner stream of eternally flowing images and feelings, he actually has to intend consciously and formally to do so.

The acme of intelligence is choosing to keep silent, restoring the soul to the imagination, and not disturbing the sweet dalliance of the young mother and her baby.

But after the golden age of its innocence, the mind only very rarely shows itself so reasonable. It wants to have sole possession of the soul, and even when the soul supposes itself alone with its innate love, the mind listens furtively and substitutes, instead of the sacred games of childhood, the mere memory of former purposes or the prospect of future ones. Yes, the mind knows how to lend a tinge of color and a fleeting warmth to these cold and hollow illusions, and through its imitative art tries to rob the innocent imagination of its most intrinsic quality.

But the youthful soul doesn't let itself be cheated by the cunning of this precocious deceiver and is always watching its darling play with the lovely images of the beautiful world. Willingly the soul allows garlands to adorn its head, garlands that the child weaves out of the flowers of life, and willingly does the soul let itself drop into a waking sleep, dreaming of the music of love and hearing the mysteriously friendly voices of the gods like the disconnected sounds of a faraway romance.

Old familiar feelings reverberate out of the depths of the past and future. Softly they touch the listener and quickly lose themselves again in the background of muted music and dimmed love. Everything loves and lives, laments and rejoices in a lovely confusion. Here at this noisy festival, the lips of all the happy open in a universal song; and here the lonely girl is mute in the presence of the friend to whom she would like to confide, denying him a kiss with a smile on her lips. Full of thoughts I strew flowers on the grave of my too soon departed son, and then give them, filled with joy and hope, to the bride of my beloved brother, while the high priestess beckons me and reaches out her hand for an earnest union, to vow, by the eternally pure fire, eternal purity and eternal inspiration. I rush from the altar and from the priestess to seize a sword and plunge into battle with an army of heroes, but soon I forget them, gazing in deepest solitude only at myself and the sky above me.

The soul that slumbers in such dreams, dreams them forever, even when it wakes. It feels itself entwined by the blossoms of love, and takes care not to destroy the loose garlands; it is gladly made a prisoner, dedicating itself to the imagination, and does not willingly let itself be ruled by the child who makes up for all the sorrows of motherhood by his sweet dalliance.

Then a fresh breath of early blossomtime and a halo of childlike bliss blows over all of life. The man worships his mistress, the mother her child, and all worship everlasting humanity.

Now the soul understands the lament of the nightingale and the smile of the newly born babe, understands the deep significance of the mysterious hieroglyphs on flowers and stars, understands the holy meaning of life as well as the beautiful language of nature. All things speak to the soul and everywhere the soul sees the loving spirit through the delicate veil.

On this festively bedecked ground the soul glides through the airy dance of life, innocent, and only concerned to follow the rhythm of companionship and friendship and not disturb the harmony of love.

And in the midst of all this: an eternal song of which the soul catches only now and then a few words that hint at ever greater wonders.

Lucinde

Always more beautifully does this magical circle encompass the soul. It can never escape, and what it forms or speaks sounds like a wonderful romance about the lovely mysteries of childhood's world of gods — a story accompanied by an enchanting music of the feelings and adorned with the most meaningful blossoms of lovely life.

Fragments of the Proposed Continuation of Lucinde

The Story of a Joke: Lucinde to Julius

LIKE you I've already learned to fuse the idea of death fearlessly with that of the highest bliss in the daring and shamelessness of love. It was love and love alone that gave me the courage to contemplate and understand this inner schism calmly, this eternal hate inherent in all existence for as long as the great spectacle of glorious forces animates the green earth with lovely fullness, and furtively and openly stirs and moves everywhere: this divine hate, this hate of climactic power and intense vitality. And love taught me also to make a heartfelt surrender to nature, and gave me the courage to feel, even at a play that often grips the spectator suddenly when he least expects it and drags him into the wild maelstrom of the unending spectacle that, just a moment ago, he was watching calmly — love gave me the courage to feel, even at the moment when it was my turn to experience what I've just been talking about, something even holier than the holy terror of dark omnipotence, because, along with the crowded fullness of the struggling earth, the bright glory of heaven too has become clear to me, because I look into myself and know that a time will come – no, won't come: is here already and always was – a time when behind his motley shell man will soar gently and purely to the light in a direct, unimpeded upward movement, as he has always hoped to do, at peace with himself, contemplating himself and the Godhead.

Yes, that's it; childish mirth and bitter pain, passionate anger and calm dreaminess, death and love, lust and piety, mad impudence and melancholy (gentle sighs that never escape me), dark grief and bright exuberance: that is what stands before me in starkly simple outline and looks at me, what lives and struggles in effusions and jokes, in stories and flirtations, in letters and dreams, conversations and speeches; that is the spirit and subject of your poem, and that is why it is so dear to me, why I press it so gladly to my heart with profound love and *awe*: for here I've found the clearest image of my own (most intense) longing.

Oh, if there were only words to express it! But nobody has ever understood himself yet. Find the words for me: I know the song. And when that too dies away, then, pointing at the colors of the pictures before us, we will signify mutely what we could not say.

Of the Nature of Friendship

Julius. I understand it. I even believe it. A joke can make a joke about everything: a joke is free and universal. But I'm against it. There are places in my being, the deepest ones in fact, where for that reason an ordinary hurt is unimaginable. And in these places a joke is intolerable to me.

Lorenzo. So the seriousness of these places is probably not completely perfect yet. Otherwise there would be irony there by now. But for that very reason irony exists. You'll only have to wait awhile.

Julius. You're taking the words out of my mouth. I don't mind the sensual corporeal joke; but I do object precisely to the most spiritual, delicate, and deliberate, the holiest element in them. You used the word yourself: it's irony that has often disturbed me in the music of friendship with its distinctly discordant note.

Lorenzo. So the note was probably put in too often, or in the wrong place. But that's not the fault of the note. Still, you may be right. And who knows if that isn't the irony of irony, that in the end one grows to dislike it.

Julius. The final irony, I think, is to be found rather in that it seems to be becoming impossible for you to talk about irony without being ironic.

Lorenzo. I'm afraid that it's exactly the other way around. Where's the irony, when in bitter earnest one doesn't know where one's at? And the more I think about it, the more incomprehensible it becomes.

Julius. What's the name of the riddle?

Lorenzo. That of all things you should find friendship incompatible with irony.

Julius. Well?

Lorenzo. Well, if irony isn't the real essence of friendship, then perhaps the gods know what it really is, or irony itself knows. I don't.

Julius. And irony does know when its essence is in harmony with its purpose.

Lorenzo. That is, when the friends know it.

Julius. No. They often don't know, but irony does.

Lorenzo. How do you know that, my friend?

Julius. When I myself still wasn't aware, and didn't imagine what this divine quality and struggle in me was, irony already knew where it was tending to and to what end — and irony showed by its actions that it knew. It attached itself profoundly only to what was just and, after a brief experiment, despised all that was unjust; it affirmed itself, expanded, became clear and conscious of its power, became wise, just as everything that is human becomes wise, through action. For surely you don't want to restrict knowledge to everything that can be said.

To Maria

In Lucinde's love the earth shone for me with a fresh and bright radiance. Your eyes remind me of the sky, your song tempts me into the depths.

––––––– ◇ –––––––

I can only entrust my joys to the night, and in the night will I carefully hide them. For I feel they'll wilt when the day comes.

Guido's Death

Yes, I want to, and so let me take up for the first and certainly the last time my simple pen before my trembling hand denies even this small service to the departed, or before my disordered senses become completely confused. Let me try to remind myself and my own of myself and my love, so that perhaps some lucky chance might bear these mortal pages from afar to the light of those eyes that shone lovingly on others, and for me alone ruinously illuminated for a few moments the night of my life like a stroke of lightning, only to deliver it up to its own darkness forever.

I would welcome pain if I could feel you! If pity can suffer, then let it kill me. But as it happens, I see down into the darkest depths what it is that lacerates others, and this clear intuition soon escapes me in loud songs so that all hearts weep. But what my disordered heart has endured no song may yet express harmoniously. On the mute page, in the confusion of the unfeeling strokes of the pen, there it may listen furtively and terrifyingly, like the snake plotting ruin.

I've loved, but I haven't lived. I'm well aware of that, for life to me was only a wearisome feeling of approaching death, and so, in future memories of me, that dark name may well be always associated with mine.

Oh, there is a melodious spirit that dwells in sounds and words, and one could love life because of it. It drags one down, deep, deep, and ever deeper. Then everything is quiet and friendly and beautiful; one can't even express what it's like.

A Novel

It wasn't always that way. Because that time when the lovely light touched my heart was also the first time I really felt music, the first time I felt it distinctly. Then everything was new: there was sound everywhere and, amazed and mystified, I heard myself in my own sounds. Now music is in a bad way, for I'm only an instrument for another to play. But now no one can play it. So what's the good of it? It has to be broken, this instrument.

Sometimes I'm afraid; but I can't be mad, for otherwise how would I know what had hurt me? Alas, I still remember quite well how it was when I lived with that glorious woman. She had everything I lacked: light and joy and strength. But as deeply as I loved her and as warmly as she loved me, we were strangers to each other. That drove me away; that is why I had to flee from you, Lucinde; that is why you couldn't save me, Julius, friend unlike any other friend: unique, sincere, beloved.

Afterwards everything was completely different. I was violently startled: I had met someone who was like me. Why wasn't I able to hide my happiness?

I got what I deserved; I shouldn't have revealed the secret. I should have hid them carefully in darkest night, those joys of the night. They withered because day came, the day: they couldn't tolerate the day.

Oh I could say a great deal about it, but now there's no more time, for they've been waiting for me a long time already. After Maria died I no longer thought of you two. I've only remembered just now. You must forgive that; I will try to forgive what I can.

Farewell, Julius; these are the last words from your friend. Farewell, both of you. You'll find the songs with the child. I hid them.

Juliane

I'd like to remain silent and yet I have to speak; my heart is full and yet I don't know of anything I have to say; and if I knew, where would there be anyone who'd want to listen — I seem dissatisfied, and I am grateful. I know it. And yes, you'll hear me, but

135

no one, not even you, will hear my suffering. And why should anyone? If something can be said it's no longer worth saying. I feel that; I see it; and still something forces me to talk. Everything is disconnected, and yet I know in my heart that the underlying connection is only too real.

You are good, you are Lucinde, you are all light and love. How like each other we are in our feelings! You often frighten me, you know my innermost thoughts so well! I'm well aware that you feel differently about men, but even that can't bother me. You're the one who's courageous, full of life, the one who's still unique for me. Oh if I'd only given you the children and died young! But it wasn't to be. My greatest love came too late.

———◇———

Do you think I want to speak of the children? Oh no, I can't do that: it would be good if I could. That's over with, I won't cry anymore; they carried my tears along with them into the grave. Where my little girl rests, where my boy smiles and holds his hand out to me, that's where my tears are. I live mutely and without joy.

———◇———

Oh, I've always watched glorious people rising up out of the masses: what is it they're rushing off to do? Everyone is rushing to destroy himself and everyone else. Yes, it's a sign that man has achieved understanding and maturity, that he's flourishing mightily, when he begins to inflame himself within himself, and rage against himself. As with individuals, so with entire generations; and if the world should ever reach the point of beginning to recollect itself, would it be any different? The man who raises his hand against himself is free. Self-destruction when the time has come; that's the destiny of man! Look, that's the story of the world and of life; you can paint it and mold it, adorn it and polish it, but it will always stay the same. That's how it is, how it was, and how it will be. (I'll gladly stay in my simple, little hut, though you build one palace of art on top of another.) After much preparation, one plants the seed in the earth; the little plant strains and labors to make a little room for itself, and finally it pushes itself up into the open air. Then the sun shines, the rain falls, and springtime blows over the earth. The little plant thrives in all its parts and grows ever lovelier; everything goes well and properly and slowly; and everyone who sees it, finds pleasure in it. Then the blossom comes. For a few moments the whole plant is transfigured, and then it withers. Now, what was the destiny of this flower; to bloom or to wither? I contend that people are partial to flowers that are still in bloom; they let themselves be carried away by the pleasurable aroma. But there's more truth in the withered flowers. Flowers exist to bloom and then to wither. Fruits have to fall to the ground. Eyes exist to shine and weep. And the heart? Well, it must beat — first calmly, then quickly (and more quickly), then slowly again, until it finally bleeds to death. Each heart is just as it must be, for each must obey its destiny; and that heart is best which obeys most willingly. This is how I live, and how I would have lived with the children. I say this because I think you feel it would have been different with me if the children were still alive. Sometimes in the spring, when I see the young plants and how they all longingly rear their heads, I think of myself again and a deep feeling of pity comes over me. Probably the infinite mother of all things likes it when her children do what she wants them to. She is a mother too, just as we are: children should do what they're told and be obedient. But someone who knows he is fulfilling his destiny and nothing more is better still, though perhaps the great mother doesn't like that. But even if she doesn't, I do it nevertheless.

And there's nothing to complain about in that either. That's the way it must be, and precisely the fact that it has to be that way is man's glory. Other things cannot go back into themselves; they're simply powerless: they can't go to each other and yet they can't be alone either. How different is man in comparison, looking into himself and never finding the end of his wealth. He can concern himself forever with himself and forever find new matter to occupy him: he plays with himself, lives on himself, and so feeds on himself, and feeds until he has finally consumed himself. And, to be sure, what should one do with oneself if not eat oneself into oneself? That's the desire of everyone who has a desire, and as yet no one has ever desired anything else. Just as every animal is attracted to its own native element as soon as it reaches maturity, so man's instinct leads him into his own depths; there he must be destroyed, perhaps by plunging headlong downwards, perhaps by sinking down calmly and beautifully. How they go is a matter of indifference, but go down they must, all of them. For a human being who is a human being, there is no death other than his own self-induced death, his suicide.

How I dislike people who strive only for happiness and maintain in all good faith that they too have already endured some deep suffering. Oh, if you knew what suffering was, if you had tasted of the forbidden fruit, if a spark of true eternity had ever entered your souls, how you would despise yourselves, your happiness, your pleasures, and whatever else those paltry things are called! But then such people, when they're still young, think that they too should love and be inspired; they've heard something about eternity and infinity, and they find all of that only too marvelous. But that soon passes, and then they think themselves wonderfully clever when they draw little pictures of blissful limitation around themselves and raise themselves with smiling self-satisfaction above everyone whose uncomprehended suffering they've not had the dimmest notion about in all their silver-plated lives. These good souls are limited, to be sure, but they've gotten their story wrong. I know better what's happened to them. They aren't limited because they want to be, because they forswore the opposite possibility voluntarily; they are limited rather because they are that way, because they always were, and because, I think, they probably always will be. They may be happy too, for all I know. I don't envy them.

Oh, these poor people who are afraid of suffering, and don't know what awareness is!

But even the best make images of the truth for themselves. When they've seen that happiness and life aren't the important things, then they turn the thing around and make death beautiful and relate everything to death, and lose themselves in death. But what is that but playing with the shadow of an old error?

Oh no, I don't fool myself, I know that dying is terrible and that death is not beautiful. Stay away from me with your fine metaphors and fairy tales. They are words and nothing but words. Everyone hangs on for as long as he can. What does it all mean to me, all these conjectures and assumptions, these inferences from metaphors, this mist of presentiment? Keep your names; they only disturb my clear spirit: or, if I'm to speak, then I'd choose first the handiest and most childish words. For everyone knows that it's possible to lose himself. If he doesn't know, then he's never looked with a clear eye into his own heart.

I know that I'm destroying myself and I want nothing more than to consume myself in the fullness of eternal pain and eternal love.

———◇———

I want to talk about myself, for why should I deny that I relate everything to myself and to my suffering? For in the end everyone has to escape back into himself, though he might gladly wander about ever so far in restless striving! That is how mankind is, a curious race, with egoism rooted deeply in it. And if I could only speak: oh, how good that would be!

Am I one of those people who think their fate is unusual? Oh no, I can't come to terms with myself that easily. The circumstances were peculiar enough, as if something quite special had been intended; but what happened? I was married and couldn't love the father of my children. Well, that's certainly nothing unusual! Oh! And here I can perhaps praise myself: I did everything that could possibly be done. He was happy; I soon learned how to hide my tears and it wasn't long before I felt my eyes were dry. It was the first impulse of the new life that is to stay with me, stay for as long as I shall stay myself. Now I longed for death, but another, equally deep longing prevented me from satisfying it. I wanted to become clear about myself. Every point in this fullness pressed for awareness, and what pain was not dear to me if I could purchase this awareness by it! I enjoy listening to men talk, and like following their subtleties. Everything has a meaning for me, of a different sort perhaps, but still a meaning to me and to my way of thinking; and yet I know something beyond it that is not in it. You may find that strange and smile. There is something in me which is aroused and moved by those words and speeches, even if others don't understand what I mean. Where haven't I looked, and how little have I found? Among men and in nature, in books and stories, in conversation and solitary thought: everything had only the one connection.

FRAGMENTS

Critical Fragments

1. Many so-called artists are really products of nature's art.

2. Every nation wants to see represented on stage only its own average and superficial aspects; unless you provide it with heroes, music, or fools.

3. When Diderot does something really brilliant in his *Jacques,** he usually follows it up by telling us how happy he is that it turned out so brilliantly.

4. There is so much poetry and yet there is nothing more rare than a poem! This is due to the vast quantity of poetical sketches, studies, fragments, tendencies, ruins, and raw materials.

5. Many critical journals make the mistake which Mozart's music is so often accused of: an occasionally excessive use of the wind instruments.

6. People criticize Goethe's poems for being metrically careless. But are the laws of the German hexameter really supposed to be as consistent and universally valid as the character of Goethe's poetry?

7. My essay on the study of Greek poetry is a mannered prose hymn to the objective quality in poetry. The worst thing about it,

---

* *Jacques le Fataliste,* published first in German in 1792 (French edition 1796); and inspired by Laurence Sterne's *Tristram Shandy.*

Fragments

it seems to me, is the complete lack of necessary irony; and the best, the confident assumption that poetry is infinitely valuable — as if that were a settled thing.

8. A good preface must be at once the square root and the square of its book.

9. Wit is absolute social feeling, or fragmentary genius.

10. One should drill the hole where the board is thickest.

11. Up to now, nothing really solid, nothing thorough, powerful, and skillful, has been written against the ancients; especially against their poetry.

12. One of two things is usually lacking in the so-called Philosophy of Art: either philosophy or art.

13. Bodmer * likes to call every simile "Homeric" that merely happens to be lengthy. So too, one hears jokes being called "Aristophanic" that have nothing classic about them except their lack of restraint and obviousness.

14. In poetry too every whole can be a part and every part really a whole.

15. The character of the stupid master in Diderot's *Jacques* perhaps does more honor to the author's skill than the character of the foolish servant. The former is just barely brilliantly stupid. But even that was probably more difficult to achieve than a completely brilliant fool.

16. Though genius isn't something that can be produced arbitrarily, it is freely willed — like wit, love, and faith, which one day will have to become arts and sciences. You should demand genius from everyone, but not expect it. A Kantian would call this the categorical imperative of genius.

17. Nothing is more contemptible than sorry wit.

18. Novels have a habit of concluding in the same way that the Lord's Prayer begins: with the kingdom of heaven on earth.

19. Many poems are loved in the way nuns love the Saviour.

20. A classical text must never be entirely comprehensible. But

* Johann Jacob Bodmer (1698–1783), Swiss critic and poet, among the first to challenge the supremacy of Gottsched's neoclassicism in Germany; also significant for his work on medieval German literature.

those who are cultivated and who cultivate themselves must always want to learn more from it.

21. Just as a child is only a thing which wants to become a human being, so a poem is only a product of nature which wants to become a work of art.

22. The flame of the most brilliantly witty idea should radiate warmth only after it has given off light; it can be quenched suddenly by a single analytic word, even when it is meant as praise.

23. Every good poem must be wholly intentional and wholly instinctive. That is how it becomes ideal.

24. The most insignificant authors have at least this similarity to the great Author of the Heavens and the Earth: that after the day's work is done, they have a habit of saying to themselves, "And behold, what he made was good."

25. The two main principles of the so-called historical criticism are the Postulate of Vulgarity and the Axiom of the Average. The Postulate of Vulgarity: everything great, good, and beautiful is improbable because it is extraordinary and, at the very least, suspicious. The Axiom of the Average: as we and our surroundings are, so must it have been always and everywhere, because that, after all, is so very natural.

26. Novels are the Socratic dialogues of our time. And this free form has become the refuge of common sense in its flight from pedantry.

27. The critic is a reader who ruminates. Therefore he ought to have more than one stomach.

28. Feeling (for a particular art, science, person, etc.) is divided spirit, is self-restriction: hence a result of self-creation and self-destruction.

29. Gracefulness is life lived correctly, is sensuality contemplating and shaping itself.

30. In modern tragedy, fate is sometimes replaced by God the Father, more often by the devil himself. How is it that this hasn't yet inspired some scholar to formulate a theory of the diabolic genre?

31. The classification of works of art into naive and sentimental *

* An allusion to Schiller's famous essay "Über naive und sentimentalische Dichtung" ("On Naive and Sentimental Poetry") (1796). Christian Thom-

might perhaps be fruitfully applied to criticism as well. There are sentimental critiques that lack only a vignette and a motto in order to be perfectly naive. For a vignette, a postilion blowing his horn. For a motto, a phrase from old Thomasius at the close of one of his academic lectures: *Nunc vero musicantes musicabunt cum paucis et trompetis.*

32. The chemical classification of disintegration into dry and wet varieties is also applicable in a literary sense to the dissolution of writers who are doomed to sink into obscurity after reaching their greatest heights. Some evaporate, others turn to water.

33. The overriding disposition of every writer is almost always to lean in one of two directions: either not to say a number of things that absolutely need saying, or else to say a great many things that absolutely ought to be left unsaid. The former is the original sin of synthetic, the latter of analytic minds.

34. A witty idea is a disintegration of spiritual substances which, before being suddenly separated, must have been thoroughly mixed. The imagination must first be satiated with all sorts of life before one can electrify it with the friction of free social intercourse so that the slightest friendly or hostile touch can elicit brilliant sparks and lustrous rays – or smashing thunderbolts.

35. One sometimes hears the public being spoken of as if it were somebody with whom one had lunch at the Hôtel de Saxe during the Leipzig Fair. Who is this public? The public is no object, but an idea, a postulate, like the Church.

36. Whoever hasn't yet arrived at the clear realization that there might be a greatness existing entirely outside his own sphere and for which he might have absolutely no feeling; whoever hasn't at least felt obscure intimations concerning the approximate location of this greatness in the geography of the human spirit: that person either has no genius in his own sphere, or else he hasn't been educated yet to the niveau of the classic.

37. In order to write well about something, one shouldn't be interested in it any longer. To express an idea with due circumspection, one must have relegated it wholly to one's past; one must no longer

asius (1655–1728) was professor of law at the University of Halle as well as a writer on philosophical subjects. The sentence at the close of the fragment is dog Latin for "Now the musicians will really make music with kettledrums and trumpets."

be preoccupied with it. As long as the artist is in the process of discovery and inspiration, he is in a state which, as far as communication is concerned, is at the very least intolerant. He wants to blurt out everything, which is a fault of young geniuses or a legitimate prejudice of old bunglers. And so he fails to recognize the value and the dignity of self-restriction, which is after all, for the artist as well as the man, the first and the last, the most necessary and the highest duty. Most necessary because wherever one does not restrict oneself, one is restricted by the world; and that makes one a slave. The highest because one can only restrict oneself at those points and places where one possesses infinite power, self-creation, and self-destruction. Even a friendly conversation which cannot be broken off at any moment, completely arbitrarily, has something intolerant about it. But a writer who can and does talk himself out, who keeps nothing back for himself, and likes to tell everything he knows, is to be pitied. There are only three mistakes to guard against. First: What appears to be unlimited free will, and consequently seems and should seem to be irrational or supra-rational, nonetheless must still at bottom be simply necessary and rational; otherwise the whim becomes willful, becomes intolerant, and self-restriction turns into self-destruction. Second: Don't be in too much of a hurry for self-restriction, but first give rein to self-creation, invention, and inspiration, until you're ready. Third: Don't exaggerate self-restriction.

38. The only thing one can criticize about the model of Germany, which a few great patriotic authors have constructed, is its incorrect placement. It doesn't lie behind, but before us.

39. The history of the imitation of ancient poetry, especially as practiced in foreign countries, is among other things useful in permitting us to derive most easily and fully the important concepts of unconscious parody and passive wit.

40. In the sense in which it has been defined and used in Germany, aesthetic is a word which notoriously reveals an equally perfect ignorance of the thing and of the language. Why is it still used?

41. Few books can be compared with the novel *Faublas* * for social wit and social exuberance. It is the champagne of the genre.

* *Les Amours du Chevalier de Faublas* (1789–1790), a semi-licentious, semi-picaresque novel by Jean-Baptiste Louvet de Couvret (1760–1797), French writer and revolutionary.

Fragments

42. Philosophy is the real homeland of irony, which one would like to define as logical beauty: for wherever philosophy appears in oral or written dialogues — and is not simply confined into rigid systems — there irony should be asked for and provided. And even the Stoics considered urbanity a virtue. Of course, there is also a rhetorical species of irony which, sparingly used, has an excellent effect, especially in polemics; but compared to the sublime urbanity of the Socratic muse, it is like the pomp of the most splendid oration set over against the noble style of an ancient tragedy. Only poetry can also reach the heights of philosophy in this way, and only poetry does not restrict itself to isolated ironical passages, as rhetoric does. There are ancient and modern poems that are pervaded by the divine breath of irony throughout and informed by a truly transcendental buffoonery. Internally: the mood that surveys everything and rises infinitely above all limitations, even above its own art, virtue, or genius; externally, in its execution: the mimic style of an averagely gifted Italian *buffo*.

43. Hippel,* so Kant says, had a commendable maxim that urged one to add the spice of profundity to the tasty dish of a whimsical style. Why doesn't Hippel find more followers for this maxim, since after all Kant gave his approval to it?

44. You should never appeal to the spirit of the ancients as if to an authority. It's a peculiar thing with spirits: they don't let themselves be grabbed by the hand and shown to others. Spirits reveal themselves only to spirits. Probably here too the best and shortest way would be to prove one's possession of the only true belief by doing good works.

45. Observing the peculiar fondness of modern poets for Greek terminology in naming their works, one is reminded of that naive remark of a Frenchman on the occasion of proclaiming the new Republican holidays: *que pourtant nous sommes menacés de rester toujours François*. Some of the names used in classifying the poetry of the Middle Ages might give rise to future scholarly investigations similar to those which concern themselves with why Dante called his masterpiece a divine comedy. There are tragedies which, if one has got to Hellenize their names in some way, would best be called sorry mimes. They seem to be baptized according to that concept of tragedy which is to be found once only in Shakespeare

---

* Theodor Gottlieb von Hippel (1741–1796), German novelist, imitator of Sterne, and precursor of Jean Paul.

but occurs much more frequently in the history of modern art: a tragedy is a drama in which Pyramus commits suicide.

46. We are closer to the Romans and can understand them better than the Greeks; and yet a real feeling for the Romans is much rarer than for the Greeks, because there are fewer synthetic than analytic people. For one can have a feeling for nations too, for historical as well as moral individuals, and not simply for practical genres, arts, and sciences.

47. Whoever desires the infinite doesn't know what he desires. But one can't turn this sentence around.

48. Irony is the form of paradox. Paradox is everything simultaneously good and great.

49. One of the most important techniques of the English drama and novel is guineas. They're used a great deal especially in the final cadenza when the bass instruments begin to have hard work of it.

50. How deeply rooted in man lies the desire to generalize about individual or national characteristics! Even Chamfort says: *"Les vers ajoutent de l'esprit à la pensée de l'homme qui en a quelquefois assez peu; et c'est ce qu'on appelle talent."* Is this common French usage?

51. To use wit as an instrument for revenge is as shameful as using art as a means for titillating the senses.

52. Instead of description, one occasionally gets in poems a rubric announcing that here something or other should really have been described, but the artist was prevented from doing so and most humbly begs to be excused.

53. In respect to their unity, most modern poems are allegories (mysteries, moralities) or novellas (adventures, intrigues), or a mixture or dilution of these.

54. There are writers who drink the absolute like water; and books in which even the dogs refer to the infinite.

55. A really free and cultivated person ought to be able to attune himself at will to being philosophical or philological, critical or poetical, historical or rhetorical, ancient or modern: quite arbitrarily, just as one tunes an instrument, at any time and to any degree.

56. Wit is logical sociability.

57. If some mystical art lovers who think of every criticism as a dis-

section and every dissection as a destruction of pleasure were to think logically, then "wow" would be the best criticism of the greatest work of art. To be sure, there are critiques which say nothing more, but only take much longer to say it.

58. Just as mankind prefers a great to a just action, so too the artist wants to ennoble and instruct.

59. Chamfort's pet idea that wit is a substitute for an impossible happiness — a small percentage, as it were, of the unpaid debt on the greatest good for which a bankrupt nature must settle — is not much better than Shaftesbury's * idea that wit is the touchstone of truth, or the more vulgar prejudice that moral ennoblement is the highest end of the fine arts. Wit is its own end, like virtue, like love and art. This brilliant man felt, so it seems, the infinite value of wit, and since French philosophy is inadequate for an understanding of this, he sought instinctively to join what was best in him to what is first and best in that philosophy. And as a maxim, the thought that the wise man must confront fate always *en état d'épigramme* is beautiful and truly cynical.

60. All the classical poetical genres have now become ridiculous in their rigid purity.

61. Strictly understood, the concept of a scientific poem is quite as absurd as that of a poetical science.

62. We already have so many theories about poetical genres. Why have we no concept of poetical genre? Perhaps then we would have to make do with a single theory of poetical genres.

63. Not art and works of art make the artist, but feeling and inspiration and impulse.

64. There should be a new *Laokoön* to determine the limits of music and philosophy. For a proper appreciation of a number of literary works we still need a theory of grammatical music.

65. Poetry is republican speech: a speech which is its own law and end unto itself, and in which all the parts are free citizens and have the right to vote.

66. The revolutionary rage for objectivity in my early philosophical writings has something of that fundamental rage which was so

* Anthony Ashley-Cooper, Third Earl of Shaftesbury (1671–1713), English moral philosopher and one of the shaping spirits of the eighteenth century.

enormously widespread during Reinhold's * philosophical consulship.

67. In England, wit is at least a profession if not an art. There everything becomes craftsmanlike, and in that island even the *roués* are pedants. So too their *wits*: they introduce an absolute willfulness — whose illusion gives to wit its romantic and piquant quality — into reality and so manage to live wittily. Hence their talent for folly. They die for their principles.

68. How many authors are there among writers? Author means creator.

69. There is a negative feeling which is much better, but also much rarer than an absence of feeling. One can love something deeply precisely because one doesn't possess it: at least it whets the appetite and leaves no aftertaste. Even a decided incapacity of which one is completely aware, or else a strong antipathy, is an impossibility for someone who is totally deficient. It presupposes at least a partial capacity and sympathy. Like the Platonic Eros this negative sense is probably also the son of overabundance and of dearth. It is born when somebody possesses only the spirit and not the letter; or, the other way around, when he possesses only the material and formal requisites, the dry hard shell of productive genius without the kernel. In the former case, we get pure tendencies, projects that are as wide as the blue sky, or, at the very best, outlines of fantasies; in the latter, that harmoniously shaped artistic banality of which the greatest English critics are such classics. The distinguishing mark of the former type, of the negative spiritual sense, is continual desire combined with continual incapacity, of always wanting to hear, but never hearing.

70. People who write books and imagine that their readers are the public and that they must educate it soon arrive at the point not only of despising their so-called public but of hating it. Which leads absolutely nowhere.

71. A sense for the witty without the possession of wit is the ABC of tolerance.

72. Actually they rather like it when a work of art is a bit obscene, especially in the middle; except that decency mustn't be directly offended and everything must come out right in the end.

* Karl Leonhard Reinhold (1758–1823), German philosopher and follower of Kant.

Fragments

73. What is lost in average, good, or even first-rate translations is precisely the best part.

74. It's impossible to offend someone if he doesn't want to be offended.

75. Notes are philological epigrams; translations are philological mimes; some commentaries, where the text is only the point of departure or the non-self, are philological idylls.

76. There is a type of ambition which would rather be the first among the last than the second among the first. That is the ancient kind. There is another ambition which would rather, like Tasso's Gabriel,

Gabriel, che fra i primi era il secondo,*

be the second among the first than the first among the second. That is the modern kind.

77. Maxims, ideals, imperatives, and postulates have all now become the small change of morality.

78. Many of the very best novels are compendia, encyclopedias of the whole spiritual life of a brilliant individual. Works which have this quality, even if they are cast in a completely different mold — like *Nathan*† — thereby take on a novelistic hue. And every human being who is cultivated and who cultivates himself contains a novel within himself. But it isn't necessary for him to express it and write it out.

79. German books become popular because of a famous name, or because of a great personality, or because of good connections, or because of hard work, or because of mild obscenity, or because of perfect incomprehensibility, or because of harmonious banality, or because of many-sided dullness, or because of a constant striving toward the absolute.

80. I'm disappointed in not finding in Kant's family tree of basic concepts the category "almost," a category that has surely accomplished, and spoiled, as much in the world and in literature as any other. In the mind of natural skeptics it colors all other concepts and perceptions.

81. Carrying on a polemic against an individual has something petty

* "Gabriel, who among the first was the second." From Torquato Tasso's *La Gerusalemme Liberata*, Canto I, 11, 4.

† That is, Lessing's play, *Nathan der Weise* (1779).

about it, like selling retail. If an artist doesn't want to involve himself wholesale in controversy, then he should at least choose individuals who are classic and have lasting merit. When that isn't possible, as for example in the lamentable case of self-defense, then the individuals must be raised as much as possible to the level of ideal prototypes of objective stupidity and objective foolishness; for these are, like everything objective, infinitely interesting, as subjects worthy of the higher polemics ought to be.

82. Spirit is natural philosophy.

83. Manners are characteristic edges.

84. From what the moderns aim at, we learn what poetry should become; from what the ancients have done, what it has to be.

85. Every honest author writes for nobody or everybody. Whoever writes for some particular group does not deserve to be read.

86. The function of criticism, people say, is to educate one's readers! Whoever wants to be educated, let him educate himself. This is rude: but it can't be helped.

87. Since poetry is of infinite worth, I don't understand why it should be merely more valuable than something or other that is also of infinite worth. There are artists who don't think too highly of art, for that's impossible, but who aren't free enough to raise themselves above their own greatest effort.

88. Nothing is more piquant than a brilliant man who has manners or mannerisms. That is, if he has them: but not at all, if they have him. That leads to spiritual petrification.

89. Isn't it unnecessary to write more than one novel, unless the artist has become a new man? It's obvious that frequently all the novels of a particular author belong together and in a sense make up only one novel.

90. Wit is an explosion of confined spirit.

91. The ancients are not the Jews, Christians, or English of poetry. They are not an arbitrarily chosen artistic people of God; nor do they have the only true saving aesthetic faith; nor do they have a monopoly on poetry.

92. Like animals, the spirit can only breathe in an atmosphere made up of life-giving oxygen mixed with nitrogen. To be unable to tolerate and understand this fact is the essence of foolishness; to simply not want to do so, is the beginning of madness.

Fragments

93. In the ancients we see the perfected letter of all poetry; in the moderns we see its growing spirit.

94. Mediocre writers who advertise a little volume as if they were about to exhibit a great giant should be compelled by the literary police to have their book stamped with the following motto: *This is the greatest elephant in the world, except himself.**

95. Harmonious banality can be quite useful to the philosopher; it can serve as a bright beacon for the as-yet-uncharted territories of life, art, or science. The philosopher will avoid the man and the book that the harmonious bore admires and loves; and he will at least be suspicious of any opinion that is staunchly held by more than a few of the species.

96. A good riddle should be witty; otherwise nothing remains once the answer has been found. And there's a charm in having a witty idea which is enigmatic to the point of needing to be solved: only its meaning should be immediately and completely clear as soon as it's been hit upon.

97. The salt of expression is piquancy, in powdered form. It comes coarsely and finely ground.

98. The following are universally valid and fundamental laws of written communication: (1) one should have something to communicate; (2) one should have somebody to whom one wants to communicate it; (3) one should really be able to communicate it and share it with somebody, not simply express oneself. Otherwise it would be wiser to keep silent.

99. Whoever isn't completely new himself judges the new as if it were old; and the old seems ever new until one grows old oneself.

100. The poetry of one writer is termed philosophical, of another philological, of a third, rhetorical, etc. But what then is poetical poetry?

101. Affectation doesn't arise so much out of a striving to be new as out of a fear of being old.

102. To want to judge everything is a great fallacy, or a venial sin.

103. Many works that are praised for the beauty of their coherence have less unity than a motley heap of ideas simply animated by the ghost of a spirit and aiming at a single purpose. What really holds

* The sentence in italics is in English in the original.

the latter together is that free and equal fellowship in which, so the wise men assure us, the citizens of the perfect state will live at some future date; it's that unqualifiedly sociable spirit which, as the beau monde maintains, is now to be found only in what is so strangely and almost childishly called the great world. On the other hand, many a work of art whose coherence is never questioned is, as the artist knows quite well himself, not a complete work but a fragment, or one or more fragments, a mass, a plan. But so powerful is the instinct for unity in mankind that the author himself will often bring something to a kind of completion which simply can't be made a whole or a unit; often quite imaginatively and yet completely unnaturally. The worst thing about it is that whatever is draped about the solid, really existent fragments in the attempt to mug up a semblance of unity consists largely of dyed rags. And if these are touched up cleverly and deceptively, and tastefully displayed, then that's all the worse. For then he deceives even the exceptional reader at first, who has a deep feeling for what little real goodness and beauty is still to be found here and there in life and letters. That reader is then forced to make a critical judgment to get at the right perception of it! And no matter how quickly the dissociation takes place, still the first fresh impression is lost.

104. What's commonly called reason is only a subspecies of it: namely, the thin and watery sort. There's also a thick, fiery kind that actually makes wit witty, and gives an elasticity and electricity to a solid style.

105. If one looks to the spirit and not the letter, then the whole Roman nation, including the senate and all triumphant generals and Caesars, was cynical.

106. Nothing is in its origins more contemptible and in its consequences more hideous than the fear of ridicule. Hence, for example, the servitude of women and many another cancer of mankind.

107. The ancients are masters of poetical abstraction; the moderns are better at poetical speculation.

108. Socratic irony is the only involuntary and yet completely deliberate dissimulation. It is equally impossible to feign it or divulge it. To a person who hasn't got it, it will remain a riddle even after it is openly confessed. It is meant to deceive no one except those who consider it a deception and who either take pleasure in the delightful roguery of making fools of the whole world or else become

Fragments

angry when they get an inkling they themselves might be included. In this sort of irony, everything should be playful and serious, guilelessly open and deeply hidden. It originates in the union of *savoir vivre* and scientific spirit, in the conjunction of a perfectly instinctive and a perfectly conscious philosophy. It contains and arouses a feeling of indissoluble antagonism between the absolute and the relative, between the impossibility and the necessity of complete communication. It is the freest of all licenses, for by its means one transcends oneself; and yet it is also the most lawful, for it is absolutely necessary. It is a very good sign when the harmonious bores are at a loss about how they should react to this continuous self-parody, when they fluctuate endlessly between belief and disbelief until they get dizzy and take what is meant as a joke seriously and what is meant seriously as a joke. For Lessing irony is instinct; for Hemsterhuis it is classical study; for Hülsen* it arises out of the philosophy of philosophy and surpasses these others by far.

109. Gentle wit, or wit without a barb, is a privilege of poetry which prose can't encroach upon: for only by means of the sharpest focus on a single point can the individual idea gain a kind of wholeness.

110. What if the harmonious education of artists and nobility is merely a harmonious illusion?

111. Chamfort was what Rousseau liked to pretend to be: a genuine cynic, more of a philosopher in the classical sense than a whole legion of dried-up school philosophers. Though at first he made common cause with the fashionable world, he nonetheless lived and died a free and honorable man, and despised the petty fame of a great writer. He was Mirabeau's friend. His most precious legacy is his ideas and observations on the art of living: a book full of solid wit, deep feeling, delicate sensitivity, mature reason, and firm masculinity; and of suggestive traces of vital passion, and at the same time exquisitely and perfectly expressed. Without comparison, the highest and best of its type.

112. The analytic writer observes the reader as he is; and accordingly he makes his calculations and sets up his machines in order to make the proper impression on him. The synthetic writer constructs and creates a reader as he should be; he doesn't imagine him

* August Ludwig Hülsen (1765–1810), German philosopher and educator, friend of Fichte and the Schlegel brothers.

156

calm and dead, but alive and critical. He allows whatever he has created to take shape gradually before the reader's eyes, or else he tempts him to discover it himself. He doesn't try to make any particular impression on him, but enters with him into the sacred relationship of deepest symphilosophy or sympoetry.

113. Voss* is Homerian in his *Louise*; and in his translation, Homer is Vossian.

114. There are so many critical journals of varying sorts and differing intentions! If only a society might be formed sometime with the sole purpose of gradually making criticism — since criticism is, after all, necessary — a real thing.

115. The whole history of modern poetry is a running commentary on the following brief philosophical text: all art should become science and all science art; poetry and philosophy should be made one.

116. The Germans, it is said, are the greatest nation in the world in respect to their cultivation of artistic sensibility and scientific spirit. Quite so — only there are very few Germans.

117. Poetry can only be criticized by way of poetry. A critical judgment of an artistic production has no civil rights in the realm of art if it isn't itself a work of art, either in its substance, as a representation of a necessary impression in the state of becoming, or in the beauty of its form and open tone, like that of the old Roman satires.

118. Isn't everything that is capable of becoming shopworn already twisted or trite to begin with?

119. Sapphic poems must grow and be discovered. They can neither be produced at will, nor published without desecration. Whoever does so lacks pride and modesty. Pride: because he tears his inmost essence out of the holy stillness of his heart and throws it into the crowd, to be stared at, crudely or coldly — and that for a lousy *da capo* or a gold coin. And it will always be immodest to put oneself up for exhibition, like an old painting. And if lyrical poems are not completely unique, free, and true, then, as lyrical poems, they're worthless. Petrarch doesn't belong here: for the cool lover doesn't utter anything except elegant platitudes; and actually he is romantic [novelistic], not lyrical. But even if another creature existed

* Johann Heinrich Voss (1751–1826), German poet and translator of Homer; his *Luise*, a narrative poem on domestic subjects, was published in 1795.

who was so coherently beautiful and classical that she could show herself naked, like Phryne* before all the Greeks, still there no longer exists an Olympian audience to appreciate such a performance. And it *was* Phryne. Only cynics make love in the marketplace. It is possible to be a cynic and a great poet: the dog and the laurel have equal title as ornaments on Horace's statue. But Horatian is not Sapphic by far. Sapphic is never cynical.

120. Whoever could manage to interpret Goethe's *Meister* properly would have expressed what is now happening in literature. He could, so far as literary criticism is concerned, retire forever.

121. The simplest and most immediate questions, like Should we criticize Shakespeare's works as art or as nature? and Are epic and tragedy essentially different or not? and Should art deceive or merely seem to do so? are all questions that can't be answered without the deepest consideration and the most erudite history of art.

122. If anything can justify that rather exalted conception of the Germans that one meets with here and there, then it is our complete neglect of and contempt for such ordinarily good writers as every other nation would receive with pomp and circumstance into their Johnson;† and also the rather general tendency to criticize freely and be quite demanding of what we recognize to be the best and too good to be appreciated by foreigners.

123. It is thoughtless and immodest presumption to want to learn something about art from philosophy. There are many who start out that way as if they hope to find something new there, since philosophy, after all, can't and shouldn't be able to do more than order the given artistic experiences and the existing artistic principles into a science, and raise the appreciation of art, extend it with the help of a thoroughly learned history of art, and create here as well that logical mood which unites absolute tolerance with absolute rigor.

124. At the heart of the best modern poems, there is rhyme, the symmetrical repetition of similarity. Such rhyme not only rounds out a poem admirably but can also have a highly tragic effect. For example, the champagne bottle and the three glasses which old Bar-

* An Athenian courtesan of the fourth century B.C., supposedly the model of Apelles' picture, *Aphrodite Anadyomene*, and Praxiteles' statue of the Cnidian Aphrodite. According to legend, she was acquitted of a capital charge when she bared her breasts before the judges.

† That is, Samuel Johnson's *The Lives of the Poets* (1779–1781).

bara places on the table before Wilhelm during the night. I'd like to call it gigantic or Shakespearean rhyme, for Shakespeare is a master of it.

125. Sophocles already believed naively that his representations of people were better than the real thing. Where did he portray a Socrates, a Solon, an Aristides, or any number of others? How often can't we repeat this same question for other poets? Haven't even the greatest artists reduced the stature of real heroes in their creations? And yet this madness has become a common thing, from the emperors of poetry down to its lowliest bailiffs. This habit may be salutary for poets, like any consistent limitation, for condensing and concentrating their powers. But a philosopher who'd let himself be infected by it would deserve at the very least to be deported from the realm of criticism. Or could it be that there isn't an infinite variety of goodness and beauty in heaven and on earth that hasn't been dreamed of in poetry?

126. The Romans knew that wit is a prophetic faculty; they called it nose.

127. It's indelicate to be astonished when something is beautiful or great; as if it could really be any different.

From *Blütenstaub*

1. Even philosophy has blossoms. That is, its thoughts; but one can never decide if one should call them witty or beautiful.

2. If in communicating a thought, one fluctuates between absolute comprehension and absolute incomprehension, then this process might already be termed a philosophical friendship. For it's no different with ourselves. Is the life of a thinking human being anything else than a continuous inner symphilosophy?

3. If one becomes infatuated with the absolute and simply can't escape it, then the only way out is to contradict oneself continually and join opposite extremes together. The principle of contradiction is inevitably doomed, and the only remaining choice is either to assume an attitude of suffering or else ennoble necessity by acknowledging the possibility of free action.

4. In order to come to terms with vulgarity in the strong and easy way that gives rise to grace, one should — that is, if one isn't vulgar oneself — consider nothing more extraordinary than vulgarity, develop a sense for it, seek and divine a great deal in it. In this way a person who lives in entirely different circumstances can mollify ordinary people to the point of their not mistrusting him at all, and make them think of him as nothing more than what they, among themselves, would call amiable.

TRANSLATOR'S NOTE: These four fragments by Friedrich Schlegel were included in Novalis's collection of fragments, *Blütenstaub* (Pollen), published by the Schlegel brothers in the *Athenaeum*, 1798.

Athenaeum Fragments

1. Nothing is more rarely the subject of philosophy than philosophy itself.

2. Both in their origins and effects, boredom and stuffy air resemble each other. They are usually generated whenever a large number of people gather together in a closed room.

3. Kant introduced the concept of the negative into philosophy. Wouldn't it be worthwhile trying now to introduce the concept of the positive into philosophy as well?

4. The frequent neglect of the subcategories of genres is a great detriment to a theory of poetical forms. So, for example, nature poetry is divided into natural and artificial kinds, and folk poetry into folk poetry for the people and folk poetry for the nobility and scholars.

5. So-called good society is usually nothing more than a mosaic of polished caricatures.

6. *Hermann und Dorothea* has been criticized by some for being greatly deficient in delicacy because of the young man's feigned proposal to his beloved, an impoverished farmer's daughter, that

TRANSLATOR'S NOTE: Authorship, if other than Friedrich Schlegel's, is indicated by one of the following abbreviations appended to the end of a fragment: [AW] for August Wilhelm Schlegel, [S] for Schleiermacher, [N] for Novalis. Cases of mixed authorship are footnoted separately. The attributions here follow those of the *Kritische Friedrich-Schlegel-Ausgabe*, vol. 2, ed. Hans Eichner (Munich, 1967).

Fragments

she should come as a maid into the house of his worthy parents. It may be that these critics don't treat their servants very well. [AW]

7. You're always demanding new ideas? Do something new, then something new might be said about it. [AW]

8. To certain eulogists of the past ages of our literature, one can make the same intrepid reply that Sthenelos made to Agamemnon: we boast of being much better than our fathers. [AW]

9. Luckily poetry waits as little for theory as virtue does for morality; otherwise we would, to begin with, have no hopes for a poem. [AW]

10. Duty is Kant's alpha and omega. Out of a duty to be grateful, so he maintains, we should defend and admire the ancients; and only out of a sense of duty did he become a great man.

11. Gessner's* idylls pleased the Parisian beau monde in the same way that a palate accustomed to *haut goût* sometimes takes delight in dairy foods. [AW]

12. It has been said of many monarchs that they would have been admirable citizens; only as kings were they failures. Can we say the same of the Bible? Is it also just an admirable everyday book whose only fault is that it should have become the Bible?

13. When young people of both sexes know how to dance to a lively tune, it doesn't in the least occur to them to try to make a critical judgment about music just for that reason. Why do people have less respect for poetry?

14. A lovely exuberance in the recital is the only thing that can save the poetical morality of licentious stories. They bear witness to indolence and perversity if they don't reveal an overflowing abundance of vitality. The imagination must want to run riot and not be in the habit of yielding servilely to the ruling bent of the senses. And yet with us lighthearted levity is most reviled; while, on the other hand, the strongest levity is condoned when accompanied by a fantastic mysticism of sensuality. As if depravity could be compensated for by madness! [AW]

15. Suicide is usually only an accident, rarely an action. In the former case, suicide is always wrong: it's like a child trying to free itself. But if suicide is an action, then there's no question of right or

---

* Salomon Gessner (1730–1791), Swiss poet and landscape painter.

Athenaeum Fragments

wrong, only of decorum. For only the latter is subject to the will which must determine whatever cannot be determined by simple law, such as the Here and Now, and which can determine everything that doesn't destroy the free will of others and thereby itself. It is never wrong to die of one's own free will, but often indecent to live any longer.

16. If the essence of cynicism consists of preferring nature to art, virtue to beauty and knowledge; of being oblivious of the letter, to which the Stoic clings so rigidly, and focusing entirely on the spirit; of absolutely despising every economic standard and political pomp, and maintaining bravely the rights of an independent will: then Christianity is really nothing but universal cynicism.

17. It's possible to choose to write in the form of the drama out of an inclination for systematic completeness; or in order to imitate and copy people and not simply portray them; or out of laziness; or out of a liking for music; or out of the pure joy of talking and letting people talk.

18. There are meritorious authors who have labored with youthful zeal for the greater education of their people, but have then desired to arrest that education at the point where their own strength left them. In vain: whoever has once aspired, be it foolishly or nobly, to take part in the advance of the human spirit must move with it or else be no better off than a dog on a spit who doesn't want to put his paws forward. [AW]

19. The best way not to be understood or, rather, to be misunderstood, is to use words in their original meanings, especially words from the ancient languages.

20. Duclos* observes that there are few excellent works which do not come from professional writers. In France this situation has been noted respectfully for quite some time. With us, a man was considered in former times less than nothing if he was merely an author, and even now this prejudice bestirs itself here and there, but the power of respected examples must paralyze it more and more. Depending on how one does it, writing is an infamy, a debauchery, a job, a craft, an art, a science, and a virtue. [AW]

21. The Kantian philosophy resembles that forged letter which Maria puts in Malvolio's way in Shakespeare's *Twelfth Night*. With the only difference that in Germany there are countless philo-

* Charles Pinot Duclos (1704–1772), French novelist and historian.

163

sophical Malvolios who tie their garters crosswise, wear yellow stockings, and are forever smiling madly.

22. A project is the subjective embryo of a developing object. A perfect project should be at once completely subjective and completely objective, should be an indivisible and living individual. In its origin: completely subjective and original, only possible in precisely this sense; in its character: completely objective, physically and morally necessary. The feeling for projects — which one might call fragments of the future — is distinguishable from the feeling for fragments of the past only by its direction: progressive in the former, regressive in the latter. What is essential is to be able to idealize and realize objects immediately and simultaneously: to complete them and in part carry them out within oneself. Since transcendental is precisely whatever relates to the joining or separating of the ideal and the real, one might very well say that the feeling for fragments and projects is the transcendental element of the historical spirit.

23. Much is printed that would have been better left simply said, and at times something is said that it would have been more appropriate to print. If the best ideas are those that are spoken and written spontaneously, then it might well be worth one's while to check occasionally what parts of one's talk could be written down and what part of one's writings printed. Of course it's presumptuous to have ideas during one's lifetime, or to make them known. To write an entire work is much more humble, because such a work can only be put together out of other works, and because, if worst comes to worst, the idea can always take refuge, hide itself submissively in a corner, and let the subject matter itself take over. But ideas, individual ideas, are forced to have value in themselves and must lay claim to being original and having been thought out. The only thing that is to some extent consoling about this is that nothing can be more presumptuous than the mere fact of existence, or, even more, of existence in a particular, independent way. From this original basic presumption we can deduce all the others, no matter how you look at it.

24. Many of the works of the ancients have become fragments. Many modern works are fragments as soon as they are written.

25. Interpretations are frequently insertions of something that seems desirable or expedient, and many a deduction is actually a traduction — a proof that erudition and speculation are not quite so harm-

ful to the innocence of the spirit as some people would have us believe. For isn't it really childlike to marvel at the wonder of what one has created?

26. Germany is probably such a favorite subject for the general essayist because the less finished a nation is, the more it is a subject for criticism and not for history.

27. Most people are, like Leibniz's possible worlds, only equally rightful pretenders to existence. Few exist.

28. Next to the perfect representation of critical idealism (which always comes first) the following seem to be the most important desiderata of philosophy: a materialistic logic, a poetical poetics, a positive politics, a systematical ethics, and a practical history.

29. Witty ideas are the proverbs of cultivated people.

30. A lovely young girl is the most charming symbol of pure good will.

31. Prudishness is pretension to innocence, without innocence. Women will probably have to remain prudish for as long as men are sentimental, stupid, and bad enough to demand eternal innocence and ignorance from them. For innocence is the only thing which can ennoble ignorance.

32. One should have wit, but not want to have it. Otherwise, you get persiflage, the Alexandrian style of wit.

33. It's much more difficult to make others talk well than to talk well oneself.

34. Almost all marriages are simply concubinages, liaisons, or rather provisional experiments and distant approximations of a true marriage whose real essence, judged not according to the paradoxes of any old system but according to all spiritual and worldly laws, consists of the fusion of a number of persons into one person. A nice idea, but one fraught with a great many serious difficulties. For this reason, if for no other, the will should be given as much free rein as possible, since after all the will has some say in any decision of whether an individual is to remain independent or become only an integral part of a common personality. It's hard to imagine what basic objection there could be to a marriage *à quatre*. But when the state tries to keep even unsuccessful trial-marriages together by force, then, in so doing, it impedes the possibility of mar-

riage itself, which might be helped by means of new and possibly more successful experiments.

35. A *cynic* should really have no possessions whatever: for a man's possessions, in a certain sense, actually possess him.* The solution to this problem is to own possessions as if one didn't own them. But it's even more artistic and cynical not to own possessions as if one owned them.

36. Nobody judges a decorative painting and an altar screen, an operetta and a piece of church music, a sermon and a philosophical treatise, according to the same standard. Then why do people make the kind of demands on rhetorical poetry — which exists only on the stage — that can only be fulfilled by a higher dramatic art?

37. Many witty ideas are like the sudden meeting of two friendly thoughts after a long separation.

38. Patience, said S. [Schleiermacher], relates to Chamfort's *état d'épigramme* as religion does to philosophy. [S]

39. Most thoughts are only the profiles of thoughts. They have to be turned around and synthesized with their antipodes. This is how many philosophical works acquire a considerable interest they would otherwise have lacked.

40. Notes to a poem are like anatomical lectures on a piece of roast beef. [AW]

41. Those people who have made a profession of explaining Kant to us were either of the sort that lacked the capacity to gain an understanding for themselves of the subjects about which Kant has written; or else such people as only had the slight misfortune of understanding no one except themselves; or such as expressed themselves even more confusedly than he did.

42. Good drama must be drastic.

43. Philosophy is still moving too much in a straight line; it's not yet cyclical enough.

44. Every philosophical review should simultaneously be a philosophy of reviews.

45. New or not new: that's the question which is asked of a work from both the highest and the lowest points of view. From the point of view of history, and of curiosity.

* Only the first sentence is by Schlegel; the continuation is by Schleiermacher.

46. According to the way many philosophers think, a regiment of soldiers on parade is a system.

47. The philosophy of the Kantians is probably termed critical *per antiphrasin*; or else it is an *epitheton ornans*.*

48. My experience with the greatest philosophers is like Plato's with the Spartans. He loved and admired them enormously, but continually complained that they always stopped halfway.

49. Women are treated as unjustly in poetry as in life. If they're feminine, they're not ideal, and if ideal, not feminine.

50. In its origins true love should be at once completely premeditated and completely fortuitous, and seem simultaneously a result of necessity and free will. But in its character it should be both lawful and virtuous, and seem both a mystery and a wonder.

51. Naive is what is or seems to be natural, individual, or classical to the point of irony, or else to the point of continuously fluctuating between self-creation and self-destruction. If it's simply instinctive, then it's childlike, childish, or silly; if it's merely intentional, then it gives rise to affectation. The beautiful, poetical, ideal naive must combine intention and instinct. The essence of intention in this sense is freedom, though intention isn't consciousness by a long shot. There is a certain kind of self-infatuated contemplation of one's own naturalness or silliness that is itself unspeakably silly. Intention doesn't exactly require any deep calculation or plan. Even Homeric naiveté isn't simply instinctive; there is at least as much intention in it as there is in the grace of lovely children or innocent girls. And even if Homer himself had no intentions, his poetry and the real author of that poetry, Nature, certainly did.

52. There is a kind of person for whom an enthusiasm for boredom represents the beginning of philosophy.

53. It's equally fatal for the mind to have a system and to have none. It will simply have to decide to combine the two.

54. One can only become a philosopher, not be one. As soon as one thinks one is a philosopher, one stops becoming one.

55. There are classifications that are bad enough as classifications but which nonetheless have dominated whole nations and eras, and are frequently extremely characteristic — are the nuclei — of the

* Rhetorical terms signifying, respectively, the use of words in a sense opposite to the proper meaning, and a decorative phrase.

historical individuals that nations and eras are. So, for example, the Greek separation of all things into the divine and the human, something that goes all the way back to Homer. So the Roman dualism of At Home and At War. And the moderns continually speak of the world of the present and the world of the hereafter, as if there were more than one world. But, of course, for them too most things are just as isolated and separated as their present and their hereafter.

56. Since nowadays philosophy criticizes everything that comes in front of its nose, a criticism of philosophy would be nothing more than justifiable retaliation.

57. The reputation of a writer is often gained in much the same way as money or the favor of women. If you put down a good foundation, the rest follows by itself. Chance has made many men great. "Everything is luck, only luck" is true of a good many literary as well as most political phenomena.

58. Believing in tradition and always straining at new insanities; frenetically imitative and proudly independent; awkward in what is superficial and accomplished to the point of dexterity in what is profoundly or gloomily ponderous; congenitally vapid but striving to be transcendental in feeling and outlook; comfortably entrenched against wit and frivolity, and inflamed by a sacred abhorrence of these qualities. Can you guess to what great body of literature these traits correspond? [AW]

59. Bad writers complain a great deal about the tyranny of reviewers; I think the latter would be more justified in complaining. They're supposed to find beautiful, ingenious, and first-rate what is nothing of the sort; and it's only the slight circumstance of power that prevents the reviewed from treating the reviewers in the same way Dionysus treated the critics of his verses. Kotzebue* even admitted this publicly. The new productions of miniature Dionysuses of this kind might in fact be adequately advertised with the words: Lead me back to the latomies. [AW]

60. The subjects of several countries boast of having a great many freedoms, which would become wholly superfluous through the possession of freedom. It is probably for this reason only that the

---

* August von Kotzebue (1761–1819), German dramatist, author of more than two hundred plays, some of which gained an almost unprecedented popularity, but never much intellectual respectability.

beauties of many poems are emphasized so strongly — because they have no beauty. They are artistic in parts, but taken as wholes are no works of art. [AW]

61. The few attacks against Kantian philosophy which exist are the most important documents for a pathological history of common sense. This epidemic, which started in England, even threatened for a while to infect German philosophy.

62. Publishing is to thinking as the maternity ward is to the first kiss.

63. Every uncultivated person is a caricature of himself.

64. The demand for moderation is the spirit of castrated intolerance.

65. Many panegyrists reveal the greatness of their idol antithetically: that is, by exhibiting their own insignificance.

66. When an author doesn't know anymore what sort of answer to make to a critic, then he usually says: But you can't do it any better. That's like a dogmatic philosopher accusing the skeptic of not being able to create a system.

67. It would be intolerant not to assume that every philosopher is tolerant and therefore capable of being reviewed; yes, even when one knows the opposite is true. But it would be presumptuous to treat poets in the same way: except if one can produce a critique that is poetical through and through and at the same time a living, vibrant work of art.

68. The only true lover of art is the man who can renounce some of his wishes entirely whenever he finds others completely fulfilled, who can rigorously evaluate even what he loves most, who will, if necessary, submit to explanations, and has a sense for the history of art.

69. The pantomimes of the ancients no longer exist. But in compensation, all modern poetry resembles pantomimes.

70. Wherever a public prosecutor puts in an appearance, a public judge should also be at hand.

71. People always talk about how an analysis of the beauty of a work of art supposedly disturbs the pleasure of the art lover. Well, the real lover just won't let himself be disturbed!

72. Surveys of entire subjects of the sort that are now fashionable

are the result of somebody surveying the individual items, and then summarizing them.

73. Might it not be the same with the people as with the truth: where, as they say, the attempt is worth more than the result?

74. According to the corrupt manner in which language is used, Probably [*wahrscheinlich*, lit. "true-seeming"] means much the same as Almost True, or Somewhat True, or whatever might at some time perhaps come to be true. But the word, simply by the way it's formed, can't signify all these things. What seems to be true doesn't have to be true in the least degree: but it must seem to be positive. Probability is a matter for shrewdness, for those who have the ability to guess among possible alternatives the real consequences of possible free actions. It is something completely subjective. What some logicians have tried to systematize under the name of probability is actually possibility.

75. Formal logic and empirical psychology are philosophical grotesques. For whatever is interesting in an arithmetic of the four elements or in an experimental physics of the spirit can surely only derive from a contrast of form and content.

76. An intellectual point of view is the categorical imperative of any theory.

77. A dialogue is a chain or garland of fragments. An exchange of letters is a dialogue on a larger scale, and memoirs constitute a system of fragments. But as yet no genre exists that is fragmentary both in form and content, simultaneously completely subjective and individual, and completely objective and like a necessary part in a system of all the sciences.

78. Usually incomprehension doesn't derive from a lack of intelligence, but from a lack of sense.

79. Folly is to be distinguished from madness only in the sense that the former, like stupidity, is conscious. If this distinction is invalid, then it's highly unfair to lock up some fools while letting others run free. Then both states of being are different only in degree, not in kind.

80. The historian is a prophet facing backwards.

81. Most people know of no dignity other than the representative; and yet only a very few people have any sense of representative worth. Even if something is nothing in itself, still it must contribute

something to the definition of some species. And in this sense one could say that nobody is uninteresting.

82. The demonstrations of philosophy are simply demonstrations in the sense of military jargon. And its deductions aren't much better than those of politics; even in the sciences possession is nine-tenths of the law. About its definitions one could raise the same objection that Chamfort does in remarking upon the sort of friends one has in worldly life. There are three kinds of explanations in science: explanations that give us an illumination or an inkling of something; explanations that explain nothing; and explanations that obscure everything. True definitions can't be made at will, but have to come of themselves; a definition which isn't witty is worthless, and there exists an infinite number of real definitions for every individual. The necessary formalities of aesthetics degenerate into etiquette and luxury. As a way of verifying and testing virtuosity, these latter qualities have their purpose and value, like the bravura arias of singers and the Latin prose of philologists. Also they make a considerable rhetorical impression. But the main point is always to know something and say something. To want to prove or even explain it is in most cases wholly unnecessary. The categorical style of the laws of the twelve tablets and the thetical method, where we find set down the pure facts of reflection without concealment, adulteration, or artificial distortion, like texts for the study of symphilosophy, are still the most appropriate for a studied natural philosophy. In a case where one has both to propose and prove something, it's indisputably more difficult to propose than to prove. There are lots of formally splendid proofs for perverse and platitudinous propositions. Leibniz proposed and Wolff* proved. Need one say more?

83. The principle of contradiction is by no means to be equated with the principle of analysis: namely, of the absolute kind of analysis which alone deserves the name, the chemical decomposition of an individual into his simplest and most basic components.

84. Viewed subjectively, philosophy, like epic poetry, always begins in medias res.

85. Principles are to life what instructions written by the cabinet are for the general in battle.

---

* Christian von Wolff (1679–1754), German rationalistic philosopher.

86. Real sympathy concerns itself with furthering the freedom of others, not with the satisfaction of animal pleasures.

87. The first principle in love is to have a sense for one another, and the highest principle, faith in each other. Devotion is the expression of faith, and pleasure can animate and whet the senses, though it can't, as is commonly believed, create them. Therefore sensuality can deceive bad people into believing for a short time that they might love each other.

88. There are people whose whole life consists in always saying no. It would be no small accomplishment always to be able to say no properly, but whoever can do no more, surely cannot do so properly. The taste of these nay-sayers is like an efficient pair of scissors for pruning the extremities of genius; their enlightenment is like a great candle-snuffer for the flame of enthusiasm; and their reason a mild laxative against immoderate pleasure and love.

89. Criticism is the sole surrogate of the moral mathematics and science of propriety which so many philosophers have sought for in vain because it is impossible to find.

90. The subject of history is the realization of all that is practically necessary.

91. Logic is neither the preface, nor the instrument, nor the formula, nor an episode of philosophy. It is, rather, a coordinated pragmatic science opposed to poetry and to ethics and deriving from the demand for a positive truth and the premise of the possibility of a system.

92. Until philosophers become grammarians, or grammarians philosophers, grammar will not be what it was among the ancients: a pragmatic science and a part of logic. It will not even be a science.

93. The doctrine of the spirit and the letter is so interesting because, among other things, it also puts philosophy in touch with philology.

94. As yet every great philosopher has explained his predecessors — often quite unintentionally — in such a way that it seemed that before him they had been entirely misunderstood.

95. Some things philosophy must assume for the present and forever, and it may do so because it must.

96. Whoever doesn't pursue philosophy for its own sake, but uses it as a means to an end, is a sophist.

97. As a temporary condition skepticism is logical insurrection; as a system it is anarchy. Skeptical method would therefore more or less resemble a rebellious government.

98. Everything is philosophical that contributes to the realization of the logical ideal and possesses scientific organization.

99. At the words "his philosophy, my philosophy," one is always reminded of that line in *Nathan*: "Who owns God? What kind of God is that who belongs to a man?"

100. Poetic illusion is a game of impressions, and the game, an illusion of actions.

101. What happens in poetry happens never or always. Otherwise it isn't really poetry. You shouldn't think it's actually happening now.

102. Women have absolutely no sense for art, but for poetry they do; no talent for science, but for philosophy. They certainly don't lack a capacity for speculation, for inward contemplation of the infinite — but they have no sense for abstractions, something that can be learned much more easily.

103. The fact that one can annihilate a philosophy — whereat a careless person can easily annihilate himself as well — or that one can prove that a philosophy annihilates itself is of little consequence. If it's really philosophy, then, like the phoenix, it will always rise again from its own ashes.

104. The world considers anyone a Kantian who is interested in the latest German philosophical writings. According to the school definition, a Kantian is only someone who believes that Kant is the truth, and who, if the mail coach from Königsberg* were ever to have an accident, might very well have to go without the truth for some weeks. According to the outmoded Socratic concept of disciples being those who have independently made the spirit of the great master their own spirit, have adapted themselves to it, and, as his spiritual sons, have been named after him, there are probably only a very few Kantians.

105. Schelling's philosophy — which might be termed criticized mysticism — concludes like Aeschylus's *Prometheus* in earthquake and ruins.

* Birthplace and residence of Immanuel Kant, from which he rarely ventured (in fact, he never traveled outside East Prussia).

106. Moral appreciation is entirely opposed to aesthetic appreciation. In the former good intentions mean everything, in the latter nothing at all. The good intention of being witty, for example, is the virtue of a clown. The only intention in matters of wit should consist of lifting the conventional barriers and liberating the spirit. But you must consider that man wittiest who is witty not merely without intending to be so, but actually against his own intention, just as the *bienfaisant bourru* is really the most good-natured of all characters. [AW]

107. The tacitly assumed and real first postulate of all the gospel harmonies of the Kantian evangelists reads as follows: Kant's philosophy must be in agreement with itself.

108. Beautiful is what is at once charming and sublime.

109. A certain kind of micrology and belief in authority are characteristics of greatness — namely, the perfecting micrology of the artist, and the historical belief in the authority of nature.

110. It is a sublime taste always to like things better when they've been raised to the second power. For example, copies of imitations, critiques of reviews, addenda to additions, commentaries on notes. This taste is very characteristic of us Germans whenever it's a matter of making something longer; and of the French when it promotes brevity and vacuity. Their scientific education very likely tends to be an abbreviation of an extract, and the highest production of their poetical art, their tragedy, is merely the formula of a form. [AW]

111. The teachings that a novel hopes to instill must be of the sort that can be communicated only as wholes, not demonstrated singly, and not subject to exhaustive analysis. Otherwise the rhetorical form would be infinitely preferable.

112. Philosophers who aren't opposed to each other are usually joined only by sympathy, not by symphilosophy.

113. A classification is a definition that contains a system of definitions.

114. A definition of poetry can only determine what poetry should be, not what it really was and is; otherwise the shortest definition would be that poetry is whatever has at any time and at any place been called poetry.

115. That the nobility of patriotic hymns is not desecrated by be-

ing well paid for is proved by the Greeks and Pindar. But that money alone isn't enough is shown by the English, who have tried to imitate the ancients in this respect at any rate. So that beauty can't really be bought and sold in England, even if virtue can.

116. Romantic poetry is a progressive, universal poetry. Its aim isn't merely to reunite all the separate species of poetry and put poetry in touch with philosophy and rhetoric. It tries to and should mix and fuse poetry and prose, inspiration and criticism, the poetry of art and the poetry of nature; and make poetry lively and sociable, and life and society poetical; poeticize wit and fill and saturate the forms of art with every kind of good, solid matter for instruction, and animate them with the pulsations of humor. It embraces everything that is purely poetic, from the greatest systems of art, containing within themselves still further systems, to the sigh, the kiss that the poetizing child breathes forth in artless song. It can so lose itself in what it describes that one might believe it exists only to characterize poetical individuals of all sorts; and yet there still is no form so fit for expressing the entire spirit of an author: so that many artists who started out to write only a novel ended up by providing us with a portrait of themselves. It alone can become, like the epic, a mirror of the whole circumambient world, an image of the age. And it can also — more than any other form — hover at the midpoint between the portrayed and the portrayer, free of all real and ideal self-interest, on the wings of poetic reflection, and can raise that reflection again and again to a higher power, can multiply it in an endless succession of mirrors. It is capable of the highest and most variegated refinement, not only from within outwards, but also from without inwards; capable in that it organizes — for everything that seeks a wholeness in its effects — the parts along similar lines, so that it opens up a perspective upon an infinitely increasing classicism. Romantic poetry is in the arts what wit is in philosophy, and what society and sociability, friendship and love are in life. Other kinds of poetry are finished and are now capable of being fully analyzed. The romantic kind of poetry is still in the state of becoming; that, in fact, is its real essence: that it should forever be becoming and never be perfected. It can be exhausted by no theory and only a divinatory criticism would dare try to characterize its ideal. It alone is infinite, just as it alone is free; and it recognizes as its first commandment that the will of the poet can tolerate no law above itself. The romantic kind of poetry is the

only one that is more than a kind, that is, as it were, poetry itself: for in a certain sense all poetry is or should be romantic.

117. Works whose ideal doesn't have as much living reality and, as it were, personality for the artist as does his mistress or his friend are best left unwritten. At any rate, they don't become works of art.

118. It's not even a subtle but actually a rather coarse titillation of the ego, when all the characters of a novel revolve around a single figure like the planets around the sun. And this central character usually turns out to be the author's own naughty little darling who then becomes the mirror and flatterer of the delighted reader. Just as a cultivated human being isn't merely an end but also a means both to himself and others, so too in the cultivated literary work all the characters should be both ends and means. The constitution should be republican, but with the proviso that some parts can choose to be active and others passive.

119. Even those metaphors that seem simply arbitrary often have deep significance. What kind of analogy, one might wonder, exists between heaps of gold or silver and the accomplishments of the spirit that are so sure and so perfect they become arbitrary, and which sprang to life so casually they seem inborn? And yet it's obvious that one only has talents, owns them as if they were things, though they still retain their solid value even though they can't ennoble the possessor. But one can never really have genius, only be one. And there is no plural for genius, which in this case is already contained in the singular. For genius is actually a system of talents.

120. They have so little regard for wit because its expressions aren't long and wide enough, since their sensitivity is only a darkly imagined mathematics; and because wit makes them laugh, which would be disrespectful if wit had real dignity. Wit is like someone who is supposed to behave in a manner representative of his station, but instead simply *does* something.

121. An idea is a concept perfected to the point of irony, an absolute synthesis of absolute antitheses, the continual self-creating interchange of two conflicting thoughts. An ideal is at once idea and fact. If ideals don't have as much individuality for the thinker as the gods of antiquity do for the artist, then any concern with ideas is no more than a boring and laborious game of dice with hollow phrases, or, in the manner of the Chinese bonzes, a brooding con-

templation of one's own nose. Nothing is more wretched and contemptible than this sentimental speculation without any object. But one shouldn't call this mysticism, since this beautiful old word is so very useful and indispensable for absolute philosophy, from whose perspective the spirit regards everything as a mystery and a wonder, while from other points of view it would appear theoretically and practically normal. Speculation *en detail* is as rare as abstraction *en gros*, and yet it is these that beget the whole substance of scientific wit, these that are the principles of higher criticism, the highest rungs of spiritual cultivation. The great practical abstraction is what makes the ancients — among whom this was an instinct — actually ancients. In vain did individuals express the ideal of their species completely, if the species themselves, strictly and sharply isolated, weren't freely surrendered, as it were, to their originality. But to transport oneself arbitrarily now into this, now into that sphere, as if into another world, not merely with one's reason and imagination, but with one's whole soul; to freely relinquish first one and then another part of one's being, and confine oneself entirely to a third; to seek and find now in this, now in that individual the be-all and end-all of existence, and intentionally forget everyone else: of this only a mind is capable that contains within itself simultaneously a plurality of minds and a whole system of persons, and in whose inner being the universe which, as they say, should germinate in every monad, has grown to fullness and maturity.

122. When Bürger came across a book of the type that leaves one neither warm nor cold, he used to say that it deserved to be praised in the *Bibliothek der schönen Wissenschaften.** [AW]

123. Isn't poetry the noblest and worthiest of the arts for this, among other reasons: that in it alone drama becomes possible?

124. If you ever write or read novels for their psychology, then it's quite illogical and petty to shrink from even the most painstaking and thorough analysis of unnatural pleasure, horrible tortures, revolting infamy, and disgusting physical or mental impotence.

125. Perhaps there would be a birth of a whole new era of the sciences and arts if symphilosophy and sympoetry became so univer-

* Gottfried August Bürger (1748–1794), German poet, celebrated for his vivid ballads, particularly "Lenore." The *Bibliothek* was a literary journal published in Leipzig from 1757 to 1806 and a rival of the Göttingen *Musenalmanach* of which, for a time, he was the editor.

sal and heartfelt that it would no longer be anything extraordinary for several complementary minds to create communal works of art. One is often struck by the idea that two minds really belong together, like divided halves that can realize their full potential only when joined. If there were an art of amalgamating individuals, or if a wishful criticism could do more than merely wish — and for that there are reasons enough — then I would like to see Jean Paul and Peter Leberecht* combined. The latter has precisely what the former lacks. Jean Paul's grotesque talent and Peter Leberecht's fantastic turn of mind would, once united, yield a first-rate romantic poet.

126. All plays that are both national and designed to produce an effect are romanticized mimes.

127. Klopstock† is a grammatical poet and a poetical grammarian. [AW]

128. Nothing is more pitiful than to sell oneself to the devil for nothing; for example, to write lascivious poems that aren't even very good. [AW]

129. In discussing questions like the use of meter in the drama, some theoreticians forget that poetry is essentially only a beautiful lie, but for just that reason one about which it also can be said:

> Magnanima menzogna, ov' or' è il vero
> Si bello, che si possa a te preporre?‡ [AW]

130. There are grammatical mystics too. Moritz§ was one. [AW]

131. The poet can learn little from the philosopher, but the philosopher much from the poet. It's even to be feared that the night lamp of the sage may lead someone astray who is given to walking by the light of revelation. [AW]

132. Every poet is really Narcissus. [AW]

---

* A pseudonym of Ludwig Tieck who published a collection of stories under that name.

† Gottlieb Friedrich Klopstock (1724–1803), whose *Messias*, a vast epic poem based on the life of Christ, established him as the Milton of Germany and as the most notable German poet before Goethe.

‡ "Magnanimous lie, where is there a truth so beautiful as to be preferable to you?"

§ Karl Phillipp Moritz (1757–1793), German novelist, critic, and friend of Goethe.

133. It's as if women made everything with their own hands, and men everything with tools. [AW]

134. The male sex won't be improved by the female until we introduce a genealogy of names inherited from the mother, as in the kingdom of Naïri. [AW]

135. At times we really do perceive a connection between the separate and often contradictory parts of our education. So it seems that the better people in our moralistic plays are graduates of the most up-to-date pedagogy. [AW]

136. There are minds that lack flexibility despite a great application and specific focusing of their powers. They'll discover something, but not much, and will be in danger of forever repeating their favorite propositions. You don't penetrate deeply when you press a drill against a board with great force, without making it turn at the same time. [AW]

137. There is a material, enthusiastic rhetoric that's infinitely superior to the sophistic abuse of philosophy, the declamatory stylistic exercise, the applied poetry, the improvised politics, that commonly go by the same name. The aim of this rhetoric is to realize philosophy practically and to defeat practical unphilosophy and antiphilosophy not just dialectically, but really annihilate it. Rousseau and Fichte, one might add, enjoin even those who believe only what they can see from considering this ideal chimerical.

138. Tragedians almost always set the scene of their stories in the past. Why should this be absolutely necessary? Why shouldn't it also be possible to set it in the future, and in that way free the imagination at one stroke from all historical considerations and limitations? But then, of course, a nation that has to endure the humiliating spectacle of a better future would require more than a republican constitution. It would need a liberal mentality.

139. From the romantic point of view, even the vagaries of poetry have their value as raw materials and preliminaries for universality, even when they're eccentric and monstrous, provided they have some saving grace, provided they are original.

140. It seems to be a characteristic of the dramatic poet to lose himself with lavish generosity in other people, and of the lyric poet to attract everything toward himself with loving egoism. [AW]

141. We're told that there are so very many infractions of good

taste in English and German tragedies. French tragedies are made up of just one single great infraction. For what can be more contrary to good taste than writing and performing plays that are completely outside nature? [AW]

142. Hemsterhuis unites Plato's beautiful visionary flights with the strict seriousness of the systematic thinker. Jacobi doesn't have this harmonious proportion of mental powers but instead a depth and force that are all the more effective. They share an instinct for the divine. Hemsterhuis's works could be called intellectual poems. Jacobi didn't create any flawlessly perfect classical works of art; he gave us fragments full of originality, nobility, and intimacy. Perhaps Hemsterhuis's enthusiasm leaves a deeper impression because it always stays within the limits of the beautiful; on the other hand, reason immediately assumes a defensive stance when it becomes aware of the vehemence of the feeling that is intruding upon it. [AW]

143. One can't force anyone to think of the ancients as classics, or as ancient. In the final analysis, that depends on maxims.

144. The golden age of Roman literature was more brilliant and more suitable for poetry; the so-called silver age much more correct in its prose.

145. Considered as a poet, Homer is very moral because he is so natural and yet so poetical. But as a moralist, as the ancients often viewed him, despite the protestations of older and better philosophers, he is for that very reason quite immoral.

146. Just as the novel colors all of modern poetry, so satire colors and, as it were, sets the tone for all of Roman poetry, yes, even the whole of Roman literature. This poetry surely remained through all its changes a classic universal poetry, a social poetry emanating from, and created for, the center of the cultivated world. In order to have a feeling for what is most urbane, original, and beautiful in the prose of a Cicero, Caesar, or Suetonius, one has to have loved and understood the Horatian satires for a long time. They are the eternal wellsprings of urbanity.

147. To live classically and to realize antiquity practically within oneself is the summit and goal of philology. Is this possible without any kind of cynicism?

148. The greatest antithesis that ever existed is that between Caesar and Cato. Sallust's description of it is not without merit.

149. The systematic Winckelmann who read all the ancients as if they were a single author, who saw everything as a whole and concentrated all his powers on the Greeks, provided the first basis for a material knowledge of the ancients through his perception of the absolute difference between ancient and modern. Only when the perspective and the conditions of the absolute identity of ancient and modern in the past, present, and future have been discovered will one be able to say that at least the contours of classical study have been laid bare and one can now proceed to methodical investigation.

150. Tacitus's *Agricola* is a classically magnificent, historical canonization of a consular economist. According to the way of thinking that predominates in the book, man's greatest mission is to triumph by permission of the emperor.

151. Up to now everyone has managed to find in the ancients what he needed or wished for: especially himself.

152. Cicero was a great virtuoso of urbanity who wanted to be an orator, and, yes, even a philosopher, and who could have been a very brilliant antiquarian, man of letters, and polyhistorian of old Roman virtue and old Roman festivity.

153. The more popular an ancient author, the more romantic. This is the governing principle of the new anthology that the moderns have in effect made from the old anthology of the classics, or, rather, that they are still in the process of making.

154. To anyone coming fresh from Aristophanes, the Olympus of comedy, romantic persiflage seems like a long spun-out thread from the cloth of Athena, like a flake of heavenly fire of which the best part was lost on the way to earth.

155. The crude cosmopolitan efforts of the Carthaginians and other ancient peoples seem, in contrast to the political universality of the Romans, like the natural poetry of uncivilized nations compared to the classical art of the Greeks. Only the Romans were satisfied with the spirit of despotism and despised the letter; only they had naive tyrants.

156. Comic wit is a mixture of epic and iambic. Aristophanes is simultaneously Homer and Archilochus.

157. Ovid is in many ways similar to Euripides. The same power to

move, the same rhetorical brilliance and often inopportune ingenuity, the same dawdling fullness, vanity, and thinness.

158. The best in Martial is what looks like Catullus.

159. In many poems of late antiquity, for example Ausonius's *Mosella*,* antiquarianism is the only remaining ancient quality.

160. Not his Attic education, his striving for Doric harmony, the Socratic grace that endows him with an occasional amiability, or the enthralling simplicity, clarity, and peculiar sweetness of his style can hide from an unbiased mind the vulgarity that is the inmost spirit of Xenophon's life and work. The *Memorabilia* shows how incapable he was of understanding the greatness of his master, and the *Anabasis*, the most interesting and beautiful of his works, how petty a man he himself was.

161. Might not the cyclical nature of Plato's and Aristotle's supreme being be the personification of a philosophical mannerism?

162. In investigating ancient Greek mythology, hasn't too little attention been paid to the human instinct for making analogies and antitheses? The Homeric world of gods is a simple variation of the Homeric world of men, while the Hesiodic world, lacking the principle of heroic contrast, splits up into several opposing races of gods. In that old remark of Aristotle that one gets to know people through their gods, one finds not only the self-illuminating subjectivity of all theology, but also the more incomprehensible innate spiritual dualism of man.

163. The history of the first Roman Caesars is like a symphony — striking up the theme that runs through the history of all the subsequent ones.

164. The mistakes of the Greek sophists were errors more of excess than omission. Even the confidence and arrogance with which they presumed and pretended to know everything has something quite philosophical about it: not intentionally but instinctively. For surely the philosopher has only the choice of knowing either everything or nothing. And certainly no philosophy worthy of the name tries to teach only some particular thing or some mélange of things.

* Decimus Magnus Ausonius (c. 310–c. 395 A.D.), Roman poet and teacher of rhetoric. The *Mosella* is a long, rather artificial poem in praise of the river Moselle.

165. In Plato we find unmixed all the pure types of Greek prose in their classic individuality, and often incongruously juxtaposed: the logical, the physical, the mimical, the panegyrical, and the mythical. The mimical style is the foundation and general component of all the rest; the others often occur only episodically. And then he has a further type of prose that is particularly characteristic of him and makes him most Platonic: the dithyrambical. It might be called a mixture of the mythical and panegyrical if it didn't also have something of the conciseness and simple dignity of the physical.

166. To characterize nations and ages, to delineate the noble nobly, is the real talent of the poetical Tacitus. In historical portraits, the critical Suetonius is a greater master.

167. Almost all criticisms of art are too general or too specific. The critics should look for the golden mean here, in their own productions, and not in the works of the poets.

168. Cicero ranks philosophies according to their usefulness to the orator; similarly, one might ask what philosophy is fittest for the poet. Certainly no system at variance with one's feelings or common sense; or one that transforms the real into the illusory; or abstains from all decisions; or inhibits a leap into the suprasensory regions; or achieves humanity only by adding up all the externals. This excludes eudaemonism, fatalism, idealism, skepticism, materialism, or empiricism. Then what philosophy is left for the poet? The creative philosophy that originates in freedom and belief in freedom, and shows how the human spirit impresses its law on all things and how the world is its work of art.

169. Proving things a priori conveys a blissful tranquillity, whereas observation always remains something partial and incomplete. Aristotle made the world as round as a ball by pure abstraction: he didn't leave the slightest corner sticking out or in. For the same reason he also drew the comets into the atmosphere of the earth and made short shrift of the true solar systems of the Pythagoreans. How long will our astronomers, looking through Herschelian telescopes, have to labor before returning to so definitely clear and spherical a view of the world? [AW]

170. Why don't German women write more novels? What are we to conclude from this about their skill in acting out novels in real life? Are both of these arts connected, or does the former relate inversely to the latter? One might almost suspect this to be true from

the circumstance of so many novels coming from English women and so few from French. Or are intelligent and charming French women in the same position as busy statesmen, who never get down to writing their memoirs except perhaps after they've been discharged from service? And when would such a female capitalist believe she's been cashiered? With the stiff etiquette of female virtue in England and the cloistered life into which women are forced by the rudeness of male society there, the frequency of novel writing by English women seems to indicate a need for more liberal conditions. One suns oneself by moonlight when one fears darkening the skin by walking out during the day. [AW]

171. A French critic has discovered *le flegme allemand* in Hemsterhuis's writings; another, after a French translation of Müller's *History of Switzerland** appeared, thought the book contained good raw materials for a future historian. Such extravagant stupidities should be preserved in the annals of the human spirit: even with the greatest intelligence it's impossible to invent them. And they also have this similarity to ideas of genius: that every word appended as commentary would deprive them of their piquancy. [AW]

172. One can say that it's a distinguishing mark of poetical genius to know a great deal more than he knows he knows. [AW]

173. There's nothing ornamental about the style of the real poet: everything is a necessary hieroglyph. [AW]

174. Poetry is music for the inner ear, and painting for the inner eye; but faint music, evanescent painting. [AW]

175. Some people prefer to look at paintings with closed eyes, so as not to disturb their imagination. [AW]

176. It could be said quite literally of many ceilings that there's pie in the sky. [AW]

177. In general it's probably impossible to enjoin any other precept for the frequently unsuccessful art of painting word-pictures than to vary it as much as possible with a mode of representation conforming to the actual objects. Sometimes the moment described can emerge alive from a story. At times an almost mathematical exactness of topical detail is necessary. Most often the tone of the de-

* Johannes von Müller (1752–1809), German historian, the so-called Thucydides of the Germans.

scription has to do its best to communicate the "how" of it to the reader. Diderot is a master of this. Like Abt Vogler,* he sets many paintings to music. [AW]

178. If any work of German painting is worthy of being displayed in the forecourt of Raphael's temple, then certainly Albrecht Dürer and Holbein would be much closer to the inner sanctum than the scholarly Mengs.† [AW]

179. Don't criticize the limited artistic taste of the Dutch. In the first place, they know exactly what they want. Secondly, they have created their own genres for themselves. Can either of these statements be made about the dilettantism of the English?

180. Greek sculpture is extremely modest wherever the purity of the sublime is concerned. In the nude figures of gods and heroes, for example, earthly necessity is suggested in only the most discreet way. But it is, of course, incapable of false delicacy and therefore displays the bestial lusts of the satyrs without any kind of concealment. Everything must remain true to its kind. Because of their shapes, these untamable creatures were outcasts from humanity to begin with. Similarly it was perhaps not merely a sensual but a moral refinement that created the hermaphrodites. Since sensuality had somehow happened to move off in that direction, people imagined specific beings originally created for the purpose. [AW]

181. Rubens's composition is often dithyrambical while his figures remain inert and disjointed. The fire of his temperament is at war with the leadenness of the climate. If his paintings stand in need of greater inward harmony, then he should either have been less vital, or else not Flemish. [AW]

182. To have a Diderot describe an art exhibition for you is a truly imperial luxury. [AW]

183. Hogarth painted ugliness and wrote about beauty. [AW]

184. Pieter Laer's bambocciades are Dutch colonists in Italy. Though the warmer climate seems to have tanned their complexions, it has ennobled their character and expression by giving them more robust strength. [AW]

* Georg Joseph Vogler (1749–1814), usually called Abt (abbé), German composer and musician.
† Anton Raphael Mengs (1728–1779), German painter and collaborator of Winckelmann's.

Fragments

185. The thing itself can make us forget about its size: it wasn't felt to be improper that Olympian Jove couldn't stand up because he would have smashed the roof in; and Hercules carved on a stone still appears to be superhumanly large. Only dimensions that are scaled down may be deceptive. When something is ordinary, a colossal treatment only serves, as it were, to multiply its ordinariness. [AW]

186. We're right to laugh at the Chinese who, looking at European portraits done in light and shadow, asked if these people were really so bespotted. But would we dare smile at an ancient Greek who, having been shown a painting in Rembrandtian chiaroscuro, would innocently remark: Is this how they paint in the country of the Cimmerians? [AW]

187. No medicine is more powerful against base lust than the worship of beauty. Hence all higher sculpture is chaste, no matter what the subject; it purifies the senses, as tragedy, according to Aristotle, purifies the passions. Its chance effects are irrelevant in this respect, because even a Vestal virgin can arouse lust in filthy souls. [AW]

188. Certain things have never been equaled because the circumstances of their achievement were too degrading. If some drunken innkeeper like Jan Steen* doesn't happen to become a painter, then you can't very well expect some artist to become a drunken innkeeper. [AW]

189. The small worthless part of Diderot's *Essai sur la Peinture* is its sentimentality. But because of his incomparable impudence, he manages himself to set right any reader whom this could lead astray. [AW]

190. Nature at its flattest and most monotonous is the best teacher of a landscape painter. Consider the wealth of Dutch art that comes under this heading. Poverty makes one thrifty: there comes from it a sense of frugality that is gladdened by even the slightest hint of higher life in nature. When later during his travels the artist gets to know romantic scenes, they make an even greater impression on him. The imagination too has its antitheses: the greatest painter of horrific wastelands, Salvator Rosa, was born in Naples. [AW]

* Jan Steen (1626–1679), Dutch painter of realistic and humorous scenes; for a time a tavern-keeper who is thought by some to have drunk too much of his own.

191. The ancients, it seems, loved eternity in miniatures as well: the gem-carver's art is the miniature of the sculptor's. [AW]

192. Ancient art per se simply won't be resurrected, no matter how unremittingly scholarship labors at the accumulated treasures of nature. Of course, it often seems so; but there's always something lacking, namely precisely what derives from life alone and no model can provide. For all that, the fortunes of ancient art do return with literal precision. It's as if the spirit of Mummius,* who exercised his connoisseurship so strenuously on the art treasures of Corinth, were now arisen from the dead. [AW]

193. If you don't let yourself be blinded by aesthetic terminology and learned allusions, then you find that a sense for the plastic arts is a much rarer accomplishment among ancient and modern poets than you might expect. Pindar, before all others, can be called the most plastic of poets, and the delicate style of old vase-paintings reminds one of his Dorian softness and gentle splendor. Propertius, who in eight lines could portray as many artists, is an exception among the Romans. Dante reveals great talent for painting in his treatment of the visible world, but he has greater precision of draftsmanship than he has perspective. He lacked subjects on which to practice this faculty, for the new art was then in its childhood and the old was still in the grave. But then, what could paintters teach a man from whom Michelangelo could learn? There are marked traces in Ariosto's work to show that he lived in the most flourishing period of painting; his descriptions of beauty and his taste for it sometimes carried him beyond the limits of poetry. This is never the case with Goethe. At times he makes the plastic arts the subject of his poems, but otherwise all mention of them is either irrelevant or farfetched. The fullness of calm possession doesn't thrust itself into the light of day, nor does it hide itself. All such passages aside, the poet's love for painting and his insight are unmistakable in the grouping of his figures, in the simple grandeur of his outlines. [AW]

194. To prove that ancient coins are genuine, numismatists look for so-called noble rust [verd-antique]. The art of counterfeiting has managed to imitate everything except this minting of time. There's

---

* Lucius Mummius (fl. second century B.C.), Roman consul who defeated the Achaean League, captured Corinth, killed its inhabitants, sent its art treasures to Rome, and razed the city to the ground.

also noble rust on people, heroes, philosophers, poets. Müller is a superb numismatist of humanity. [AW]

195. Condorcet built a monument to himself by writing, while encompassed by mortal dangers, his book on the *Progrès de l'esprit humain*. Isn't it a more beautiful one than any he could have constructed, during his brief respite, out of his own limited individuality? How could he have appealed better to posterity than by forgetting himself while dealing with it? [AW]

196. Pure autobiographies are written either by neurotics who are enthralled by their own egos — a class that includes Rousseau; or out of robust artistic or adventurous self-love, like that of Benvenuto Cellini; or by born historians who consider themselves nothing more than the raw materials of historical art; or by women who are playing the coquette with posterity as well as with their contemporaries; or by worrisome people who want to clean up the least little speck of dust before they die and who can't bear letting themselves depart this world without explanations. Or else they are to be viewed as nothing more than *plaidoyers* before the public. A sizable proportion of autobiographers are actually autopseudists.

197. Hardly any literature other than ours can exhibit so many monstrosities born of a mania for originality. Here too are we proved Hyperboreans. For among the Hyperboreans asses were sacrificed to Apollo, who would then take delight in their marvelous leaps. [AW]

198. In former times nature used to be preached among us, now it's exclusively the ideal. We forget too often that these two things are profoundly compatible, that in a beautiful description nature should be ideal, and the ideal natural. [AW]

199. The notion that the English national character is sublime is unquestionably the doing, in the first instance, of innkeepers; but novels and plays have fostered it and thereby made a by no means contemptible contribution to the science of sublime ridiculousness. [AW]

200. "Nay, I'll ne'er believe a madman," says a very clever madman in Shakespeare, "till I see his brains." One might expect certain self-styled philosophers to fulfill this precondition of belief; and I would wager that one would find they had made papier-mâché out of Kant's writings. [AW]

201. In the *Fatalist*, in the *Essays on Painting*, and wherever he is really Diderot, Diderot is true to the point of shamelessness. He has often surprised nature when she was dressed only in a charming nightgown, and occasionally has also seen her relieving herself. [AW]

202. Ever since the need for the ideal in art has been so earnestly enjoined, one can observe students guilelessly chasing after this particular bird to put, as soon as they can get close enough to it, the salt of aesthetics on its tail. [AW]

203. Moritz loved how the Greeks used neuter adjectives as abstract nouns. He divined something mysterious in it. One could say in the language of his *Mythology* and *Anthusa* that here the human seeks to approximate the divine in every respect, and here too thought seeks to recognize itself in symbol, but sometimes doesn't even understand itself. [AW]

204. No matter how good a lecture delivered from the height of the podium might be, the best of it is dissipated because one can't interrupt the speaker. So too with the didactic writer. [AW]

205. They have a habit of calling themselves Criticism. They write coldly, superficially, pretentiously, and beyond all measure vapidly. Nature, feeling, nobility, and greatness of spirit simply don't exist for them, and yet they act as if they could summon these things to appear before their judgment-stools. Imitations of the outdated French fashion of society verses are the furthest reaches of their lukewarm admiration. For them correctness is equivalent to virtue. Taste is their idol: a fetish that can only be worshiped joylessly. Who doesn't recognize in this portrait the priests of the temple of *belles lettres* who have the same sex as those of *Cybele*? [AW]

206. A fragment, like a miniature work of art, has to be entirely isolated from the surrounding world and be complete in itself like a porcupine.

207. Freethinking always proceeds in the following sequence: first the devil is attacked, then the Holy Spirit, next the Lord Christ, and finally God the Father. [AW]

208. There are days when one is in a very good mood and able to formulate new projects easily, but when one is as incapable of communicating them as of really creating anything. These aren't ideas, only the souls of ideas. [AW]

Fragments

209. Should a language bound by conventions like the French not be able to republicanize itself by having recourse to the power of the general will? The mastery of language over spirit is manifest: but its sacred inviolability follows as little from this domination as does the admission in natural law of the divine origin formerly imputed to all sovereign state power. [AW]

210. The story goes that Klopstock met the French poet Rouget de Lisle, who was paying him a visit, with this greeting: how did he dare appear in Germany after his *Marseillaise* had cost the lives of fifty thousand brave Germans? This was an undeserved reproach. Didn't Samson defeat the Philistines with the jawbone of an ass? And even if the *Marseillaise* really does have a share in the victories of France, then Rouget de Lisle exhausted the murderous power of his poetry in this one piece: with all the others put together you couldn't kill a fly. [AW]

211. To disrespect the masses is moral; to honor them, lawful.

212. Perhaps no people deserves freedom, but that is a matter for the *forum dei.*

213. A state only deserves to be called aristocratic when at least the smaller mass that despotizes the larger has a republican constitution.

214. A perfect republic would have to be not just democratic, but aristocratic and monarchic at the same time; to legislate justly and freely, the educated would have to outweigh and guide the uneducated, and everything would have to be organized into an absolute whole.

215. Can legislation be called moral which punishes attacks on the honor of citizens less severely than attacks on their lives?

216. The French Revolution, Fichte's philosophy, and Goethe's *Meister* are the greatest tendencies of the age. Whoever is offended by this juxtaposition, whoever cannot take any revolution seriously that isn't noisy and materialistic, hasn't yet achieved a lofty, broad perspective on the history of mankind. Even in our shabby histories of civilization, which usually resemble a collection of variants accompanied by a running commentary for which the original classical text has been lost; even there many a little book, almost unnoticed by the noisy rabble at the time, plays a greater role than anything they did.

217. Archaism of the words, novelty in their placement, compelling brevity and digressive fullness, reproducing even the inexplicable features of the individuals it delineates: these are the essential characteristics of the historical style. Most essential of all are nobility, splendor, dignity. The historical style is distinguished by the homogeneity and purity of its native words of true ancestry, and by the selection of the most significant, weighty, and precious words; by a nobly outlined and clearly — rather too rigidly than not clearly enough — articulated periodic structure, like that of Thucydides; by spare solidity, august alacrity, and superb joviality of tone and color after the manner of Caesar; but particularly by that innate and exalted cultivation of Tacitus, which poetizes, civilizes, and philosophizes the dry facts of pure empiricism, refines and generalizes them so that they seem to have been apprehended and variously sifted by someone who is at once a perfect thinker, artist, and hero, who has achieved this without allowing raw poetry, pure philosophy, or isolated wit to disturb the harmony of the whole at any point. All of this must be blended into history, just as images and antitheses must only be hinted at or dissolved again, so that the brooding, flowing expression should match the living actualization of the moving shapes.

218. It's always a strange, rather suspicious feeling when one thinks one knows that such and such is going to happen. And yet it's really quite as strange that we should be able to know that such and such is as it is — which no one ever notices because it always happens.

219. In Gibbon the common, English, pedantic bigotry in matters relating to the classics has been exalted to the level of sentimental epigrams about the ruins of a past grandeur, but still it hasn't been able to divest itself entirely of its native character. He shows us repeatedly that he had absolutely no understanding of the Greeks. And what he loves in the Romans is actually only their materialistic pomp, but particularly — in the style of a country divided between mercantilism and mathematics — he loves quantitative nobility. The Turks, it appears, would have served his purpose just as well.

220. If wit in all its manifestations is the principle and the organ of universal philosophy, and if all philosophy is nothing but the spirit of universality, the science of all the eternally uniting and dividing sciences, a logical chemistry: then the value and importance of that absolute, enthusiastic, thoroughly material wit is infinite, that wit

wherein Bacon and Leibniz, the chief representatives of scholastic prose, were masters, the former among the first, chronologically speaking, the latter among the greatest. The most important scientific discoveries are bon mots of this sort — are so because of the surprising contingency of their origin, the unifying force of their thought, and the baroqueness of their casual expression. But they are, of course, in respect to content, much more than the unsatisfied and evanescent expectation of purely poetical wit. The best ones are *echappées de vue* into the infinite. Leibniz's whole philosophy consists of a few fragments and projects that are witty in this sense. It may be that Kant — the Copernicus of philosophy — has even more natural syncretistic spirit and critical wit than Leibniz, but his situation and his education aren't as witty; and furthermore the same thing has happened to his ideas that happens to popular songs: the Kantians have sung them to death. Therefore it's quite easy to be unfair to him and think him less witty than he really is. Of course, philosophy will only be healthy when it no longer expects and counts on getting brilliant ideas, when it's able to make continuous progress, relying, naturally, on enthusiastic energy and brilliant art, but also on a sure method. But are we to despise the few still extant products of synthesizing genius because no unifying art and science exists as yet? And how could they exist as long as we still simply spell out most sciences like high schoolers and imagine that we've achieved our object when we can decline and conjugate one of the many dialects of philosophy but have no notion of syntax and can't construct even the shortest periodic sentence?

221. A. You always maintain you're a Christian. What do you mean by Christianity? B. What the Christians have been doing — or have wanted to do — for the last eighteen centuries. Christianity seems to me to be a fact. But only a fact in its beginning stages, one, that is, that can't be represented historically in a system, but can only be characterized by means of divinatory criticism.

222. The revolutionary desire to realize the kingdom of God on earth is the elastic point of progressive civilization and the beginning of modern history. Whatever has no relation to the kingdom of God is of strictly secondary importance in it.

223. The so-called History of States, which represents nothing more than a genetic definition of the phenomenon of the present political conditions of a nation, actually can't be considered a pure

art or science. It's a scientific trade that gains nobility through its candor and opposition to the idea of fashion and to the law of the strongest. Even universal history becomes sophistic as soon as it places anything above the communal education of all mankind, even if the heteronomous principle were a moral idea, and as soon as it chooses to take up the cause of any particular side of the historical universe. Nothing is more annoying in a historical work than rhetorical digressions and moral homilies.

224. In his history, Johannes Müller often looks beyond the borders of Switzerland into the history of the world; but less frequently does he examine Switzerland with the eye of a citizen of the world. [AW]

225. If a biography strives to generalize, then it is a historical fragment. If it concentrates on characterizing individuality, then it is a historical document or a work on the art of living.

226. Since people are always so much against hypotheses, they should try sometime to begin studying history without one. It's impossible to say that a thing is, without saying what it is. In the very process of thinking of facts, one relates them to concepts, and, surely, it is not a matter of indifference to which. If one is aware of this, then it is possible to determine and choose consciously among all the possible concepts the necessary ones to which facts of all kinds should be related. If one refuses to recognize this, then the choice is surrendered to instinct, chance, or fate; and so one flatters oneself that one has established a pure solid empiricism quite a posteriori, when what one actually has is an a priori outlook that's highly one-sided, dogmatic, and transcendental.

227. The illusion of anarchy in the history of man arises simply out of the collisions of heterogeneous spheres of nature, all meeting and concatenating in his experience. For otherwise the absolute will has neither constitutional nor legislative power in this area of free necessity and necessary freedom, and only an illusory title to executive and judiciary power. The rough idea of historical dynamism does Condorcet's* mind as much credit as his more than French enthusiasm for the idea of infinite perfectibility — now almost trivial — does credit to his heart.

* The Marquis de Condorcet (1743–1794), French mathematician, revolutionary, and philosopher, whose last and most famous work was the optimistic *Progrès de l'esprit humain* (*Progress of the Human Mind*) (1794), written while he was in hiding from the Revolutionary Terror.

Fragments

228. The historical tendency of his actions determines the positive morality of the statesman and citizen of the world.

229. The Arabs have highly polemical natures; they are the annihilators among nations. Their fondness for destroying or throwing away the originals when the translations are finished characterizes the spirit of their philosophy. Precisely for that reason it may be that they were infinitely more cultivated but, with all their culture, more purely barbaric than the Europeans of the Middle Ages. For barbarism is defined as what is at once anti-classical and anti-progressive.

230. The mysteries of Christianity necessarily led, because of those unceasing struggles which entangled reason with faith, either to a skeptical resignation of all nonempirical knowledge, or else to critical idealism.

231. Catholicism is naive Christianity, Protestantism sentimental Christianity. The latter, besides the merit of its polemical revolutionary services, has the further positive virtue of having — by its worship of the written word — given birth to philology, one of the essentials for a universal and progressive religion. Only Protestant Christianity is perhaps still somewhat lacking in urbanity. To travesty a few of the biblical stories into a Homeric epic, to portray others in the style of classical history with the frankness of Herodotus and the austerity of Tacitus, or to review the whole Bible as if it were the work of a single author: all this would seem paradoxical to everyone, irritating to many, and quite improper and unnecessary to a few. But should anything seem unnecessary that might make religion more tolerant?

232. Since all things that are rightly One are usually Three as well, it's hard to see why it should be any different with God. God isn't simply an idea, but at the same time a thing, as are all ideas that aren't simply delusions.

233. Religion is usually only a supplement or even a surrogate for education, and nothing is religious, strictly speaking, that is not a product of freedom. So that it is possible to say: the more free, the more religious; and the more education, the less religion.

234. It's only prejudice and presumption that maintains there is only a single mediator between God and man. For the perfect Christian — whom in this respect Spinoza probably resembles most — everything would really have to be a mediator.

235. Christ has now been repeatedly deduced by a priori methods: but shouldn't the Madonna have as much right to be an original, eternal, and necessary ideal, if not of pure, then of male and female reason?

236. It's a gross but still common misconception to believe that in order to describe an ideal one has to pack into one name as numerous a conglomeration of virtues as possible, and that one has to exhibit a whole compendium of morality in a single human being — all of which achieves nothing but the obliteration of individuality and truth. The ideal is to be found not in quantity but in quality. Grandison* is an exemplar and not an ideal. [AW]

237. Humor is, as it were, the wit of sentiment. Hence it may express itself consciously; but it ceases to be genuine as soon as one perceives intention in it. [AW]

238. There is a kind of poetry whose essence lies in the relation between ideal and real, and which therefore, by analogy to philosophical jargon, should be called transcendental poetry. It begins as satire in the absolute difference of ideal and real, hovers in between as elegy, and ends as idyll with the absolute identity of the two. But just as we wouldn't think much of an uncritical transcendental philosophy that doesn't represent the producer along with the product and contain at the same time within the system of transcendental thoughts a description of transcendental thinking: so too this sort of poetry should unite the transcendental raw materials and preliminaries of a theory of poetic creativity — often met with in modern poets — with the artistic reflection and beautiful self-mirroring that is present in Pindar, in the lyric fragments of the Greeks, in the classical elegy, and, among the moderns, in Goethe. In all its descriptions, this poetry should describe itself, and always be simultaneously poetry and the poetry of poetry.

239. The fondness of Alexandrian and Roman poets for difficult and unpoetical themes is really a result of their grand conception that all things are subject matter for poetry, though this is something that was by no means a conscious artistic intention, but a historical tendency of their works. And behind the confusion of all the artistic genres by the poetical eclectics of late antiquity there

* A reference to the virtuous hero of Samuel Richardson's novel, *The History of Sir Charles Grandison* (1754).

lies the demand that there should be only One Poetry and One Philosophy.

240. In Aristophanes immorality is, so to speak, legal, and in the great tragedians illegality is moral.

241. How convenient it is that mythological creatures signify all kinds of things that one would like to impute to oneself! By talking unceasingly about them, one contrives to make the good-natured reader believe one possesses the designated virtue. One or another of our poets would be a beaten man if there were no Graces. [AW]

242. If someone attempts a characterization of the ancients en masse, then no one considers that paradoxical; and yet so little do these people usually know their own minds that they would be surprised at the suggestion that classical poetry is an individual in the strictest and most literal sense of the word: more clearly defined in its physiognomy, more original in its manners, and more consistent in its maxims than whole masses of the phenomena whom we consider and should consider, in our legal and social relations, to be people and, yes, even individuals. Is it possible to characterize anything but individuals? Isn't whatever can't be multiplied after a certain given point just as much a historical entity as something that can no longer be divided? Aren't all systems individuals just as all individuals are systems at least in embryo and tendency? Isn't every real entity historical? Aren't there individuals who contain within themselves whole systems of individuals?

243. The mirage of a former golden age is one of the greatest obstacles to approximating the golden age that still lies in the future. If there once was a golden age, then it wasn't really golden. Gold can't rust or decompose: it emerges victoriously genuine from all attempts to alloy or decompose it. If the golden age won't last always and forever, then it might as well never begin, since it will only be good for composing elegies about its loss. [AW]

244. The comedies of Aristophanes are works of art that can be viewed from all sides. Gozzi's* plays have one point of view.

245. To become popular with the masses, a poem or a drama has to have a little of everything, has to be a kind of microcosm. A little misfortune and a little happiness, a bit of art and a bit of nature, the appropriate amount of virtue and the right dose of vice. And it must

* Count Carlo Gozzi (1720–1806), Italian poet and dramatist who defended the *Commedia dell'arte* against Goldoni's attempts at reform.

have spirit along with wit, even philosophy, and particularly morality, sprinkled with politics. If one ingredient doesn't help, then
maybe another will. And even supposing that the whole lot of them
fail, then like many medicines that deserve eternal praise for precisely this reason, they at least won't do any harm.

246. Magic, caricature, and materialism are the means by which
modern comedy can become inwardly similar to the old Aristophanic comedy, just as demagogic popularity is the outward means.
Gozzi has succeeded here to the extent of reminding us of it. But
the essence of the comic art will always remain enthusiastic spirit
and classical form.

247. Dante's prophetic poem is the only system of transcendental
poetry, and is still the greatest of its kind. Shakespeare's universality
is like the center of romantic art. Goethe's purely poetical poetry
is the most complete poetry of poetry. This is the great triple chord
of modern poetry, the inmost and holiest circle among all the broad
and narrow spheres of a critical anthology of the classics of modern
poetry.

248. The individual great figures are less isolated among the Greeks
and Romans. They had fewer geniuses but more brilliance. Everything ancient is brilliant. All of antiquity is a genius, the only genius
that could without exaggeration be called absolutely great, unique,
and unattainable.

249. The poetizing philosopher, the philosophizing poet, is a prophet. A didactic poem should be and tends to become prophetic.

250. Whoever has imagination, or pathos, or a gift for mimicry
ought to be able to learn poetry like any other mechanical art.
Imagination consists of both enthusiasm and invention; pathos, of
soul and passion; and mimicry, of penetration and expression.

251. There are so many people nowadays who are too tender and
softhearted to be able to see tragedies, and too noble and dignified
to go to comedies—a tangible proof of the delicate morality of a
century that only tried to slander the French Revolution.

252. A real aesthetic theory of poetry would begin with the absolute antithesis of the eternally unbridgeable gulf between art and
raw beauty. It would describe their struggle and conclude with
the perfect harmony of artistic and natural poetry. This is to be
found only among the ancients and would in itself constitute nothing but a more elevated history of the spirit of classical poetry. But

Fragments

a philosophy of poetry as such would begin with the independence of beauty, with the proposition that beauty is and should be distinct from truth and morality, and that it has the same rights as these: something that — for those who are able to understand it at all — follows from the proposition $I = I$. It would waver between the union and the division of philosophy and poetry, between poetry and practice, poetry as such and the genres and kinds of poetry; and it would conclude with their complete union. Its beginning would provide the principles of pure poetics; its middle the theory of the particular, characteristically modern types of poetry: the didactic, the musical, the rhetorical in a higher sense, etc. The keystone would be a philosophy of the novel, the rough outlines of which are contained in Plato's political theory. Of course, to the ephemeral, unenthusiastic dilettantes, who are ignorant of the best poets of all types, this kind of poetics would seem very much like a book of trigonometry to a child who just wants to draw pictures. Only a man who knows or possesses a subject can make use of the philosophy of that subject; only he will be able to understand what that philosophy means and what it's attempting to do. But philosophy can't inoculate someone with experience and sense, or pull them out of a hat — and it shouldn't want to do so. To those who knew it already, philosophy of course brings nothing new; but only through it does it become knowledge and thereby assume a new form.

253. In the nobler and more original sense of the word correct — meaning a conscious main and subordinate development of the inmost and most minute aspects of a work in line with the spirit of the whole — there probably is no modern poet more correct than Shakespeare. Similarly, he is also systematic as no other poet is: sometimes because of those antitheses that bring into picturesque contrast individuals, masses, even worlds; sometimes through musical symmetry on the same great scale, through gigantic repetitions and refrains; often by a parody of the letter and an irony on the spirit of romantic drama; and always through the most sublime and complete individuality and the most variegated portrayal of that individuality, uniting all the degrees of poetry, from the most carnal imitation to the most spiritual characterization.

254. Even before *Hermann und Dorothea* appeared, people compared it to Voss's *Luise*. Its publication should have put an end to comparisons, but, in the form of a letter of introduction to the pub-

lic, *Luise* still — and rightly so — is helpful to the former poem in its travels. With posterity it will be a recommendation for Luise that she stood godmother to Dorothea. [AW]

255. The more poetry becomes science, the more it also becomes art. If poetry is to become art, if the artist is to have a thorough understanding and knowledge of his ends and means, his difficulties and his subjects, then the poet will have to philosophize about his art. If he is to be more than a mere contriver and artisan, if he is to be an expert in his field and understand his fellow citizens in the kingdom of art, then he will have to become a philologist as well.

256. The basic error of sophistic aesthetics is to consider beauty merely as something given, as a psychological phenomenon. Of course, beauty isn't simply the empty thought of something that should be created, but at the same time the thing itself, one of the human spirit's original ways of acting: not simply a necessary fiction, but also a fact, that is, an eternally transcendental one.

257. German parties are serious; their comedies and satires are serious; their criticism is serious; all of their belles lettres are serious. Must anything amusing in this nation always be either unconscious or involuntary? [AW]

258. All poetry that wants to produce an effect, and all music that tries to imitate the comic or tragic excesses and exaggerations of eccentric poetry for the sake of exhibiting itself or of making an impression, is rhetorical.

259. A. You say that fragments are the real form of universal philosophy. The form is irrelevant. But what can such fragments do and be for the greatest and most serious concern of humanity, for the perfection of knowledge? B. Nothing but a Lessingean salt against spiritual sloth, perhaps a cynical *lanx satura* in the style of old Lucilius or Horace, or even the *fermenta cognitionis** for a critical philosophy, marginal glosses to the text of the age.

260. Wieland thought that his career, spanning almost half a century, began with the dawn of our literature and ended with its twilight. A really candid confession of a natural optical illusion. [AW]

261. Just as the motto "Mad but clever" of the poetical vagabond

* *Lanx satura* and *fermenta cognitionis* are Latin terms meaning, respectively, a full plate (of food) and the yeast or leaven of knowledge. *Satura* is also the Latin word for satire.

in *Claudine von Villabella** also describes the character of many a work of genius, so too the opposite slogan might be applied to witless correctness: sane but stupid. [AW]

262. Every good human being is always progressively becoming God. To become God, to be human, to cultivate oneself are all expressions that mean the same thing.

263. True mysticism is morality at its most exalted.

264. You shouldn't try to symphilosophize with everyone, but only with those who are *à la hauteur*.

265. Some people have a genius for truth; many have a talent for error — a talent that is accompanied by an equally great industry. As with many a tasty tidbit, the ingredients for a single error are often gathered together with tireless effort from all the continents of the human spirit.

266. Couldn't we have a provisional philosophy right now, even before drafting a logical constitution? And isn't every philosophy provisional until that constitution has been sanctioned by acceptance?

267. The more one knows, the more one still has to learn. Ignorance increases in the same proportion as knowledge — or rather, not ignorance, but the knowledge of ignorance.

268. A so-called happy marriage is to love as a correct poem is to an improvised song.

269. W. [August Wilhelm Schlegel] said of a young philosopher: he has a theory ovarium in the brain and, like a hen, lays a theory every day; and that's his only possible time of rest in his continual movement of self-creation and self-destruction — which could be a tiresome maneuver. [AW]

270. As is well known, Leibniz went to Spinoza to have his glasses made; and that's the only contact he had with him or his philosophy. If only he had also ordered his eyes there, so that he might have gazed at least from a distance into that continent of philosophy that was unknown to him and where Spinoza has his home.

271. Perhaps one has to be arch-modern in order to gain a transcendental perspective on antiquity. Winckelmann felt the Greeks like a Greek. Hemsterhuis, on the other hand, knew how to circumscribe modern amplitude beautifully with ancient simplicity, and

* *Claudine von Villabella* (1776), a "singspiel" by Goethe.

from the height of his culture he cast, as if from a free frontier, equally meaningful glances into the old and the new world. [AW]

272. Why shouldn't there be immoral people as well as unphilosophical and unpoetical ones? Antipolitical or unlawful people are the only ones who shouldn't be tolerated.

273. Mysticism is what the eye of the lover alone sees in his beloved. Anyone can have his own mysticism, but he must keep it to himself. There are doubtless a great many people who parody the beauty of antiquity, but surely some too who mystify it, and therefore have to keep it to themselves. Both attitudes are removed from the sense of its pure enjoyment, and the way it can be regained.*

274. Every philosophy of philosophy that excludes Spinoza must be spurious.

275. People are always complaining that German authors write for such a small circle, and even sometimes just for themselves. That's how it should be. This is how German literature will gain more and more spirit and character. And perhaps in the meantime an audience will spring into being.

276. Leibniz was such a passionate moderate that he even wanted to fuse the I and the not-I, as well as Catholicism and Protestantism. And he thought of activity and passivity as differing only in degree. This is to exaggerate harmony and pursue moderation to the point of parody.

277. To believe in the Greeks is only another fashion of the age. People are rather fond of listening to declamations about the Greeks. But if someone were to come and say, here are some, then nobody is at home.

278. Much seeming stupidity is really folly, which is more common than one might think. Folly is an absolute wrongness of tendency, a complete lack of historical spirit.

279. Leibniz's *Method of Jurisprudence* is, for all practical purposes, a general display of his intentions. He designed it for everyone: for the practical man, the chancery clerk, the professor, the tutor. Its uniqueness consists merely in its combination of juristic substance with theological form. His *Theodicy*, on the other hand,

* The last sentence of this fragment is by Friedrich Schlegel; the rest by his brother, August Wilhelm.

is a lawyer's writ in God's defense against Bayle and accomplices. [S]

280. People think it unfortunate that there's no specific feeling to indicate physical health, but that for illness there is. The wisdom of this arrangement of nature can be seen from the state of the sciences, where the situation is reversed and where someone suffering from dropsy, consumption, or jaundice believes, when he compares himself with a healthy man, that there's no difference between them, other than the one between fat and thin, or brunet and blond. [S]

281. Fichte's theory of knowledge is a philosophy about the subject matter of Kant's philosophy. He doesn't say much about form because he is a master of it, but if the essence of the critical method is that the theory of the determining ability and the system of determined affective impressions should be intimately united in it, like object and idea, in a pre-stabilized harmony, then it might very well be that even formally he is a Kant raised to the second power, and the theory of knowledge much more critical than it seems to be. Especially the new version of the theory of knowledge is always simultaneously philosophy and philosophy of philosophy. There may be valid meanings of the word critical that don't apply to every work of Fichte's, but in Fichte one has to look as he does — without paying attention to anything else — only at the whole and at the one thing that really matters. Only in this way can one see and understand the identity of his philosophy with Kant's. And besides, one can never be too critical.

282. When man can't progress any further, he resorts to some dictatorial command or despotic act or rash decision. [N]

283. Whoever seeks will doubt. But a genius discloses unabashedly and confidently what he sees going on in himself, because he isn't embarrassed to describe himself and so in turn his description isn't embarrassed by him. On the contrary, his perception and the thing perceived seem to harmonize and unite freely into a single work. When we speak of the outer world, when we describe real objects, then we act as the genius does. Without genius none of us would even exist at all. Genius is necessary for all things. But what is usually called genius, is the genius of genius. [N]

284. The spirit comes equipped with an eternal proof of its own existence. [N]

285. A transcendental perspective on this life still awaits us. Only then will it become really meaningful for us. [N]

286. The life of a truly canonical person must be thoroughly symbolic. Isn't every death, according to this premise, a redemptory death? More or less, it goes without saying. And couldn't a number of extremely interesting inferences be drawn from this? [N]

287. Only then do I show that I've understood an author: when I can act in his sense, when I can translate him and transform him in diverse ways, without diminishing his individuality. [N]

288. We are close to waking when we dream about dreaming. [N]

289. Truly sociable wit has no punch. There's a species of it that's only a magical play of colors in the higher spheres. [N]

290. Inspiration is something wherein the spirit reveals itself endlessly, at any rate often reappears in a new shape; and not simply once, at some point near the beginning, as in many philosophical systems. [N]

291. There are Germans everywhere. Germanism is confined to a particular state as little as Romanism, Hellenism, or Britannism are; these are universal characteristics of humanity that have only on occasion achieved perfect universality. Germanism is genuine popularity and therefore an ideal. [N]

292. Death is a triumph over the self that, like all self-mastery, procures a new and easier existence. [N]

293. Is the reason why we need so much strength and effort for something common and vulgar perhaps to be found in the fact that nothing is more uncommon for the real man than wretched commonness? [N]

294. Brilliant subtlety is the subtler use of subtlety. [N]

295. The famous prize competition of the Berlin Academy of Sciences on the topic of the progress of metaphysics elicited answers of all sorts: one that was hostile, one favorable, one unnecessary, another one, then one that was dramatic, and even a Socratic one by Hülsen. A little bit of enthusiasm, even if crude, a certain touch of universality, can hardly fail to make an impression and gain an audience for a paradox. But a feeling for pure genius is a rarity even among cultivated people. No wonder then that there are only a few who are aware that Hülsen's work is one of those that always has been and still is extremely rare in philosophy: a work in the strictest

Fragments

sense of the word, a work of art, all of one cloth, second only to Fichte in dialectic virtuosity. And that a first essay originally intended only as an occasional piece. Hülsen is wholly master of his thought and expression: he proceeds surely and calmly; and this calm, noble circumspection combined with comprehensive vision and pure humanity is precisely what a historical philosopher, in his antiquarian and now unfashionable dialect, would call Socratic: a term, however, that an artist who has so much philological spirit will simply have to put up with.

296. Though he is such an idyllic character, Fontenelle is still strongly hostile to instinct; he compares pure talent, which he considers impossible, with the pointless artistic industry of beavers. How hard it is not to overlook oneself! For when Fontenelle says, *la gêne fait l'essence et le mérite brillant de la poésie*, it seems almost impossible to define French poetry better in fewer words. But a beaver who was an *academicien* would probably have been hard put to hit on the right phrase with a more perfect lack of awareness.

297. A work is cultivated when it is everywhere sharply delimited, but within those limits limitless and inexhaustible; when it is completely faithful to itself, entirely homogeneous, and nonetheless exalted above itself. Like the education of young Englishmen, the most important thing about it is *le grand tour*. It should have traveled through all the three or four continents of humanity, not in order to round off the edges of individuality, but to broaden its vision and give its spirit more freedom and inner versatility; and thereby greater independence and self-sufficiency.

298. In vain do the orthodox Kantians seek the principle of their philosophy in Kant. It's to be found in Bürger's* poems, and reads: "The words of the Emperor shouldn't be twisted and turned."

299. I rather doubt if the philosophers are very far behind the poets in their sublime lack of awareness.

300. When reason and unreason touch, there's an electric shock. It's called polemics.

301. Philosophers still admire only Spinoza's consistency, just as the English only praise Shakespeare's truth.

* The quotation is from Bürger's ballad "Die Frauen von Weinsberg" ("The Women of Weinsberg").

302. Jumbled ideas should be the rough drafts of philosophy. It's no secret how highly these are valued by connoisseurs of painting. For a man who can't draw philosophical worlds with a crayon and characterize every thought that has a physiognomy with a few strokes of the pen, philosophy will never be an art and consequently never a science. For in philosophy the way to science lies only through art, just as the poet, on the other hand, finds his art only through science.

303. To penetrate ever deeper and to climb ever higher are what philosophers like to do most. And they do it, if we are to believe every word they say, with astonishing rapidity. Moving forward is, however, a rather slow process for them. They compete especially in respect to height, outbidding each other remarkably, like two agents at an auction who have unlimited authority to continue the bidding. But perhaps all philosophy that is philosophical is infinitely high and infinitely deep. Or does Plato occupy a rather lower position than modern philosophers do?

304. Philosophy too is the result of two conflicting forces – of poetry and practice. Where these interpenetrate completely and fuse into one, there philosophy comes into being; and when philosophy disintegrates, it becomes mythology or else returns to life. The wisdom of the Greeks was created out of poetry and law. The most sublime philosophy, some few surmise, may once again turn to poetry; and it is in fact a common occurrence that ordinary people only begin to philosophize according to their own lights after they've stopped living. It seems to me that Schelling's real vocation is to describe better this chemical process of philosophizing, to isolate, wherever possible, its dynamic laws and to separate philosophy – which always must organize and disorganize itself anew – into its living, fundamental forces, and trace these back to their origins. On the other hand, his polemics, particularly his literary critique of philosophy, seem to me to represent a false tendency; and his gift for universality is probably still not sufficiently developed to be able to discover in the philosophy of physics what it seeks.

305. Intention taken to the point of irony and accompanied by the arbitrary illusion of its self-destruction is quite as naive as instinct taken to the point of irony. Just as the naive plays with the contradictions between theory and practice, so the grotesque plays with the wonderful permutations of form and matter, loves the illusion of the random and the strange and, as it were, coquettes with infi-

Fragments

nite arbitrariness. Humor deals with being and nonbeing, and its true essence is reflection. Hence its closeness to the elegy and to everything transcendental; and hence its arrogance and its bent for the mysticism of wit. Just as genius is necessary to naiveté, so too an earnest, pure beauty is a requisite of humor. Most of all humor likes to hover about the gently and clearly flowing rhapsodies of philosophy or poetry, and abhors cumbersome masses and disconnected parts.

306. The story of the Gadarene swine is probably a symbolical prophecy from the period of the masterminds, who have now happily plunged themselves into the sea of forgetfulness.

307. When I talk about my antipathy toward cats, I except Peter Leberecht's puss 'n boots.* His tomcat has claws and whoever has been scratched by these has, quite reasonably, cursed him; but others are amused how he, so to speak, takes his walks on the roof of dramatic art.

308. The thinker needs precisely the same sort of light as the painter: bright, without direct sunshine or blinding reflections, and, wherever possible, falling straight down from above.

309. What kind of ideas must those theorists have had who excluded portraiture from the province of the properly fine, liberal, and creative arts. It's just as if one were to refuse to consider something poetical in which a poet praises his actual mistress. The art of the portrait is the foundation and the touchstone of historical painting. [AW]

310. Recently the unexpected discovery was made that the hero in the Laocoön group is represented as dying: and specifically of apoplexy. It's now impossible to develop connoisseurship any further in this direction, unless somebody were to tell us that Laocoön is really already dead, something that would indeed be quite true in respect to the expert. When any occasion offers, Lessing and Winckelmann are taken to task: not beauty, as the former maintains (actually both do and Mengs along with them), nor the latter's calm grandeur and noble simplicity, are supposed to constitute the fundamental law of Greek art, but rather truth of characterization. Surely all human sculpture, down to the wooden idols of the Kamchadales, tries to characterize. But if one wants to capture the spirit of an object in one stroke, then one doesn't point to

* Ludwig Tieck's "Der gestiefelte Kater" (1794).

what is self-evident and what the object has in common with other objects, but rather to what constitutes its essential individuality. It's impossible to imagine characterless beauty; it always possesses, if not a moral, then certainly a physical character — the beauty of a certain age and sex — or reveals definite physical habits, like the bodies of wrestlers. Ancient art created its forms under the guidance of mythology and conceived them not only in their highest and noblest sense, but joined to every characteristic of form and expression that degree of beauty which it could tolerate without being destroyed. That they also knew how to make this possible where a barbarous taste wouldn't even have been capable of conceiving the idea is almost palpable in, for example, ancient busts of the Medusa. If comic or tragic representations were really an objection to this universal aspiration for beauty, then it would have been too obvious to escape the eyes of such connoisseurs of antiquity as Mengs and Winckelmann. Compare the grossest debauchery of ancient Satyrs and Bacchantes with similar performances from the Flemish school, and you would have to be totally unhellenic yourself not to feel what's still Hellenic in them. It's something completely different to wallow in the filth of vulgar sensuality or, like a god in the shape of an animal, to debase oneself out of wanton lust to that level. In the selection of horrible subjects too, everything still depends on the treatment that can diffuse over such subjects the moderating breath of beauty, and has actually done so in Greek art and poetry. Precisely in the warring elements, in the seemingly insoluble contradiction between the nature of what is represented and the law of representation, the inner harmony of the spirit appears most divine. Or is one going to deny the calm grandeur and noble simplicity of the tragedies of Sophocles, simply because they are so very tragic? Winckelmann very definitely recognized that in the body of Laocoön is expressed the most violent state of suffering and struggle; yet the face, he maintains, reveals the indomitable soul of the hero. Now we are given to understand that Laocoön does not scream because he can no longer scream. Of course he can't scream; otherwise he would raise his voice against such a distorted portrayal and misconception of his heroic grandeur. [AW]

311. If the English taste in painting is going to spread even further into the continent, as the mechanical elegance of their engravings gives reason to fear, then one would like to propose that we aban-

don the name "historical painting," which is in any case rather unsuitable, and introduce in its stead "theatrical painting." [AW]

312. In answer to the reproach that the captured Italian paintings in Paris are being treated badly, the man who has been restoring them has offered to exhibit one of Carracci's pictures half restored and half in its original state. An ingenious idea! In the same way, one often sees during some sudden hubbub in the streets a half-shaved face peering out of a window; and, carried out with French vivacity and impatience, this business of restoration may very well have a great deal in common with the barber's art.

313. The delicate femininity of thought and imagination that adheres to the pictures of Angelika Kauffmann* at times insinuates itself illicitly into her figures; you can read in the eyes of her youths that they would so terribly much like to have girlish bosoms and, if possible, hips as well. Perhaps women painters among the Greeks were conscious of this barrier or gulf imposed on their talents. Of the few that Pliny mentions, he cites for Timarate, Irene, and Lala only pictures with female subjects. [AW]

314. Since the demand everywhere now is for practical applications of moral principles, the usefulness of portraiture will also have to be demonstrated by a reference to domestic bliss. Many a man who has gotten rather bored with looking at his wife will rediscover his pristine feelings when gazing at the purer features of her portrait. [AW]

315. The origin of the Greek elegy, it is said, lies in the Lydian double flute. Won't it be looked for soon in the human spirit as well?

316. For empiricists, who are sometimes capable of raising themselves to the level of an aspiration to thoroughness and a belief in great men, Fichte's theory of knowledge still will surely never mean more than the third issue of the *Philosophical Journal*†: the constitution.

317. If nothing too much means a little of everything, then Garve‡ is the greatest German philosopher.

---

* Angelika Kauffmann (1741–1807), German painter who, in part because she had been a child prodigy, was internationally famous.

† The *Philosophisches Journal* (1795–1800), to which Fichte contributed occasionally.

‡ Christian Garve (1742–1798), German philosophical popularizer.

318. Heraclitus said that reason can't be learned by trying to know everything. Nowadays it seems more necessary to remember that pure reason alone doesn't make one educated.

319. In order to be one-sided, we at least need to have one side. This is by no means the case with those people who (like the true rhapsodists in Plato's description of the species) have an understanding only of one thing, not because it's everything to them but because it's the only thing they have, and a thing they're forever repeating. It isn't so much that their mind is enclosed in narrow limits as that it stops altogether, and where it stops, empty space immediately begins. Their whole being is like a dot that still retains some resemblance to gold: namely, that it can be hammered into unbelievably thin and large sheets of foil.

320. Why is an entry for the ridiculous always missing in those fashionable catalogues of all possible principles of morality? Perhaps because this principle is generally valid only in practice?

321. No mere amateur would dare pass judgment on even the slightest exemplar of ancient craftsmanship. But anybody who can produce some sort of conjecture or commentary, or who perhaps has been to Italy, thinks he has a right to talk about classical poetry and philosophy. Here for once they've put too much faith in instinct: for it may very well be one of the demands of reason that every human being should be a poet and a philosopher, and reason's demands, they say, bring faith in their wake. This particular species of the naive could be called the philological naive.

322. The continual repetition of a theme in philosophy is a result of two distinct causes. Either the author has discovered something, but he doesn't yet know himself quite what; and in this sense Kant's writings are rather musical. Or else the author has heard something new, but hasn't understood it properly; and in this sense the Kantians are the greatest musicians of literature.

323. That a prophet isn't heeded in his own country must be the reason why clever writers so often avoid having a homeland in the realm of the arts and sciences. They prefer to concentrate instead on traveling and on writing travel books, or else on reading and translating travelogues; and for that they receive the accolade of universality.

324. All genres are good, says Voltaire, except the one that's boring. But what is the boring genre? It may be bigger than all the rest,

Fragments

and many paths may lead to it. But the shortest probably is when a work itself is unsure of its own proper genre. Did Voltaire never follow this path?

325. Just as Simonides called poetry a talking picture, and painting a mute poem, so might one say that history is philosophy in the state of becoming, and philosophy completed history. But Apollo, who neither speaks nor keeps silent but intimates, no longer is worshipped; and wherever a Muse shows herself, people immediately want to carry her off to be cross-examined. How perversely even Lessing treats this clever Greek's beautiful insight, who perhaps had no opportunity to think of "descriptive poetry," * and who would have considered it quite unnecessary to remember that poetry is spiritual music also, since it would never have occurred to him that the two arts could be separated.

326. Once seized by the rage for progress, ordinary people who usually have no feeling for the future really go at it literally. With head forward and eyes closed they march into the four corners of the world as if the spirit of progress had arms and legs. And if they don't succeed in breaking their necks, then one of two things usually happens: either they become restive, or else they turn tail. The latter class of people has to be dealt with in the manner of Caesar who, in the heat of battle, had the habit of grabbing cowardly soldiers by the throat and turning their faces to the enemy.

327. Masters working in related fields are often those who understand each other least, and even spiritual closeness has a habit of causing dislike. Hence it isn't unusual for generous and cultivated people, who all write, think, or live in a godlike fashion — though approaching God in their own individual ways — to deny each other's religion: not because of any party or system, but through lack of understanding for religious individuality. Religion is quite simply as vast as nature, and even the best priest has only a little piece of it. There are infinite varieties of religion which nonetheless seem to fall of themselves under a few main headings. Some people have a great gift for worshipping the Saviour, for miracles and visions. These are the ones whom the common man calls either dreamers or poets. Another person perhaps knows more about God the Father and is adept at mysteries and prophecies. He is a philosopher and, like the healthy man who rarely talks about health, won't have much to say about religion, least of all his own. Others

* English in the original.

believe in the Holy Spirit and whatever is connected with it — revelations, inspirations, etc. — but in nothing else. These are the artistic people. It's very natural and even unavoidable to want to unite all the different types of religion in oneself. But in attempting to do so, the same thing happens as when one tries to mix the different genres of poetry. Whoever believes really instinctively both in the Saviour and in the Holy Spirit is already practicing religion as an isolated art, and that's one of the most wretched professions an honorable man can have. What would someone who believed in all three have to endure!

328. Only someone who risks himself can risk others. So too only someone who annihilates himself has a right to annihilate another. [S]

329. It's childish to want to persuade people of something for which they have no feeling. Pretend they aren't there and show them what they should learn to see. This is both highly cosmopolitan and highly moral; very polite and very cynical. [S]

330. Many people have spirit or feeling or imagination. But because singly these qualities can only manifest themselves as fleeting, airy shapes, nature has taken care to bond them chemically to some common earthly matter. To discover this bond is the unremitting task of those who have the greatest capacity for sympathy, but it requires a great deal of practice in intellectual chemistry as well. The man who could discover an infallible reagent for every beautiful quality in human nature would reveal to us a new world. As in the vision of the prophet, the endless field of broken and dismembered humanity would suddenly spring into life. [S]

331. There are people who take no interest in themselves: some because they are simply incapable of taking any interest, even in others; others because they are sure of their uniform progress and because their self-creating power no longer requires any reflected sympathy, because in them freedom in all its noblest and most beautiful manifestations has, as it were, become natural. So that here in appearance too, the lowest and the highest meet. [S]

332. Among people who move with the times there are some who, like running commentaries, don't want to stop at the difficult places.

333. According to Leibniz, God exists because nothing prevents

Fragments

the possibility of his existence. In this respect, Leibniz's philosophy is quite godlike.

334. The age isn't ready for it, they always say. Is that a reason why it shouldn't happen? If something can't yet be, then it must at least always continue to become. [S]

335. If the world is the aggregate of all that is dynamically affective, then the cultivated man will never succeed in living in just one world. This single world should be the best: one that can only be sought and never found. But the belief in it is as sacred as the belief in the uniqueness of friendship and love. [S]

336. A man who can be the life of a party with his way of offhandedly cutting out little silhouettes of himself in various poses and handing them around, or who is ready at the slightest hint to transform himself into a cicerone and display what he has inside himself to everyone who stops at his door (like a country squire showing the tangled grounds of his English garden): this kind of man they call open. For those who don't leave their laziness behind when they go out into society, and who have an incidental bent for examining and classifying whatever they see around them, this quality is unquestionably convenient. And there are enough people like this, people constructed exactly like garden houses: where every window is a door and everyone is urged to sit down in the supposition that they won't expect to find more than a thief could clean out in one night without making himself particularly rich in the process. A true human being has something more in him than these wretched household items and won't, of course, expose himself in the same way, because it would be futile in any case to try to get to know him from even the best and most intelligent descriptions of himself. There is no knowledge of character except through observation. You yourselves have to find the point of view from which you can survey the whole man and must know how to infer his inner self from appearances, according to fixed laws and sure intuitions. So that for any real purpose, this kind of self-explanation is superfluous. And to require openness in this sense is as presumptuous as it is ignorant. Who could dissect himself and, like the subject of an anatomical lecture, tear the individual limb out of the context that alone makes it beautiful and intelligible, and, as it were, squirt out with words whatever is most subtle and delicate in it, so that the whole is distorted into a monstrosity? The inner life vanishes under such treatment; it's the most wretched kind of sui-

cide. A human being should be like a work of art which, though openly exhibited and freely accessible, can nevertheless be enjoyed and understood only by those who bring feeling and study to it. A man should be unencumbered and move himself in accordance with his nature, without asking who is looking at him and how. It's only this serene unconcern that really deserves the name of openness: for open is where everyone can enter without resort to violence; though it goes without saying that even what isn't nailed down and bolted should be treated with consideration. That's the extent of the hospitality a human being must provide within his own heart; everything else is not out of place only in the effusions and delights of intimate friendship. In order even to find this narrower circle, a more privileged communication is of course necessary, a diffident, shy openness that discovers its inmost existence here and there through the slight pressure of its springs, and thereby reveals its tendency toward love and friendship. But this is no permanent condition; rather, like a divining rod, it comes to life only at the point where the instinct of friendship hopes to salvage the treasure. Loving souls are led beyond and to either side of this narrow line of moral beauty only through misunderstanding: by the unsuccessful attempts of this beautiful instinct to get at that attractive reserve which doesn't want to disguise but only hide itself, and which is so magically intriguing to anyone who is able to divine excellence; by sanguine hopes and an excitability set in motion by even the slightest affinity and leading to that naïve cordiality which, like the Freemasons, believes that at least the lowest rank can't be conferred on too many people. These are delightful and interesting phenomena because they are still at the borderline of what is the best and only the uninitiated would confuse them with the mannerisms that arise out of pure incapacity. Just as we'd rather deny merit to any book we don't understand, so many people are reserved only because they want to avoid questions about themselves; and in the same way that many people can't read without at the same time saying the words out loud, so many people can't look at themselves without immediately telling us what they see. But this reserve is timid and childishly unsure of itself, and this merely apparent openness doesn't care if someone is there and who it is, but simply pours forth its substance into the void and in all directions like an electric discharge. Another species of boring openness, one that caters more to the listener, is that of the enthusiasts who lecture, explicate, and translate themselves because they consider themselves exemplars

Fragments

in whom everything is instructive and edifying. Heinrich Stilling* is very likely the most perfect specimen of this type; and how is it that he's now sunk so low? With whatever we merely possess, we can afford without much danger to be much more generous than we are. No one should want to keep completely to himself experiences and insights that depend on local and temporal circumstances; they must always be accessible to every honorable man. Of course, there's also a not exactly enviable way of having opinions, feelings, and principles just sort of by the way, and whoever is in that position naturally has much more scope for his insignificant openness. Whereas, those people whose idiosyncrasy of feeling or character always comes into play are very badly off. One has to allow them to be more reserved even toward what others are usually only loosely attached to, until a complete knowledge of themselves and others gives them an unfailing tact for separating entirely the thing that these people are really concerned with from their own individual conception of it, and for discovering for every substance the mutually shared form that is so alien to them, but so much desired by others. In this way, notes and criticisms can be communicated without alluding to ideas and without profaning sensations; and the sanctity of feeling can be preserved without denying to anyone what might even remotely be his due. Whoever has reached this point can be open to anyone according to the measure of his deserts. Everyone would think to have and know him, but only an equal or someone to whom he had conferred the gift of himself would really possess him. [S]

337. A man is arrogant who possesses both intellect and character, and who lets us know every now and then that this combination is useful and good. Whoever demands both from women too is a misogynist. [S]

338. Only the external formative and creative power of man is changeable and subject to the seasons. Change is a word for the physical world only. The ego loses nothing and engulfs nothing; it lives together with all that belongs to it, its thoughts and feelings, in the lordly freedom of immortality. You can only lose something that you've put now in one place, then in another. In the ego, all things are created organically and everything has its proper place.

* Heinrich Stilling or Jung-Stilling, but actually Johann Heinrich Jung (1740–1817), German pietistic and spiritualist writer and sentimental novelist.

What you can lose never belonged to you. This is true even of individual thoughts. [S]

339. Feeling that is aware of itself becomes spirit; spirit is inner conviviality, and soul, hidden amiability. But the real vital power of inner beauty and perfection is temperament. One can have a little spirit without having any soul, and a good deal of soul without much temperament. But the instinct for moral greatness which we call temperament needs only to learn to speak to have spirit. It needs only to move and love to become all soul; and if it is mature, it has a feeling for everything. Spirit is like a music of thoughts; where soul is, there feelings too have outline and form, noble proportions, and charming coloration. Temperament is the poetry of elevated reason and, united with philosophy and moral experience, it gives rise to that nameless art which seizes the confused transitoriness of life and shapes it into an eternal unity.

340. What's often called love is merely a peculiar kind of magnetism. It begins with a tiresomely titillating placement *en rapport*, consists of disorganization, and concludes with revolting clearsightedness and much fatigue. Ordinarily one's also sober during the process. [S]

341. Whoever has discovered a higher viewpoint for himself than that of his external existence is able to remove himself from the world for brief moments. Similarly, those who haven't yet found themselves are thrust into the world only for brief moments, as if by magic, to see if perhaps they might not discover themselves. [S]

342. A beautiful spirit smiling at itself is a thing of beauty; and the moment when a great personality looks at itself calmly and earnestly is a sublime moment. But greater still is when two friends perceive at the same time, clearly and completely, what is holiest in each other's hearts, and when, mutually happy in the assurance of their mutual worth, they can sense the presence of their limitations only by the knowledge of having been made whole through the existence of the other person. That's the intellectual conception of friendship.

343. If you happen to be an interesting philosophical phenomenon and an excellent writer as well, then you can be quite sure of gaining a reputation as a great philosopher. Often one gets it even without the latter prerequisite.

344. Philosophy is a mutual search for omniscience.

Fragments

345. It would be a good thing if a transcendental Limné were to classify the various egos and publish an exact description of them, accompanied in each case by a colored etching. Then the philosophizing ego would no longer be so commonly confused with the philosophized ego.

346. The renowned *salto mortale* of the philosophers is often only a false alarm. In their thoughts they take a frightfully long approach run and then congratulate themselves on having braved the danger; but if one only looks a little more closely, they're still sitting on the same old spot. It's like Don Quixote's flight on the wooden horse. Jacobi too seems to me someone who, though he can never stop moving, always stays where he is: caught in a squeeze between two kinds of philosophy, the systematic and the absolute, between Spinoza and Leibniz, where his delicate spirit has gotten to be rather pinched and sore.

347. It's a good deal more risky to assume that someone is a philosopher than to maintain that he's a sophist: if the latter should never be allowed, then the former is even less admissible.

348. There are elegies of a heroically lamentable sort that might be explained as follows: they are the feelings of wretchedness at the thought of the silliness of the relationship of dullness to folly.

349. Tolerance has no object other than destructiveness. Whoever has no desire to destroy anything has no need to be tolerated. The range between these two extremes is where tolerance exercises the full scope of its powers. For if you can't be intolerant, tolerance would be meaningless. [S]

350. No poetry, no reality. Just as there is, despite all the senses, no external world without imagination, so too there is no spiritual world without feeling, no matter how much sense there is. Whoever only has sense can perceive no human being, but only what is human: all things disclose themselves to the magic wand of feeling alone. It fixes people and seizes them; like the eye, it looks on without being conscious of its own mathematical operation. [S]

351. Have you ever been able to touch the whole extent of another person, including all his rough spots, without causing him pain? Then both of you need furnish no further proof of being cultivated human beings. [S]

352. It's an invention of historians of nature that her creative powers labored long in vain exertions and that, after exhausting them-

selves in forms that could have no lasting life, conceived still others that, though living, were doomed to perish because they lacked the strength to reproduce themselves. The self-creative power of mankind is still at this level. Few live, and most of those who do only have fleeting existence. If they have found their egos in a propitious moment, then they still lack the strength to procreate them out of their own selves. Death is their habitual state, and if they once come to life, they imagine themselves transported into another world. [S]

353. That story about a Frenchman of the *ancien régime* who delivered his patents of nobility to the courts in order to ask for their return after he'd made a small fortune in trade is an allegory about modesty. Whoever would like to be reputed to have this virtue will have to act likewise with his inner nobility. First, let him deliver it *ad depositum* to public opinion and thereby gain the right to demand it back again, so that he may then manage with good luck and hard work an export-import business in other people's services, talents, and ideas: first-rate and medium quality, just as the customer likes it. [S]

354. Whoever wants to fuse tolerance and rigorism would need to be more than self-denying in the former and more than one-sided in the latter. But is this permitted? [S]

355. Pitiful, to be sure, is what the pragmatic philosophy of the French and English is, though they are considered to be so well versed in the knowledge of what man is, despite their failure to speculate on what he should be. Every organic being has its rules, its duties; and if one doesn't know them, how can one possibly understand that being? Where do they get the organizing principle of their scientific descriptions, and what standard do they use to measure man? But at least they're just as good as those who begin and end with the concept of duty. The latter class aren't aware that the moral man rotates around his axis freely by means of his own power. They've discovered the point outside earth that only a mathematician should try to find, but they've lost the earth itself. In order to say what a man should do, one has to be a man, and know it too. [S]

356. Knowing the world means knowing that one doesn't signify much on it, means believing that no philosophical dream can be realized in it, and means hoping that it will never be otherwise, or at best only somewhat flimsier. [S]

Fragments

357. Of a good bible Lessing demands adumbrations, hints, assays; he also approves of tautologies that sharpen one's acumen, and of allegories and parables that put the abstract in didactic dress; and he is confident that the mysteries of revelation are destined to be transformed into the truths of reason. According to this ideal, what book is more fit to be chosen by the philosophers for their bible than the *Critique of Pure Reason?*

358. At one point in describing the action and essence of a monad, Leibniz uses the remarkable phrase: *Cela peut aller jusqu'au sentiment.* It's tempting to apply this to Leibniz himself. If someone goes about making physics more universal, treating it as if it were a part of mathematics, and treating that as if it were a game of charades, and if he then sees that he has to bring theology in as well, whose mysteries appeal to his sense of diplomacy and whose confused controversies tempt his surgical abilities: *cela peut aller jusqu'à la philosophie,* even if he has even more instinct than Leibniz. But surely such a philosophy must always remain a muddled, incomplete something, much like Leibniz's idea of the primeval elemental substance which, in the manner of geniuses, has a habit of endowing particular objects in the external world with the form of its inner being.

359. Friendship is a partial marriage, and love is friendship from all sides and in all directions: universal friendship. The consciousness of necessary limits is the most essential and rarest thing in friendship.

360. If any art exists that could be called the black art, then it must be the art of making nonsense fluent, clear, and flexible, and of organizing it into a mass. The French possess masterpieces of this kind. Every great calamity is at its deepest root a serious grimace, a *mauvaise plaisanterie.* Therefore, all hail and honor to those heroes who never tire of struggling against a folly that often carries in its most trivial aspects the germ of an endless succession of horrible devastations! Lessing and Fichte are the princes of peace of future centuries.

361. Leibniz views existence as an office in court that one has to hold in fee. His God isn't merely the feudal liege lord of existence but also, as his royal prerogative, has sole possession of freedom, harmony, and synthetic power. To steal from the divine privy chancellory a title of nobility for a slumbering monad is a fruitful affair.

218

362. The ability to find for any given end the means which will satisfy that end most fully, without regard for any other consequences, and the ability to select the means in such a way that, aside from its relation to the particular end, nothing else will ensue from it which could either frustrate another one of our ends or else preclude thereby some object from our future exertions: these are two quite different talents, even though language prescribes the word intelligence for both. One shouldn't waste it on just anyone who knows how to display a sense of propriety only in the most ordinary circumstances, or who has acquired, by means of a little self-observation, a certain degree of knowledge about human nature, something that's neither very difficult nor particularly praiseworthy. The concept of intelligence really does make one imagine something meaningful and important, and a talent for making the most expedient choice out of a set list of means is something so trivial that even the most ordinary mind is equal to it and could only be led astray by some mad passionate delusion. To go to great expense for such an object with so imposing a word is surely not worth the trouble. And furthermore, common linguistic usage doesn't justify it. One never ascribes intelligence to nature or to the supreme being, despite the fact that one praises this faculty very highly in all their works. It would be better, therefore, to retain the word only to describe the latter quality. While striving to achieve one particular end, to consider at the same time all real and possible ends, and calculate the incidental natural consequences which each and every action can have, is indeed something great, something that could be said of only a few people. That in common usage something like this is really meant by the word intelligence is also evident from the feeling which is aroused when one uses a certain tone in calling somebody intelligent. Our first reaction is to think the man impressive, and the second, to search him for signs of sympathy and irony, and find him hateful if we don't discover both qualities in him. The latter is perhaps as common as the former, and is certainly quite as natural the moment we define intelligence in this sense. For in fact we expect everyone to be more or less available for our own purposes, and at the same time we want him to become for us, by the free, natural play of his disposition and his artless and unguarded expressions, an object of sympathy and, as occasion warrants, of amusement or innocent mockery as well. With others we're fairly certain of gaining these two objectives even against their will. But the extraordinarily in-

telligent man, who regulates his actions so that they can result in nothing but what he's already foreseen, renders us dependent on his good will for both; and if he isn't sympathetically disposed to entering consciously and freely into the intentions of others, and if he lacks the irony that might cause him to raise himself consciously outside his intelligence and, by renouncing it, offer himself up as one of nature's creatures to whatever use society may find for him, then it's natural for us to want to have the place he occupies in our group filled by someone else. [S]

363. To idolize the object of love is in the nature of the lover. But it's something else to use one's strained imagination to substitute a new image and then admire it as absolute perfection, when it only seems perfect to us because we aren't cultivated enough to perceive the infinite fullness of human nature and the harmony of its contradictions. Laura is the product of her poet. And yet the real Laura may very well have been a woman of whom a less one-sided lover might have made both something less and something more than a saint.

364. Idea for a catechism of reason for noble ladies. The Ten Commandments. (1) Thou shalt have no other lover before him, but thou shalt be capable of friendship without toying with the shadow of love and without coquetry or idolization. (2) Thou shalt not make unto thee any ideal, neither of an angel in heaven, nor of a hero in a poem or novel, nor one that is dreamed up or imagined: rather shalt thou love a man as he is. For nature, your mistress, is a jealous divinity and visits the infatuations of the girl upon the third and upon the fourth generation of the feelings of the woman. (3) Thou shalt not profane even the smallest of the shrines of love: for that woman shall lose her tender feeling who desecrates her favor and delivers herself up for gifts and chattels, or merely in order to become a mother in peace and security. (4) Remember the sabbath day of your heart, to keep it holy, and if they hold you, then break free or perish. (5) Honor the individuality and the will of your children, that they may prosper and live vigorously on earth. (6) Thou shalt not conceive life intentionally. (7) Thou shalt not contract a marriage that may have to be broken. (8) Thou shalt desire to be loved where thou dost not love. (9) Thou shalt not bear false witness for men; thou shalt not extenuate their barbarity in word or deed. (10) Covet the education, art, wisdom, and honor of men. The Credo. (1) I believe in immortal humanity, which was before

it assumed the garment of masculinity and femininity. (2) I believe that I do not live to obey commands or to seek diversions, but rather to be and to become; and I believe in the power of the will and of education to make me draw near once more to the infinite, to deliver me from the chains of miseducation, and to make me independent of the restraints of sex. (3) I believe in inspiration and virtue, in the honor of art and the charm of science, in the friendship of men and the love for my country, in vanished glory and future progress. [S]

365. Mathematics is, as it were, sensual logic. It relates to philosophy as the material arts, music and sculpture, relate to poetry.

366. Understanding is mechanical, wit is chemical, genius is organic spirit.

367. People often think they can insult writers by comparing them to factories. But why shouldn't a real writer be a manufacturer as well? Shouldn't he devote all his life to the business of shaping literary substance into forms that are practical and useful on a grand scale? How well many bunglers could use only a small fraction of the industry and precision that we hardly notice anymore in the most ordinary tools!

368. There already have been and are doctors who want to philosophize about their art. Only businessmen make no show even about this and are quite quaintly modest.

369. A deputy is something quite different from a representative. Representative means only someone who, whether elected or not, portrays in his person a political whole that is, as it were, identical with himself; he is like the visible world-soul of the state. This idea apparently often constituted the spirit of past monarchies and was perhaps nowhere so purely and consistently put into practice as in Sparta. The Spartan kings were at once the supreme priests, generals, and presidents of public education. They had little to do with actual administration; they were quite simply nothing more than kings in the representative sense. The power of the priest, general, and educator is by its very nature undefined, universal, more or less a kind of lawful despotism. Only by virtue of the spirit of representation can it be softened and legitimized.

370. What is it, if not absolute monarchy, when all essential decisions are made secretly by a cabinet, and when the parliament is allowed to discuss and quarrel about the forms openly and osten-

Fragments

tatiously? In this way an absolute monarchy might very well have a kind of constitution that to the uninitiated might even appear to be republican.

371. In order to determine the difference between a duty toward oneself and a duty toward others, it would probably be hard to find other criteria than the ones a certain simpleton recommended for distinguishing between tragedy and comedy. If you laugh and get something out of it at the end, then think of it as a duty toward yourself; if you're closer to crying and someone else gets the benefit of it, then think of it as a duty toward your neighbor. It is obvious that in the final analysis the whole classification amounts to this, and obvious too that it's really a completely immoral distinction. Out of it emerges the notion that there are, as it were, two completely different and conflicting attitudes that either ought to be kept carefully apart or else artificially reconciled by means of some petty arithmetic. And out of this there arise the phantoms of dedication, sacrifice, magnanimity, and every other sort of moral mischief. In fact, the whole morality of all systems is anything but moral. [S]

372. In the works of the greatest poets there often breathes the spirit of a different art. Might not this be the case with painters too? Doesn't Michelangelo in a certain sense paint like a sculptor, Raphael like an architect, Correggio like a musician? And surely they aren't for this reason lesser painters than Titian, who was only a painter.

373. Philosophy was *in ecclesia pressa** among the ancients, as art is among the moderns. Morality, however, has always had a difficult time of it; utility and legality even begrudge the fact of its existence.

374. If one doesn't look at Voltaire's artistry but simply at the message of his book, namely that ridiculing the universe is philosophy and quite the proper thing to do, then one could say that the French philosophers use *Candide* in the same way that women use their femininity — they find an application for it everywhere.

375. Of all things, energy in particular least needs to prove what it can do. If circumstances require, it can quite easily make a show of being passive and be believed. It's satisfied to do its work silently, without accompaniment and without gesticulations. The virtuoso,

* "In the service of the church."

222

the genius, want to carry out some particular intention, create some work, etc. The energetic man always makes use of only the moment, and is always ready and infinitely flexible. He has an infinite number of projects, or none at all; for energy is really more than mere agility: it is effective, certainly externally effective, but it is also universal power, through which the whole man shapes himself and acts.

376. Passive Christians usually regard their religion from a medical, active Christians from a mercantile point of view.

377. Does the state have a right to sanction change, purely arbitrarily, as being more valid than other treaties, and thereby deprive these of their force?

378. It's not unusual for someone who has long seemed and been considered cold to astonish the whole world later with the most violent explosions of passion, brought on by extraordinary provocations. This is a truly sensitive person whose first impressions aren't strong but have lasting effects, penetrating deeply into his heart and growing there secretly, nourished by their own strength. Always to react immediately is a sign of weakness. That inner crescendo of feelings is the mark of an energetic personality. [S]

379. The Satan of Italian and English poets may be more poetical, but the German Satan is more satanic; and to that extent one might say that Satan is a German invention. Unquestionably he is a favorite of German poets and philosophers. So he probably must have his good side, and even if his character consists of unlimited willfulness and scheming, and a fondness for destroying, confusing, and leading astray, one still finds him not infrequently in the very best society. But isn't it possible that up to now people have been mistaken about his real proportions? A great Satan always has something rough and robust about him; at best he only suits the pretensions to impiety of those caricatures who can't get beyond a mere affectation of intelligence. Why are the "Satanisks," the lesser Satans, not present in Christian mythology? There exists perhaps no fitter word and image for those vices *en miniature* which innocence is fond of feigning, and for the charmingly grotesque music of colors, consisting of the most sublime and most delicate mischief which so delights in playing about the surface of greatness. The classical Cupids are only a different species of these Satanisks.

Fragments

380. Reading aloud and declaiming are not one and the same thing. The latter demands a really superlative, the former a moderately good elocution. Declamation belongs in the distance, not in a room. The loud voice to which it must raise itself in order to produce the required variation offends the sensitive ear. The whole effect is lost in the deafening noise. Combined with gesticulations it becomes repulsive, like all demonstrations of extreme passion. A refined sensitivity can tolerate it only at a distance that, as it were, casts a veil upon it. In order to gain its effect by different means, the tone, instead of rising, has to be kept muted and low, and the accent indicated only in such a way that a comprehension of what one is reading is suggested without being fully expressed. Particularly with epic poems and novels, the reader should never seem to be carried away with his subject, but rather maintain the calm superiority of the author himself, standing above his work. Altogether, it's quite necessary to practice reading aloud so as to establish the custom more generally, and quite necessary to establish it so as to practice it all the better. With us, poetry at any rate remains dumb, and nevertheless anyone who hasn't, for example, read *Wilhelm Meister* aloud, or heard it read, has only studied its music in the notes. [AW]

381. Many of the chief founders of modern physics should not be considered philosophers, but artists.

382. Instinct speaks darkly and metaphorically. If it is misunderstood, a false tendency ensues. This happens to ages and nations as often as it does to individuals.

383. There is a kind of wit which, because of its solidity, thoroughness, and symmetry, one is tempted to call architectonic wit. Expressed satirically, it produces the only real sarcasms. It has to be properly systematic, and then again it doesn't; with all its completeness, something should still seem to be missing, as if torn away. This baroque quality may very well be the source of the grand style in wit. It plays an important role in the novella, for surely a story can remain forever new only by virtue of this sort of uniquely beautiful rarity. This seems to be the direction in which the little understood point of the *Conversations of Emigrants** is moving. It's certainly not at all strange that an understanding for pure novellas has practically ceased to exist; and yet it wouldn't be a bad

* Goethe's *Unterhaltungen deutscher Ausgewandeter* (1795).

thing to revive it, since, among other things, one can never understand the form of the Shakespearean drama without it.

384. Every philosopher has his impulsive moments that frequently are real limitations for him, and to which he accommodates himself, etc. Hence those obscure places in a system for the investigator who isolates the system and doesn't study the philosophy historically and as a whole. Many of the confused controversies of modern philosophy are like the legends and gods of classical poetry. They recur in every system, but always in a new form.

385. In the transactions and regulations that are essential to the legislative, executive, or judiciary powers for achieving their aims, something absolutely arbitrary, something unavoidable often happens that can't be deduced from the concept of those powers, and over which they therefore seem to have no lawful authority. Isn't the authority for such extraordinary cases actually derived from the constitutive power and shouldn't that power therefore also have to have a veto and not merely a right of interdiction? Don't all absolutely arbitrary decisions in the state happen by virtue of the constitutive power?

386. The dull person judges all other people like people but treats them like things, and is absolutely incapable of understanding that they are human beings distinct from himself.

387. Critical philosophy is always thought of as if it had fallen from the sky. It would have originated in Germany even without Kant, and might have done so in a variety of ways. Still, it's better the way it is.

388. Transcendental is what is, should be, and can be high up; transcendent what tries to be high up, but can't or shouldn't be. It would be slanderous nonsense to believe that humanity could exceed its own aim, overtax its own powers, or that philosophy oughtn't to be able to do something it wants to do and can do.

389. If every purely arbitrary or purely random connection of form and matter is grotesque, then philosophy has its grotesques as well as poetry; only it knows less about them and has not yet been able to find the key to its own esoteric history. There are works of philosophy that are a tissue of moral discords from which one could learn disorganization, or in which confusion is properly constructed and symmetrical. Many a philosophical quasi chaos of this kind has had stability enough to outlast a Gothic church. In

our century, construction has been less ambitious in the sciences as well as elsewhere, though no less grotesque. There is no lack of Chinese garden houses in literature. So, for example, English criticism, which surely consists of nothing but applying the philosophy of common sense (which is itself only a permutation of the natural and scholastic philosophies) to poetry without any understanding for poetry. For in Harris, Home,* and Johnson, the *coryphaei* of the species, there isn't even the faintest trace of a feeling for poetry.

390. There are law-abiding and agreeable people who think and talk about humanity and life as if they were discussing the best way of breeding sheep, or buying and selling land. These are the economists of morality, and really all morality without philosophy, no matter how sophisticated and sublimely poetical, always retains a certain intolerant and economical hue. Some economists are fond of building, others prefer to patch things up, or always have to be getting something, or drift as the stream carries them, or make a try at everything and hold on wherever they can, or put things in order and divide things up neatly, or watch how it's done and imitate it. All imitators in poetry and philosophy are actually economists *manqués*. Every human being has his economic instinct that needs to be trained quite as much as orthography and metrics deserve to be learned. But there are economic zealots and pantheists who heed nothing but pressing needs and are happy about nothing but their usefulness. Wherever they appear, everything becomes dull and craftsmanlike, and even religion, the ancients, and poetry on their lathe turn into nothing more noble than flax comb.

391. To read means to satisfy the philological drive, to make a literary impression on oneself. To read out of an impulse for pure philosophy or poetry, unaided by philology, is probably impossible.

392. Many musical compositions are merely translations of poems into the language of music.

393. In order to translate perfectly from the classics into a modern language, the translator would have to be so expert in his language that, if need be, he could make everything modern; but at the same time he would have to understand antiquity so well that he would be able not just to imitate it but, if necessary, re-create it.

394. It's a great mistake to try to restrict wit to society. By their

* James Harris (1709–1780), English philologist and aesthetician. Henry Home (1696–1782), English critic.

overwhelming power, their infinite content, and their classical form, the best ideas often cause an embarrassing pause in the conversation. It's just that real wit is still conceivable only in written form, like laws; one has to value one's products according to weight, just as Caesar carefully estimated the comparative weight of pearls and precious stones by balancing them in his hands. Their value increases quite disproportionately to their size; and some that possess, besides an enthusiastic spirit and a baroque exterior, also animated accents, fresh coloration, and a certain crystalline transparency comparable to the water of diamonds, are impossible to appraise.

395. In true prose, everything has to be underlined.

396. Caricature is a passive conjunction of the naive and the grotesque. The poet can use it equally well for tragic or comic purposes.

397. Since nature and man contradict each other so often and so sharply, philosophy perhaps can't avoid doing the same.

398. Mysticism is the cheapest and most moderate of all philosophical ravings. Only credit one of its absolute contradictions, and you will thereby supply all its needs and even allow it to live in the lap of luxury.

399. Polemical totality is, to be sure, a necessary consequence of assuming and demanding unlimited communicability and communication, and it can no doubt destroy one's opponents completely. Still, it does not suffice to legitimize the philosophy of its possessor so long as that philosophy is directed only at externals. Only when applied to the inner world, when a philosophy criticizes its own spirit and creates its own letter on the whetstone and with the file of polemics, only then can it lead to logical correctness.

400. As yet there is no skepticism worthy of the name. Real skepticism would have to begin and end with the assertion of and demand for an infinite number of contradictions. The fact that skeptical consistency would bring with it absolute self-annihilation is nothing characteristic. This is a trait which this logical disease shares with all unphilosophy. A respect for mathematics and a falling back to common sense are the diagnostic symptoms of the quasi-genuine skepticism.

401. In order to understand someone who only partially understands himself, you first have to understand him completely and

better than he himself does, but then only partially and precisely as much as he does himself.

402. In trying to see if it's possible to translate the classical poets, the important thing is to decide whether or not even the most faithful German translation isn't still Greek. To judge by the reaction of the most sensitive and intelligent laymen, there are valid grounds for such a suspicion.

403. A real review should be the solution of a critical equation, the result and description of a philological experiment and a literary investigation.

404. One has to be born for philology just as for poetry and philosophy. There is no philologist without philology in the original sense of the word; that is, without interest in grammar. Philology is a logical emotion, the counterpart of philosophy, enthusiasm for chemical knowledge; for grammar is surely only the philosophical part of the universal art of dividing and joining. By the artistic development of this sense, we arrive at criticism, whose substance can only be the classical and absolutely eternal; otherwise the philologists, almost all of whom reveal the usual unmistakable signs of unscientific virtuosity, might just as easily display their skill on works other than those of classical antiquity, where, as a rule, they have neither any interest nor understanding. But this necessary limitation is all the less to be blamed or regretted since here too only artistic perfection leads to knowledge, and a purely formal philology must move toward a material theory of antiquity and a humane history of mankind. And that is better than a so-called application of philosophy to philology in the usual style of those who compile rather than combine the sciences. The only way to apply philosophy to philology, or, what is much more important, philology to philosophy, is by being both philologist and philosopher. But even without this, the art of philology can assert its rights. To devote oneself exclusively to developing some original instinct is as good and wise as the best and noblest task a man can choose to make the business of his life.

405. Charity is the ignominious virtue that's always made to pay in novels and plays when a common person is elevated into a noble character, or even, as in Kotzebue's plays, when some other extraneous baseness is to be compensated for. Why don't they take advantage of the charitable mood of the moment to pass the hat around the house? [AW]

406. If every infinite individual is God, then there are as many gods as there are ideals. And further, the relation of the true artist and the true human being to his ideals is absolutely religious. The man for whom this inner divine service is the end and occupation of all his life is a priest, and this is how everyone can and should become a priest.

407. The most important part of good breeding is to have the cheek to attribute it intentionally to those one knows don't have it; the most difficult is to intuit and discover the essential commonness beneath the veneer of general good manners. [S]

408. Cute vulgarity and refined bad manners are called delicacy in the language of good society.

409. In order to be called moral, feelings have to be not only beautiful but also wise, appropriate to the structure of the whole, and in the highest sense decorous.

410. Triviality — economy — is the necessary supplement of all people who aren't absolutely universal. Often talent and education are lost entirely in this surrounding element.

411. The scientific ideal of Christianity is to portray God in an infinite series of variations.

412. Ideals that seem unattainable to themselves are for that reason not ideals but mathematical phantoms of a merely mechanical mind. Whoever has a sense for the infinite and knows what he wants to do with it sees here the result of eternally separating and uniting powers, conceives of his ideals at least as being chemical, and utters, when he expresses himself decisively, nothing but contradictions. This is the point that the philosophy of our age has reached, but not the philosophy of philosophy; for even chemical idealists often have only a one-sided, mathematical ideal of philosophy. Their theses in this regard are quite true, that is, philosophical; but the antitheses are missing. The time doesn't seem to have arrived yet for a physics of philosophy, and only a perfect mind could conceive of ideals organically.

413. A philosopher must talk about himself just as the lyrical poet does.

414. If there is an invisible church, then it is the church of the great paradox that is inseparable from morality and that still has to be kept quite distinct from the merely philosophical church. People who are eccentric enough to be quite seriously virtuous under-

Fragments

stand each other everywhere, discover each other easily, and form a silent opposition to the ruling immorality that happens to pass for morality. A certain mysticism of expression, combined with romantic imagination and grammatical understanding, can be something quite attractive and good, and it often serves them as a symbol for their beautiful mysteries.

415. Whoever conceives of poetry or philosophy as individuals has a feeling for them.

416. Depending on how you see it, you need either the fullest expert knowledge for philosophy, or none at all.

417. One shouldn't try to seduce or talk anyone into philosophy.

418. Even by the most ordinary standards, a novel deserves to become famous when it portrays and develops a thoroughly new character interestingly. *William Lovell** undeniably does this, and the fact that all the rest of its staging and scenery is either commonplace or a failure, just like the great stage manager behind it all, and the further fact that what's extraordinary about it is only the ordinary turned inside out would probably not have done the book a great deal of damage, except that unfortunately the character was poetical. Lovell, like his insufficiently differentiated alter ego, Balder, is a complete phantast in every good and every bad, every beautiful and every ugly sense of the word. The whole book is a struggle between prose and poetry, in which prose is trodden underfoot and poetry stumbles and breaks its neck. Besides, it suffers from the fault of many first productions: it wavers between instinct and intention because it doesn't have enough of either. Hence the repetitions whereby the description of sublime boredom at times shifts into a communication of the thing itself. This is the reason why the absolute imaginativeness of this novel could have been misunderstood even by the initiates of poetry and disdained as mere sentimentalism. And this is the reason too why the reasonable reader, who likes to be moderately moved in return for his money, didn't like at all — in fact thought quite mad — the sentimentality of the novel. Tieck has perhaps never again portrayed a character so profoundly and thoroughly. But *Sternbald* combines

* *William Lovell* (1793–1796) and *Franz Sternbalds Wanderungen* (1798) are novels by Ludwig Tieck. Together with Wilhelm Wackenroder, he also wrote the curious religious, aesthetic, historical production entitled *Herzensergiessungen eines kunstliebenden Klosterbruders* (1797), or "Effusions from the Heart of an Art-loving Monk."

the seriousness and vitality of *Lovell* with the artificial religiosity of the *Klosterbruder* and with everything that, taken as a whole, is most beautiful in those poetical arabesques he fabricated out of old fairy tales: namely their fantastic richness and facility, their sense of irony, and particularly their intentional variety and uniformity of coloration. Here too everything is clear and transparent, and the romantic spirit seems to be daydreaming pleasantly about itself.

419. The world is much too serious, but seriousness is nevertheless a rather rare phenomenon. Seriousness is the opposite of play. It has a particular purpose, the most important of all possible purposes; it is incapable of trifling or of deceiving itself; it pursues its aims tirelessly until it has achieved them. For this it needs energy, a mental power of absolutely unlimited extension and intensity. If there's no absolute height and breadth for man, then the word *greatness* is superfluous in the moral sense. Seriousness is greatness in action. Great is what simultaneously possesses enthusiasm and genius, what is both divine and complete. Complete is what is at the same time natural and artificial. Divine is what wells up out of love into pure eternal being and becoming, what is higher than any poetry and philosophy. There is a kind of serene divinity that lacks the crushing power of the hero and the creative activity of the artist. Whatever is simultaneously divine, complete, and great is perfect.

420. Whether or not a cultivated woman — and it's only of such that we can speak in moral terms — is corrupt or pure is a question that perhaps can be answered with considerable certainty. If she follows the general trend, if energy of spirit and character — their external appearance and whatever else relates to it — are her be-all and end-all, then she is corrupt. If she knows of something greater than greatness, if she can smile at her natural liking for energy, if she is, in a word, capable of enthusiasm, then she is innocent in the moral sense. In this respect, one can say that all womanly virtue is religious. But that women should, as it were, believe more in God or Christ than men do, that some good and beautiful habit of free-thinking should suit them less than it does men, is probably only one of the infinite number of commonly accepted platitudes which Rousseau built into a real systematic theory of womankind; and in which nonsense is so improved and developed that it simply had to gain universal acclaim.

421. Perhaps the great mass likes Friedrich Richter's novels only because of their apparent adventurousness. All in all he is probably

Fragments

interesting in the greatest variety of ways and for the most contradictory reasons. Although the educated businessman sheds quanti-
ties of noble tears while reading him, and the exacting artist hates
him as the bloody symbol of the triumphant unpoetry of his nation
and his age, the man of universal tendency can idolize his arbitrariness or else find great pleasure in those grotesque porcelain figures
that his pictorial wit drums together like imperial soldiers. Richter
is a unique phenomenon: an author who hasn't mastered the first
principles of his art, who can't express a bon mot properly and
can't tell a story in a better than average way, and yet someone
who — if only because of a humorous dithyramb like the mulish,
pithy, tense, and magnificent Leibgeber's letter to Adam — cannot
justly be denied the name of a great poet. Even if his works don't
have a great deal of cultivation, they are nonetheless cultivated.
The whole is like the part, and vice versa; in short, he is accomplished. It is a great advantage of *Siebenkäs* that its execution and
descriptions are even better than those of his other works; and it
has the far greater advantage of having so few Englishmen in it. To
be sure, his Englishmen are ultimately Germans too, but in idyllic
surroundings and with sentimental names; still, they always have a
strong resemblance to Louvet's Poles and so belong with those
false tendencies he is so given to. In the same category is also where
his women, philosophy, the Virgin Mary, delicacy, ideal visions,
and self-criticism belong. His women have red eyes and are para-
gons, puppets who serve as occasions for psycho-moralistic reflections on womanhood or infatuation. In fact, he almost never comes
down to the level of portraying his characters; it is enough for him
to have thought of them, and now and then to say something striking about them. And so he sides with the passive humorists, the
people who are actually nothing more than humorous objects; the
active ones seem more self-sufficient, but they share too much of a
family likeness amongst themselves and with the author to make us
think of their self-sufficiency as a merit. His decor consists of
leaden arabesques in the Nuremberg style. It is here that the
monotony of his imagination and intelligence — bordering almost
on destitution — becomes most noticeable; but here too do we find
that charming dullness of his, and that piquant tastelessness which
we can censure only on the grounds that he doesn't seem to be
aware of it. His madonna is a sentimental sexton's wife, and his
Christ is cast in the role of an enlightened student of divinity. The
more moral his poetical Rembrandts are, the more common and or-

dinary they become; the funnier, the closer to the good; the more dithyrambical and provincial, the more divine: for he conceives of the village primarily as the City of God. His humorous poetry is separating itself more and more from his sentimental prose; often it appears, like interpolated songs, as an episode, or else it destroys the book in the shape of an appendix. But at times large masses of it still escape from him into the universal chaos.

422. Mirabeau played a great role in the Revolution because his character and mind were revolutionary; Robespierre because he obeyed the Revolution absolutely, devoted himself entirely to it, worshipped it, and considered himself its god; Bonaparte because he can create and shape revolutions, and destroy himself.

423. Isn't it true that the modern French national character actually begins with Cardinal Richelieu? His strange and rather tasteless universality reminds one of many of the most remarkable French phenomena which came after him.

424. The French Revolution may be regarded as the greatest and most remarkable phenomenon in the history of states, as an almost universal earthquake, an immeasurable flood in the political world; or as a prototype of revolutions, as the absolute revolution per se. These are the usual points of view. But one can also see it as the center and apex of the French national character, where all its paradoxes are thrust together; as the most frightful grotesque of the age, where the most profound prejudices and their most brutal punishments are mixed up in a fearful chaos and woven as bizarrely as possible into a monstrous human tragicomedy. Now only a few isolated traces remain that might serve to develop these historical insights.

425. The first impulse of morality is to oppose positive legality and conventional justice, and to be boundlessly irritable in temper. If one adds to this the negligence so peculiar to independent and strong minds, and the passion and clumsiness of youth, then it is unavoidable that there should be excesses with incalculable consequences which can often poison a whole life. And so it happens that the rabble considers some people criminals or examples of immorality whom a truly moral person would class among the extremely rare exceptions who may be regarded as creatures of his own kind, as fellow citizens of his world. Who doesn't think in this connection of Mirabeau and Chamfort?

426. It's natural that the French should more or less dominate the age. They are a chemical nation and in them the chemical sense is most widely developed, and they always conduct their experiments — not least in moral chemistry — on a grand scale. Likewise, the age is also a chemical one. Revolutions are universal, chemical not organic movements. Big business is the chemistry of a great economy, and there's probably an alchemy of the same kind, too. That the novel, criticism, wit, sociability, the most recent rhetoric, and all previous history have a chemical makeup is self-evident. But until we have reached the stage of being able to characterize the universe and classify mankind, we have to be content with brief notes on the prevailing mood and individual mannerisms of the age, without even being able to draw a profile of the giant. For how would we go about finding out if the age is really an individual or perhaps only the collision point of other ages without this kind of preliminary knowledge? Where exactly does it begin and where does it end? How is it possible to understand and punctuate the contemporary period of the world correctly, if one can't even foresee the general outlines of the subsequent one? By analogy to what I said before, an organic age will follow a chemical one, and then the citizens of the next solar revolution will probably think much less of us than we do now, and consider a great deal of what we now simply marvel at as only the necessary preliminary exercises of humanity.

427. A so-called investigation is a historical experiment. The subject and result thereof are a fact. Every fact must have a strict individuality, be both a mystery and an experiment, that is, an experiment of creative Nature. Everything is secretive and mysterious that can only be apprehended by enthusiasm and philosophical, poetical, or moral understanding.

428. Even language behaves badly toward morality. It's never so rude and beggarly as when it comes to classifying moral concepts. As an example, let me cite the three types of character that can be constructed out of the various relations between ends and means. There are people with whom everything they consider a means turns mysteriously into an end. They dedicate themselves to a branch of science in order to make their fortune, and are captivated by its charms. They look up one of its devotees, and they begin to love him. They frequent his circle of friends in order to be with him, and they become the most fervent members of that

circle. They write, or dabble in the fine arts, or dress themselves better in order to be liked by these new friends, and suddenly they discover, quite independently of being liked or not being liked, a profound pleasure in their writing, their study of art, their elegance. This is a very specific type of character that is easily recognizable anywhere. But does language have a name for it? A great variety of activities can be run through in this way, and even language is generous with the adjectives "variegated" or "many-sided." But this variety is only a fraction of the manifestations of this mode of thinking, and a fraction shared by several other modes. People of this type transform the finite space of a specific moment into an infinite and infinitely divided greatness until they have reached their particular end. The man who is always delighted by this knack of treating the finite as if it were something infinite would like to call it by its name; but that is only to describe an impression. For the essence of this kind of character — namely that easy and habitual shifting from an interest in something as a means into a direct and immediate interest — language has no word. There are other people who take the opposite course and quite readily treat something that was for them at the outset an end as the means to something else; who, after they have enthusiastically read an author, finish by writing a critical sketch of him; who, after they have labored long in a science, soon raise themselves to the level of philosophy of science; and who, even when bound by personal attachment, are in danger of treating a beautiful friendship as the means to gaining new insight into human nature, or to philosophizing about love on the basis of their own experiments. Someone give me a name for that in German! To talk about the effect and impression of such a character is easy: you can say how noble it is to cast the finite aside because one is pursuing the infinite; or how original it is to tear down barriers where others are deterred; or to open up new channels where others imagine a dead end; or to run through great passions at a torrential pace and construct great works of art almost in passing (for these are the natural expressions of this kind of a character if he doesn't burn out). To portray all this, language has plenty of words. There is a third type of character who combines the other two; who, as long as he has an end before his eyes, reshapes all means into ends belonging to the system of that primary end, but who still, while enjoying this finite pleasure, does not forget to strive for higher things and in the midst of making his giant strides, again and again remembers the end he started out with. He combines a talent for discovering his own limits easily, and for not attempting anything he cannot do, with a gift for enlarging his ends while at the same time enlarging his powers; he combines the wisdom and calm resignation of an inwardly directed mind with the energy of a completely elastic and expansive spirit that makes use of the slightest opening to escape and to occupy, in a moment, a much larger area than before. He never makes a futile attempt to escape the recognized limitations of the moment, and yet always burns with a longing to augment himself still further; he never struggles against fate, but forever challenges it to provide him with a broader existence; he always keeps close watch over everything a man can ever become or hope to be, but he never goes after something until the right moment. That this kind of character is a perfect practical genius, that everything is design in him and everything instinct, everything will and everything nature, can all be said, but it is useless to look for a word to describe his essence. [S]

429. Just as the novella has to be new and striking at every point of its substance and development, so perhaps the poetical tale and especially the romance has to be infinitely bizarre. For the romance tries not only to interest the imagination, but also to enchant the mind and stimulate the feelings; and the essence of the bizarre seems to consist precisely in certain arbitrary and strange connections and confusions of the processes of thinking, poetizing, and acting. There is a kind of bizarreness of enthusiasm that is compatible with the greatest refinement and freedom, and that not only intensifies tragedy but makes it beautiful and, as it were, deifies it: like Goethe's *Bride of Corinth*,* which is an epoch in the history of poetry. What moves one in that work lacerates and nevertheless is seductively fascinating. Some parts could almost be called burlesque, and it is precisely in these parts that the horrible seems overwhelmingly great.

430. There are unavoidable situations and relationships that one can tolerate only by transforming them by some courageous act of the will and seeing them as pure poetry. It follows that all cultivated people should be capable of being poets if they have to be; and from this we can deduce equally well that man is by nature a poet, and that there is a natural poetry, or vice versa.

* A ballad written in 1797.

431. To sacrifice to the Graces means, when said to a philosopher, as much as: create irony and aspire to urbanity.

432. There are works, particularly rather comprehensive historical works, that in all their individual component parts are beautifully and attractively written, but as wholes are unpleasantly monotonous. To avoid this, the coloration, tone, and even the style would have to be changed and made strikingly different in each of the various large blocks that make up the whole; in this way, the work would become not only more variegated, but also more systematic. It is clear that this kind of regular alternation is not the result of chance; here the artist has to know precisely what he wants to do in order to be able to do it. But it is equally clear that it would be premature to call a work of poetry or prose art before these works have reached the point of being completely structured. The possibility that genius could be made superfluous by this requirement is something that needn't worry us, since the leap from the most vivid recognition and clearest perception of what needs to be done to its actual accomplishment will always be infinite.

433. The essence of the poetical sense, it may be, consists in being impressionable to the point of losing self-awareness, in getting emotionally wrought up about nothing and moved to daydreaming for no reason at all. Moral sensitivity is quite compatible with a total lack of poetical sense.

434. Should poetry simply be divided up? Or should it remain one and indivisible? Or fluctuate between division and union? Most of the ways of conceiving a poetical world are still as primitive and childish as the old pre-Copernican ideas of astronomy. The usual classifications of poetry are mere dead pedantry designed for people with limited vision. Whatever somebody is capable of producing, or whatever happens to be in fashion, is the stationary earth at the center of all things. But in the universe of poetry nothing stands still, everything is developing and changing and moving harmoniously; and even the comets obey invariable laws of motion. But until the course of these heavenly bodies can be calculated and their return predicted, the true world system of poetry won't have been discovered.

435. Some grammarians seem to want to introduce into language that principle in the old law of nations that says every stranger is an enemy. But a writer who knows how to manage even without foreign words will always have a right to use them wherever the

Fragments

demands of his genre require or make desirable a coloration of universality; and a historical mind will have a respectful and loving interest in old words and will occasionally rejuvenate them. After all, they often have not only more experience and understanding, but also more vitality and unity than many so-called human beings or grammarians.

436. Its contents quite aside, the *Fuerstenspiegel** is as good a model of the *bon ton* in written conversation as can, with only a few exceptions, be met with in German prose; and a writer who wants to put philosophy and the life of society *en rapport* with each other should learn from it how to raise the decorum of convention to the niveau of natural propriety. Actually everyone should know how to write in this style who has occasion to print something without wanting for that reason to be an author.

437. How can a science pretend to scientific rigor and perfection when it is usually regulated and arranged *in usum delphini*† or according to the system of accidental causation, like mathematics?

438. Urbanity is wit of harmonious universality, and that is the beginning and the end of historical philosophy and Plato's most sublime music. The humanities are the gymnastics of this art and science.

439. A critical sketch is a critical work of art, a *visum repertum* of chemical philosophy. A review is an applied and applying critical sketch with respect to the contemporary state of literature and the reading public. Surveys and literary annals are sums or series of critical sketches. Literary parallels are critical groups. By joining both together we get a selection of the classics, the critical world system for a given sphere of philosophy or poetry.

440. All pure, unselfish education is gymnastic or musical; its aim is the development of each particular power and the combined harmony of all. The Greek dichotomy of education is more than just another one of the paradoxes of antiquity.

441. Tolerance means being almost unaware of being free in all di-

* A *Fuerstenspiegel* is a "Mirror for Princes," that is, a manual of conduct for the nobility, like Machiavelli's *The Prince*. There may also be a reference here to Wieland's poetical novel, *Der goldene Spiegel* (*The Golden Mirror*).
† The notice on the series of translations of classics ordered by Louis XIV for the Dauphin's use.

rections and from all sides; means living one's whole humanity; means holding sacred whatever acts, is, and develops, according to the measure of one's power; means taking part in all aspects of life and not letting oneself be seduced by limited opinions into a hatred or contempt for life.

442. Even those call themselves philosophical lawyers who, along with their other, frequently unlawful rights, also have a natural right that is often even more unlawful.

443. To deduce a concept is to provide the genealogical proof of its descent from the intellectual perception of a science. For every science has its genealogical proofs.

444. Many people find it strange and ridiculous when musicians talk about the ideas in their compositions; and it often happens that one perceives they have more ideas in their music than they do about it. But whoever has a feeling for the wonderful affinity of all the arts and sciences will at least not consider the matter from the dull viewpoint of a so-called naturalness that maintains music is supposed to be only the language of the senses. Rather, he will consider a certain tendency of pure instrumental music toward philosophy as something not impossible in itself. Doesn't pure instrumental music have to create its own text? And aren't the themes in it developed, reaffirmed, varied, and contrasted in the same way as the subject of meditation in a philosophical succession of ideas?

445. Dynamics is the macrology of energy which, in astronomy, is applied to the organization of the universe. To that extent both could be called historical mathematics. Algebra demands the most wit and enthusiasm, that is, of the mathematical sort.

446. Consistent empiricism ends in contributions toward settling misunderstandings, or in a subscription to truth.

447. False universality is either theoretical or practical. The theoretical type is the universality of a bad lexicon, of a record office. The practical type originates in a totality of involvement.

448. These are the intellectual insights of criticism: the feeling of the infinitely subtle analytic quality of Greek poetry, and that of the infinitely rich mixture of Roman satire and Roman prose.

449. As yet there has been no moral author who could be compared with the great masters of poetry and philosophy. Such a writer would have to combine the sublime antiquarian politics of Müller

with Forster's great universal economics and Jacobi's moral gymnastics and music; and combine in his language, too, the weighty, dignified, and enthusiastic style of the first with the fresh hues, the lovable delicacy of the second, and the refined sensitivity — so like a distant, ghostly concertina — of the third.

450. Rousseau's polemic against poetry is really only a bad imitation of Plato. Plato is more against poets than he is against poetry; he thought of philosophy as the most daring dithyramb and the most monodic music. Epicurus is the real enemy of art, for he wants to root out imagination and retain sense only. Spinoza might be viewed as the enemy of poetry in quite a different way: because he demonstrates how far one can get with philosophy and morality unaided by poetry, and because it is very much in the spirit of his system not to isolate poetry.

451. Universality is the successive satiation of all forms and substances. Universality can attain harmony only through the conjunction of poetry and philosophy; and even the greatest, most universal works of isolated poetry and philosophy seem to lack this final synthesis. They come to a stop, still imperfect but close to the goal of harmony. The life of the Universal Spirit is an unbroken chain of inner revolutions; all individuals — that is, all original and eternal ones — live in him. He is a genuine polytheist and bears within himself all Olympus.

Ideas

1. The calls for and even the beginnings of a morality that might be more than the practical part of philosophy are becoming increasingly obvious. Already there is talk even of religion. It's time to tear away the veil of Isis and reveal the mystery. Whoever can't endure the sight of the goddess, let him flee or perish.

2. A priest is someone who lives only in the invisible world and for whom everything visible possesses only the truth of an allegory.

3. Only in relation to the infinite is there meaning and purpose; whatever lacks such a relation is absolutely meaningless and pointless.

4. Religion is the all-animating world-soul of culture, the fourth invisible element besides philosophy, morality, and poetry, which like the hearth-held fire gives off gentle warmth to all around it, and only breaks out into terrible destruction when subjected to forcible external interference.

5. The mind understands something only insofar as it absorbs it like a seed into itself, nurtures it, and lets it grow into blossom and fruit. Therefore scatter holy seed into the soil of the spirit, without any affectation and any added superfluities.

6. Eternal life and the invisible world are to be found only in God. All spirits dwell in him. He is an abyss of individuality; he alone is infinitely full.

7. Liberate religion and a new race of men will be born.

Fragments

8. The mind, says the author of the *Talks on Religion*,* can understand only the universe. Let imagination take over and you will have a God. Quite right: for the imagination is man's faculty for perceiving divinity.

9. A true priest always feels something greater than sympathy.

10. Ideas are infinite, independent, unceasingly moving, godlike thoughts.

11. Only through religion does logic become philosophy; only from it comes everything that makes philosophy greater than science. And instead of an eternally rich, infinite poetry, the lack of religion gives us only novels or the triviality that now is called art.

12. Is there such a thing as enlightenment? We should only be entitled to use this term if we could arbitrarily and without interference set going, if not artificially create, a principle in the mind of man that would play the same role in it that light plays in the universe.

13. Only someone who has his own religion, his own original way of looking at infinity, can be an artist.

14. Religion is not merely a part of culture, a limb of humanity: it is the center, it is always first and foremost. It is originality per se.

15. Every particular conception of God is mere gossip. But the idea of God is the Idea of ideas.

16. The priest as such exists only in the invisible world. In what guise is it possible for him to appear among men? His only purpose on earth will be to transform the finite into the infinite; hence he must be and continue to be, no matter what the name of his profession, an artist.

17. When ideas become gods, then the consciousness of harmony will become devotion, humility, and hope.

18. The spirit of the moral man is everywhere suffused with religion; it is his element. And this bright chaos of divine thoughts and feelings we call enthusiasm.

19. To have genius is the natural state of humanity. Nature endowed even humanity with health, and since love is for women

* Schleiermacher's *Reden über die Religion* (*On Religion. Talks to the Educated among Those Who Despise It*) (1799).

242

what genius is for men, we must conceive of the golden age as a time when love and genius were universal.

20. Everyone is an artist whose central purpose in life is to educate his intellect.

21. The need to raise itself above humanity is humanity's prime characteristic.

22. What are the few remaining mystics doing? More or less ordering the raw chaos of already extant religion, but only in isolation, on a small scale, in ineffectual attempts. Let us do it on a large scale everywhere and in every possible way; let us awaken all religions from their graves and through the omnipotence of art and science reanimate and reorganize those that are immortal.

23. Virtue is reason transformed into energy.

24. The symmetry and organization of history teach us that mankind, for as long as it existed and developed, has really always been and has always become an individual, a person. In the great person of mankind, God became a man.

25. The life and power of poetry consist in its ability to step out of itself, tear off a fragment of religion, and then return into itself and absorb it. So too with philosophy.

26. Wit is the appearance, the outward lightning bolt of the imagination. Hence the divinity and witty appearance of mysticism.

27. Plato's philosophy is a worthy preface to the religion of the future.

28. Man is Nature creatively looking back at itself.

29. Man frees himself by bringing forth God or making him visible, and this is how he becomes immortal.

30. Religion is absolutely unfathomable. One can sound it anywhere and still penetrate more deeply into the infinite.

31. Religion is the centripetal and centrifugal force of the human spirit, and the power that unites the two.

32. Can we expect the world to be saved by scholars? I don't know. But it's time for all artists to join together as comrades into an eternal brotherhood.

33. The morality of a work is not to be found in its subject or in the relation of the speaker to his audience, but in the spirit of its execu-

tion. If this is infused with the whole wealth of humanity, then the work is moral. If it is only the product of a particular ability or art, then it is not.

34. Whoever has religion will speak in poetry. But to seek and find religion, you need the instrument of philosophy.

35. As the generals of antiquity used to address their soldiers before a battle, so too the moralist ought to address mankind in the battle of the times.

36. Every complete human being has some sort of genius. True virtue is genius.

37. Culture is the greatest good and it alone is useful.

38. In the world of language or, what is much the same, the world of art and culture, religion necessarily assumes the guise of a mythology or a bible.

39. The Kantians' conception of duty relates to the commandment of honor, the voice of God and of one's calling in us, as the dried plant to the fresh flower on the living stem.

40. A definite relationship to God must seem as intolerable to the mystic as a particular conception or notion of God.

41. There is no greater need of the age than the need for a spiritual counterweight to the Revolution and to the despotism which the Revolution exercises over people by means of its concentration of the most desirable worldly interests. Where can we find such a counterweight? The answer isn't hard: unquestionably in ourselves, and whoever has seen that the center of humanity lies there will also have discovered in the same place the center of modern culture and the harmony of all the hitherto isolated and conflicting sciences and arts.

42. If one is to believe the philosophers, then what we call religion is simply intentionally popular or instinctively artless philosophy. The poets, however, seem to prefer to think of it as a variety of poetry which, unsure of its own lovely playfulness, takes itself too seriously and too one-sidedly. Still, philosophy already admits and begins to recognize that it must start with religion and achieve perfection in religion, and poetry strives only for the infinite and despises worldly practicality and culture as the real opposites of religion. Hence eternal peace among artists is no longer a distant prospect.

43. What men are among the other creatures of the earth, artists are among men.

44. We cannot see God but we can see godlikeness everywhere — first and foremost in the heart of a thoughtful man, in the depths of a living human creation. Nature, the universe, can be felt and conceived of without mediation: but not God. Only a man among men can write divine poetry, think divine thoughts, and live religiously. No one can be the direct mediator for even his own spirit because the mediator must be purely objective, and necessarily centered on a point outside himself. One can select and appoint one's mediator, but only a mediator who has already appointed himself as such. A mediator is one who perceives the divinity within himself and who self-destructively sacrifices himself in order to reveal, communicate, and represent to all mankind this divinity in his conduct and actions, in his words and works. If this impulse is not present, then what was perceived was not divine or not really his own. To mediate and to be mediated are the whole higher life of man and every artist is a mediator for all other men.

45. An artist is someone who carries his center within himself. Whoever lacks such a center has to choose some particular leader and mediator outside of himself, not, to be sure, forever, but only to begin with. For a man cannot live without a vital center, and if he does not yet have one within himself, then he can only seek it in another man, and only a man and a man's center can stimulate and awaken his own.

46. Poetry and philosophy are, depending on one's point of view, different spheres, different forms, or simply the component parts of religion. For only try really to combine the two and you will find yourself with nothing but religion.

47. God is everything that is purely original and sublime, consequently the individual himself taken to the highest power. But aren't nature and the world also individuals?

48. Where philosophy stops, poetry has to begin. An ordinary point of view, a way of thinking, natural only in opposition to art and culture, a mere existing: all these are wrong; that is, there should be no kingdom of barbarity beyond the boundaries of culture. Every thinking part of an organization should not feel its limits without at the same time feeling its unity in relation to the whole.

Fragments

For example, one ought to contrast philosophy not simply with unphilosophy, but with poetry.

49. To give the brotherhood of artists a particular purpose would mean substituting a shabby institute for an eternal union, or debasing the community of saints into a state.

50. You marvel at the age, at the ferment of its gigantic power, at its violent convulsions, and don't know what new births to expect. You should understand yourselves and answer for yourselves the question whether something can happen to mankind which does not have its origins in mankind. Doesn't all motion have to come from the center, and where is the center? The answer is obvious, and therefore these events also point to a great rebirth of religion, a universal metamorphosis. To be sure, religion is per se eternal, consistent, and unchanging, as God is; but for precisely this reason its appears forever newly shaped and transformed.

51. We won't know what a man is until we have learned from the nature of man why there should be some men who have intellect and spirit, and others who don't.

52. Pretending to represent a religion is even more sacrilegious than trying to establish one.

53. No occupation is so human as one that simply supplements, joins, fosters.

54. The artist should have as little desire to rule as to serve. He can only create, do nothing but create, and so help the state only by making rulers and servants, and by exalting politicians and economists into artists.

55. Versatility consists not just in a comprehensive system but also in a feeling for the chaos outside that system, like man's feeling for something beyond man.

56. Just as the Romans were the only nation that was completely national, so our age is the first true age.

57. You will find a wealth of culture in our best poetry; but seek the profundity of man among the philosophers.

58. Even the so-called national teachers whom the state has hired should become priests again, and mindful of the spirit: but they can do so only by attaching themselves to higher culture.

59. Nothing is wittier and more grotesque than classical mythology and Christianity — because they are so mystical.

60. Individuality is precisely what is original and eternal in man; personality doesn't matter so much. To pursue the cultivation and development of this individuality as one's highest calling would be a godlike egoism.

61. The power of the letter has been talked about for quite some time without anyone's really understanding what is being said. It's time for it to be taken seriously, for the mind to awaken and grasp once again the forgotten magic wand.

62. You only have as much morality as you have philosophy and poetry.

63. The really central insight of Christianity is sin.

64. Artists make mankind an individual by connecting the past with the future in the present. Artists are the higher organ of the soul where the vital spirits of all external humanity join together, and where inner humanity has its primary sphere of action.

65. Only by being cultivated does a human being, who is wholly that, become altogether human and permeated by humanity.

66. The original Protestants wanted to live faithfully according to scripture, take it absolutely seriously, and annihilate everything else.

67. Religion and morality are symmetrically opposed, like poetry and philosophy.

68. If you cast your life into a human mold, you've done enough; but you'll never reach the heights of art and the depths of science without some portion of divinity.

69. Irony is the clear consciousness of eternal agility, of an infinitely teeming chaos.

70. Music is more closely related to morality, history to religion; for rhythm is the idea of music, but history deals with the primitive.

71. Confusion is chaotic only when it can give rise to a new world.

72. Vainly do you search through your so-called aesthetics for the harmonious fullness of humanity, the beginning and end of culture. Try to recognize the elements of humanity and culture, and worship them, particularly fire.

73. There is no dualism without primacy; and therefore morality is not equal to religion, but subordinate to it.

Fragments

74. Join the extremes and you will find the true middle.

75. As the finest flower of a particular kind of organization, poetry is a very localized thing. Philosophy, on the other hand, may possibly be not very dissimilar even on different planets.

76. Morality without a sense for paradox is vulgar.

77. Honor is the mysticism of justice.

78. The thinking of a religious person is etymological; it traces all concepts back to the original insight, to whatever is characteristic.

79. There is only a single sense incorporating all the others. The most spiritual sense is the most original; all others derive from it.

80. We agree on this point because we are of one sense; but here we disagree because you or I am lacking in sense. Who is right, and how are we to settle the matter? Only by virtue of a culture that broadens every particular sense into a universal, infinite sense, and by faith in this sense or in religion. Then we will agree before we can agree to agree.

81. Every relation of man to the infinite is religion; that is, man in the entire fullness of his humanity. When a mathematician calculates what the infinitely great number is, that of course isn't religion. The infinite conceived of in such fullness is God.

82. You live only insofar as you live according to your own ideas. Your principles are only the means, your calling the end in itself.

83. Only through love and the consciousness of love does man become man.

84. The pursuit of morality is probably the greatest waste of time, with the exception of the rituals of piety. Can you make a habit of having a soul and a mind? So too with religion and morality; neither should influence the economy and politics of life without mediation.

85. The kernel, the center of poetry, is to be found in mythology and the mysteries of antiquity. Satiate the feeling of life with the idea of infinity, and you will understand both the ancients and poetry.

86. Beautiful is what reminds us of nature and thereby stimulates a sense of the infinite fullness of life. Nature is organic, and whatever is most sublimely beautiful is therefore always vegetal, and the same is true of morality and love.

87. A true human being is one who has penetrated to the center of humanity.

88. There is a beautiful kind of openness that unfolds like a flower to breathe forth its fragrance.

89. Why should morality belong only to philosophy, since the greatest part of poetry is concerned with the art of living and the knowledge of human nature! Is morality then independent of both and something unto itself? Or is it perhaps like religion, which ought never to appear in isolation?

90. You wanted to destroy philosophy and poetry in order to have more room for religion and morality, both of which you misunderstood; but you've managed to destroy nothing but yourself.

91. All life is in its ultimate origins not natural, but divine and human; for it must arise out of love, just as there can be no understanding without spirit.

92. The only significant opposition to the religion of man and artist now springing up everywhere is to be expected from the few remaining real Christians. But they too, when the sun really begins to dawn, will fall down and worship.

93. Polemics can only sharpen the mind, and ought to exterminate irrationality. Polemics are thoroughly philosophical. Boundless religious wrath and fury lose their dignity when they become polemical, when they are focused in a specific direction and on a particular object or purpose.

94. The few revolutionaries who took part in the Revolution were mystics as only Frenchmen of our age could have been mystics. They legislated their characters and their actions into religion. But future historians will consider it the greatest honor and destiny of the Revolution that it was the strongest stimulus to a slumbering religion.

95. The new, eternal gospel that Lessing prophesied will appear as a bible: but not as a single book in the usual sense. Even what we now call the Bible is actually a system of books. And that is, I might add, no mere arbitrary turn of phrase! Or is there some other word to differentiate the idea of an infinite book from an ordinary one, than Bible, the book per se, the absolute book? And surely there is an eternally essential and even practical difference if a book is merely a means to an end, or an independent work, an individual, a

personified idea. It cannot be this without divine inspiration, and here the esoteric concept is itself in agreement with the exoteric one; and, moreover, no idea is isolated, but is what it is only in combination with all other ideas. An example will explain this. All the classical poems of the ancients are coherent, inseparable; they form an organic whole, they constitute, properly viewed, only a single poem, the only one in which poetry itself appears in perfection. In a similar way, in a perfect literature all books should be only a single book, and in such an eternally developing book, the gospel of humanity and culture will be revealed.

96. All philosophy is idealism, and there exists no true realism except that of poetry. But poetry and philosophy are only extremes. If one were to say that some people are pure idealists and others very definitely realists, then that remark would be quite true. Stated differently, it means that there as yet exist no wholly cultivated human beings, that there still is no religion.

97. A happy omen: that even a physicist — the profound Baader* — has raised himself up from the depths of physics to the level of intuiting poetry, honoring the elements as organic individuals, and pointing out the divinity at the heart of matter!

98. Conceive of something finite formed into something infinite, and you have a man.

99. If you want to penetrate into the heart of physics, then let yourself be initiated into the mysteries of poetry.

100. We will know man when we know the center of the earth.

101. Wherever there are politics or economics no morality exists.

102. The first man to have an intellectual conception of morality, to recognize and, with divine inspiration, reveal the prototype of perfected man in the forms of art and antiquity was the holy Winckelmann.

103. Whoever doesn't come to know Nature through love will never come to know her.

104. Original love never appears in a pure state, but in manifold forms and disguises, as trust, humility, devotion, cheerfulness, loyalty, shame, and gratitude; but mostly as yearning and secret melancholy.

* Franz Baader (1765–1841), German Catholic philosopher and theosophist; also a student of the natural sciences and technology.

105. So Fichte is supposed to have attacked religion? If an interest in the world beyond the senses is the essence of religion, then his whole doctrine is religion in the form of philosophy.

106. Don't waste your faith and love on the political world, but, in the divine world of science and art, offer up your inmost being in a fiery stream of eternal creation.

107. In undisturbed harmony, Hülsen's muse formulates beautiful, sublime ideas about culture, humanity, and love. This is morality in its highest sense; but morality suffused with religion, and moving from the artificial flux of syllogism into the free stream of the epic.

108. Whatever can be done while poetry and philosophy are separated has been done and accomplished. So the time has come to unite the two.

109. Imagination and wit are everything to you! Explain a beautiful illusion and take playfulness seriously, and you will apprehend what is at the center and rediscover your revered art in a more sublime light.

110. The difference between religion and morality is to be found quite simply in the old classification of all things into divine and human, if only it were understood properly.

111. Your goal is art and science, your life love and culture. Without knowing it, you're on the way to religion. Realize the fact and you'll be sure of achieving your goal.

112. In our age or any other, nothing more to the credit of Christianity can be said than that the author of the *Talks on Religion* is a Christian.

113. The artist who doesn't reveal himself completely is a contemptible slave.

114. No artist should be the only, the sole artist among artists, the central one, the director of all the others; rather, all artists should be all of these things, but each one from his own point of view. No artist should be merely the representative of his genre, but should relate himself and his genre to the whole, and thereby influence and control it. Like the Roman senators, true artists are a nation of kings.

115. If you want to achieve great things, then inspire and educate women and young men. Here, if anywhere, fresh strength and

health are still to be found, and this is the way that the most important reformations have been accomplished.

116. Outward nobility in the man is to genius as beauty in women is to their capacity to love, to their temperament.

117. Philosophy is an ellipse. The one center, which we are closer to at present, is the rule of reason. The other is the idea of the universe, and it is here that philosophy and religion intersect.

118. What blindness to talk of atheism! Are there any theists? Did any human mind ever encompass the idea of divinity?

119. All honor to the true philologists! They accomplish a godlike task, for they disseminate the artistic sense throughout the whole region of scholarship. No scholar should be a simple workman.

120. The spirit of the old heroes of German art and science will remain ours for as long as we are Germans. The German artist either has no character at all or else that of an Albrecht Dürer, Kepler, Hans Sachs, or of a Luther and Jacob Böhme. Righteous, guileless, thorough, precise, and profound is this character, but also innocent and somewhat clumsy. Only with the Germans is it a national characteristic to worship the arts and sciences simply for their own sakes.

121. If you only listen to me now and realize why you can't understand each other, then I'll have achieved my purpose. When the sense of harmony has been awakened, then it's time to express more harmoniously the One Thing that will always have to be repeated.

122. Wherever artists make up a family there we have the original convocations of humanity.

123. False universality is what rubs the edges off all individual kinds of culture and takes as its basis the mediocre average. With true universality, on the other hand, art, for example, would become even more artificial than it is in its pure state, poetry would become more poetical, criticism more critical, history more historical, and so on. This universality can come into being when the simple light of religion and morality touches a chaos of combinative wit and fertilizes it. Then the most sublime poetry and philosophy burst into flower by themselves.

124. Why does all that is highest nowadays reveal itself so often as a false tendency? Because nobody understands himself who doesn't understand his fellows. Therefore you first have to believe you're

not alone, you always have to intuit everything infinitely and never tire of cultivating the intellect until you've finally found what's original and essential. Then the Genius of the Age will appear to you and gently intimate what is proper and what isn't.

125. Whoever feels a noble impulse stirring deeply within himself and doesn't know how to explain it, let him read the *Talks on Religion*, and what he felt will become so clear to him that he will be able to formulate it precisely.

126. A family can only be formed around a loving woman.

127. Women have less need for the poetry of poets because their very essence is poetry.

128. Mysteries are female; they like to veil themselves but still want to be seen and discovered.

129. In religion it's always morning and the rosy light of dawn.

129a. You're not really supposed to understand me, but I want very much for you to listen to me.*

130. Only a man who is at one with the world can be at one with himself.

131. The hidden meaning of sacrifice is the annihilation of the finite because it is finite. In order to demonstrate that this is its only justification, one must choose to sacrifice whatever is most noble and most beautiful: but particularly man, the flower of the earth. Human sacrifices are the most natural sacrifices. But man is more than the flower of the earth; he is reasonable, and reason is free and in itself nothing but an eternal self-destination into the infinite. Hence man can only sacrifice himself, and he does so in an omnipresent sanctity the mob knows nothing of. All artists are Decians,† and to become an artist means nothing but consecrating oneself to the gods of the underworld. In the enthusiasm of annihilation, the meaning of the divine creation is revealed for the first time. Only in the midst of death does the lightning bolt of eternal life explode.

132. If you separate religion entirely from morality, then you'll get the real energy of evil in man, the horrible, cruel, raging, and inhu-

* This fragment – though contained in the manuscript of the *Ideas* – was not printed in the *Athenaeum*.

† The Decii, a noted Roman family in which grandfather, father, and son freely gave their lives for the greater glory of Rome.

man principle that has dwelt in his spirit from the very beginning. Here the division of the indivisible is punished most terribly.

133. To begin with, I speak only to those who are already facing the Orient.

134. You suspect something greater even in me and ask why I keep silent precisely at the threshold? It's because it's still so early in the day.

135. Not Hermann and Odin are the national gods of the Germans, but art and science. Think again of Kepler, Dürer, Luther, Böhme; and then of Lessing, Winckelmann, Goethe, Fichte. Virtue is applicable not only to morals; it also holds good for the arts and sciences, which have their own rights and duties. And this spirit, this power of virtue, is precisely what differentiates the German from everyone else in his treatment of the arts and the sciences.

136. What am I proud of, and what can I be proud of as an artist? Of the decision that separated and isolated me forever from everything ordinary; of the work that divinely surpasses every intention, and whose intention no one will ever probe entirely; of the ability to worship the perfection I have encountered; of the awareness that I can stimulate my fellows to do their best, and that everything they create is my gain.

137. The piety of philosophers is theory, pure contemplation of the divinity, calm and gay in silent solitude. Spinoza is the ideal of the species. The religious state of the poet is more passionate and more communicative. At the root of things lies enthusiasm, and at the end there remains mythology. Whatever stays at the midpoint possesses the character of life to the point of sexual differentiation. Mysteries are, as I said before, female; and orgies seek, in the happy exuberance of their male strength, to overcome everything around them or fertilize it.

138. Precisely because Christianity is a religion of death, it could be treated with the greatest realism, and could have its orgies just as the old religion of nature and life did.

139. There is no self-knowledge except historical self-knowledge. No one knows what he is if he doesn't know what his contemporaries are, particularly the greatest contemporary of the brotherhood, the master of masters, the genius of the age.

140. One of the most important concerns of the brotherhood is to

remove all outsiders who have insinuated themselves into its ranks. Bunglers should be thrown out.

141. Oh, how wretched are your conceptions of genius (I mean the best among you). Where you see genius, I often see a wealth of false tendencies, the very center of incompetence. A little talent and a lot of humbug are things everyone praises, and which even lead everyone to proclaim that genius is incorrect, must be incorrect. So, this idea is gone too? Isn't the thoughtful man the one who is fittest to perceive the language of the spirit? Only the spiritual man has a spirit, a genius, and every genius is universal. Whoever is merely representative, merely has talent.

142. Like the merchants in the Middle Ages, the artists of today should band together into a Hansa in order to defend themselves.

143. There is no great world but the world of artists. They live nobly, though they still lack a proper sense of decorum. But decorum would develop wherever everybody expressed themselves openly and cheerfully, and felt the value of others completely.

144. You demand, once and for all, original understanding from a thinker, and even allow a certain measure of inspiration to a poet. But do you really know what that means? Without being aware of it, you have trespassed on holy ground; you are ours.

145. All human beings are somewhat ludicrous and grotesque simply because they are human; and in this respect too, artists probably are doubly human. So it is, so it was, so it will be.

146. Even in their outward behavior, the lives of artists should differ completely from the lives of other men. They are Brahmins, a higher caste: ennobled not by birth, but by free self-consecration.

147. What constitutes the free human being per se, what to the unfree man is the standard of all things, is his religion. There is a profound meaning in the expression that something or other is his God or his idol, and in other expressions of the sort.

148. Who unlocks the magic book of art and frees the imprisoned holy spirit? Only a kindred spirit.

149. Without poetry, religion becomes murky, false, and evil; without philosophy, extravagant in its lewdness and lustful to the point of self-emasculation.

150. You can neither explain nor understand the universe, but only contemplate and reveal it. Only stop calling the system of empiri-

cism the universe, and if you haven't yet understood Spinoza, discover for the present the true religious conception of the universe in the *Talks on Religion*.

151. Religion can assume all the aspects of feeling. Here wild rage and the sweetest melancholy touch, devouring hate and the childish smile of happy compliance.

152. If you want to see complete humanity, then look for a family. In the family, minds organically grow into a unit, and for precisely that reason, the family is pure poetry.

153. All self-sufficiency is radical, is original, and all originality is moral, is originality of the whole man. Without originality, there is no energy of reason and no beauty of disposition.

154. Absolutely candid, carefree, but straightforward speech becomes possible for the first time when one speaks of the highest.

155. I have expressed a few ideas pointing toward the heart of things, and have greeted the dawn in my own way, from my own point of view. Let anyone who knows the road do likewise in his own way, from his own point of view.

156. *To Novalis*: You don't stay at the threshold of things. On the contrary, your spirit is deeply suffused with poetry and philosophy. It was closest to me in these images of uncomprehended truth. What you've thought I think; what I've thought you will think or have already thought. There are misunderstandings that only serve to confirm the greatest shared understanding. Every doctrine of the eternal Orient belongs to all artists. I name you instead of all the others.

ON INCOMPREHENSIBILITY

On Incomprehensibility

BECAUSE of something either in them or in us, some subjects of human thought stimulate us to ever deeper thought, and the more we are stimulated and lose ourselves in these subjects, the more do they become a Single Subject, which, depending on whether we seek and find it in ourselves or outside of ourselves, we designate the Nature of Things or the Destiny of Man. Other subjects perhaps would never be able to attract our attention if we were to withdraw into holy seclusion and focus our minds exclusively on this subject of subjects, and if we did not have to be together with people and hence busy our minds with real and hypothetical human relationships which, when considered more carefully, always become more numerous and complex and thereby make us diverge into directions contrary to this single subject.

Of all things that have to do with communicating ideas, what could be more fascinating than the question of whether such communication is actually possible? And where could one find a better opportunity for carrying out a variety of experiments to test this possibility or impossibility than in either writing a journal like the *Athenaeum* oneself or else taking part in it as a reader?

On Incomprehensibility

Common sense which is so fond of navigating by the compass of etymologies — so long as they are very close by — probably did not have a difficult time in arriving at the conclusion that the basis of the incomprehensible is to be found in incomprehension. Now, it is a peculiarity of mine that I absolutely detest incomprehension, not only the incomprehension of the uncomprehending but even more the incomprehension of the comprehending. For this reason, I made a resolution quite some time ago to have a talk about this matter with my reader, and then create before his eyes — in spite of him as it were — another new reader to my own liking: yes, even to deduce him if need be. I meant it quite seriously and not without some of my old bent for mysticism. I wanted for once to be really thorough and go through the whole series of my essays, admit their frequent lack of success with complete frankness, and so gradually lead the reader to being similarly frank and straightforward with himself. I wanted to prove that all incomprehension is relative, and show how incomprehensible Garve, for example, is to me. I wanted to demonstrate that words often understand themselves better than do those who use them, wanted to point out that there must be a connection of some secret brotherhood among philosophical words that, like a host of spirits too soon aroused, bring everything into confusion in their writings and exert the invisible power of the World Spirit on even those who try to deny it. I wanted to show that the purest and most genuine incomprehension emanates precisely from science and the arts — which by their very nature aim at comprehension and at making comprehensible — and from philosophy and philology; and so that the whole business shouldn't turn around in too palpable a circle I had made a firm resolve really to be comprehensible, at least this time. I wanted to focus attention on what the greatest thinkers of every age have divined (only very darkly, to be sure) until Kant discovered the table of categories and there was light in the spirit of man: I mean by this a real language, so that we can stop rummaging about for words and pay attention to the power and source of all activity. The great frenzy of such a Cabala where one would be taught the way the human spirit

On Incomprehensibility

can transform itself and thereby perhaps at last bind its transforming and ever transformed opponent in chains — I simply could not
portray a mystery like this as naively and nakedly as, when with
the thoughtlessness of youth, I made *Lucinde* reveal the nature of
love in an eternal hieroglyph. Consequently I had to think of some
popular medium to bond chemically the holy, delicate, fleeting,
airy, fragrant, and, as it were, imponderable thought. Otherwise,
how badly might it have been misunderstood, since only through
its well-considered employment was an end finally to be made of
all understandable misunderstandings? At the same time, I noted
with sincere pleasure the progress of our country — not to speak
of our age! The same age in which we too have the honor to live;
the age that, to wrap it all up in a word, deserves the humble but
highly suggestive name of the Critical Age, so that soon now everything is going to be criticized, except the age itself, and everything
is going to become more and more critical, and artists can already
begin to cherish the just hope that humanity will at last rise up in a
mass and learn to read.

Only a very short while ago this thought of a real language occurred to me again and a glorious prospect opened up before my
mind's eye. In the nineteenth century, so Girtanner* assures us, in
the nineteenth century man will be able to make gold; and isn't it
now more than mere conjecture that the nineteenth century is
shortly going to begin? With laudable confidence and some huffing
and puffing, the worthy man says: "Every chemist, every artist will
make gold; the kitchen utensils are going to be made of silver, of
gold." How gladly all artists will now resolve to go on being hungry for the slight, insignificant remainder of the eighteenth century, and in future no longer fulfill this sacred duty with an ag-
grieved heart; for they know that in part they themselves, and in
part also (and all the more certainly) their descendants will shortly
be able to make gold. That he should specify precisely kitchen
utensils is due to the fact that what this ingenious prophet finds

* Christoph Girtanner (1760–1800), German physician, author of various
essays on medicine and chemistry.

On Incomprehensibility

really beautiful and great in this catastrophe is that we won't be swallowing so much vile vinegary wine out of ordinary, ignoble, base metals like lead, copper, iron, and suchlike.

I saw the whole thing from another point of view. I had often secretly admired the objectivity of gold, I might say even worshipped it. Among the Chinese, I thought, among the English, the Russians, in the island of Japan, among the natives of Fez and Morocco, even among the Cossacks, Cheremis, Bashkirs, and Mulattoes, in short, wherever there is even a little enlightenment and education, silver and gold are comprehensible and through them everything else. When it comes to pass that every artist possesses these materials in sufficient quantity, then he will be allowed only to write his works in bas-relief, with gold letters on silver tablets. Who would want to reject so beautifully printed a book with the vulgar remark that it doesn't make any sense?

But all these things are merely chimeras or ideals: for Girtanner is dead and consequently for the moment so far removed from being able to make gold that one might extract with all possible artistry only so much iron out of him as might be necessary to immortalize his memory by way of a little medallion.

Furthermore, the complaints of incomprehensibility have been directed so exclusively and so frequently and variously at the *Athenaeum* that my deduction might start off most appropriately right at the spot where the shoe actually hurts.

A penetrating critic in the *Berliner Archiv der Zeit* has already been good enough to defend the *Athenaeum* against these attacks and in so doing has used as an example the notorious fragment about the three tendencies. What a marvelous idea! This is just the way one should attack the problem. I am going to follow the same procedure, and so as to let the reader perceive all the more readily that I really think the fragment good, I shall print it once more in these pages:

The French Revolution, Fichte's philosophy, and Goethe's *Meister* are the greatest tendencies of the age. Whoever is offended by this juxtaposition, whoever cannot take any revolution seriously that

On Incomprehensibility

isn't noisy and materialistic, hasn't yet achieved a lofty, broad perspective on the history of mankind. Even in our shabby histories of civilization, which usually resemble a collection of variants accompanied by a running commentary for which the original classical text has been lost; even there many a little book, almost unnoticed by the noisy rabble at the time, plays a greater role than anything they did.

I wrote this fragment with the most honorable intentions and almost without any irony at all. The way that it has been misunderstood has caused me unspeakable surprise because I expected the misunderstanding to come from quite another quarter. That I consider art to be the heart of humanity and the French Revolution a marvelous allegory about the system of transcendental idealism is, to be sure, only one of my most extremely subjective opinions. But I have let this opinion be known so often and in so many different ways that I really might have hoped the reader would have gotten used to it by now. All the rest is mere cryptology. Whoever can't find Goethe's whole spirit in *Wilhelm Meister* won't be able to find it anywhere else. Poetry and idealism are the focal points of German art and culture; everybody knows that. All the greatest truths of every sort are completely trivial and hence nothing is more important than to express them forever in a new way and, wherever possible, forever more paradoxically, so that we won't forget they still exist and that they can never be expressed in their entirety.

Up to this point I have not been ironical and by all rights I ought not to be misunderstood; and yet it has happened, to the extent in fact of having the well-known Jacobin, Magister Dyk of Leipzig,* even find democratic leanings in it.

To be sure, there is something else in the fragment that might in fact be misunderstood. This lies in the word *tendencies* and this is where the irony begins. For this word can be understood to mean that I consider the *Theory of Knowledge*, for example, to be merely a tendency, a temporary venture like Kant's *Critique of*

---

* Johann Dyk (1750–1813), proprietor of the Dyk Bookstore in Leipzig and translator of a number of French light comedies.

On Incomprehensibility

Pure Reason which I myself might perhaps have a mind to continue (only rather better) and then bring to completion; or else that I wish to use the jargon that is most usual and appropriate to this kind of conception, to place myself on Fichte's shoulders, just as he placed himself on Reinhold's shoulders, Reinhold on Kant's shoulders, Kant on Leibniz's, and so on infinitely back to the prime shoulder. I was perfectly aware of this, but I thought I would like to try and see if anyone would accuse me of having had so bad an intention. No one seems to have noticed it. Why should I provide misunderstandings when no one wants to take them up? And so I now let irony go to the winds and declare point-blank that in the dialect of the *Fragments* the word means that everything now is only a tendency, that the age is the Age of Tendencies. As to whether or not I am of the opinion that all these tendencies are going to be corrected and resolved by me, or maybe by my brother or by Tieck, or by someone else from our group, or only some son of ours, or grandson, great-grandson, grandson twenty-seven times removed, or only at the last judgment, or never: that I leave to the wisdom of the reader, to whom this question really belongs.

Goethe and Fichte: that is still the easiest and fittest phrase for all the offense the *Athenaeum* has given, and for all the incomprehension it has provoked. Here too probably the best thing would be to aggravate it even more: when this vexation reaches its highest point, then it will burst and disappear, and then the process of understanding can set to work immediately. We haven't gotten far enough in giving offense; but what is not yet may still come to be. Yes, even those names are going to have to be named again — more than once. Just today my brother wrote a sonnet which I can't resist passing along to the reader because of the charming puns which he (the reader) loves almost more than he loves irony:

> Go, admire idols* that are finely made
> And leave us Goethe to be master, guide and friend:
> When his spirit's rosy dawns do fade
> Apollo's golden day no joy will send.

* *Götzen* in the original. The reference is to *Götz von Berlichingen*.

On Incomprehensibility

He lures no new spring green from barren trunks,
But cuts them down to give us warmth and fire.
And so the time will come when all the Muse's clunks
Will curse themselves to stone and stiffened mire.

Not to know Goethe means to be a Goth.
Fools are first blinded by every new, bright flame,
Then too much light kills them, like the moth.

Goethe, you who by the mercy of the gods came
To us, an angel from the stars: we are not loth
To call you godly in form, look, heart, and name.

———— ◇ ————

A great part of the incomprehensibility of the *Athenaeum* is unquestionably due to the *irony* that to a greater or lesser extent is to be found everywhere in it. Here too I will begin with a text from the *Lyceum* [*Critical*] *Fragments*:

Socratic irony is the only involuntary and yet completely deliberate dissimulation. It is equally impossible to feign it or divulge it. To a person who hasn't got it, it will remain a riddle even after it is openly confessed. It is meant to deceive no one except those who consider it a deception and who either take pleasure in the delightful roguery of making fools of the whole world or else become angry when they get an inkling they themselves might be included. In this sort of irony, everything should be playful and serious, guilelessly open and deeply hidden. It originates in the union of *savoir vivre* and scientific spirit, in the conjunction of a perfectly instinctive and a perfectly conscious philosophy. It contains and arouses a feeling of indissoluble antagonism between the absolute and the relative, between the impossibility and the necessity of complete communication. It is the freest of all licenses, for by its means one transcends oneself; and yet it is also the most lawful, for it is absolutely necessary. It is a very good sign when the harmonious bores are at a loss about how they should react to this continuous self-parody, when they fluctuate endlessly between belief and disbelief until they get dizzy and take what is meant as a joke seriously and what is meant seriously as a joke. For Lessing irony is instinct; for Hemsterhuis it is classical study; for Hülsen it arises out of the philosophy of philosophy and surpasses these others by far.

On Incomprehensibility

Another one of these fragments recommends itself even more by its brevity:

Irony is the form of paradox. Paradox is everything which is simultaneously good and great.

Won't every reader who is used to the *Athenaeum* fragments find all this simply trifling — yes, even trivial? And yet at the time it seemed incomprehensible to many people because of its relative novelty. For only since then has irony become daily fare, only since the dawn of the new century has such a quantity of great and small ironies of different sorts sprung up, so that I will soon be able to say, like Boufflers,* of the various species of the human heart:

> J'ai vu des coeurs de toutes formes,
> Grands, petits, minces, gros, médiocres, énormes.

In order to facilitate a survey of the whole system of irony, we would like to mention here a few of the choicest kinds. The first and most distinguished of all is coarse irony. It is to be found in the real nature of things and is one of the most widespread of substances; it is properly at home in the history of mankind. Next there is fine or delicate irony; then extra-fine. Scaramouche employs the last type when he seems to be talking amicably and earnestly with someone when really he is only waiting for the chance to give him — while preserving the social amenities — a kick in the behind. This kind of irony is also to be found in poets, as well as straightforward irony, a type that flourishes most purely and originally in old gardens where wonderfully lovely grottoes lure the sensitive friend of nature into their cool wombs only to be-splash him plentifully from all sides with water and thereby wipe him clean of delicacy. Further, dramatic irony; that is, when an author has written three acts, then unexpectedly turns into another man and now has to write the last two acts. Double irony, when two lines of irony run parallel side-by-side without disturbing each

---

* Stanislas, Chevalier de Boufflers (1738–1815), French poet, noted primarily for his *vers de société*.

On Incomprehensibility

other: one for the gallery, the other for the boxes, though a few little sparks may also manage to get behind the scenes. Finally, there is the irony of irony. Generally speaking, the most fundamental irony of irony probably is that even it becomes tiresome if we are always being confronted with it. But what we want this irony to mean in the first place is something that happens in more ways than one. For example, if one speaks of irony without using it, as I have just done; if one speaks of irony ironically without in the process being aware of having fallen into a far more noticeable irony; if one can't disentangle oneself from irony anymore, as seems to be happening in this essay on incomprehensibility; if irony turns into a mannerism and becomes, as it were, ironical about the author; if one has promised to be ironical for some useless book without first having checked one's supply and then having to produce it against one's will, like an actor full of aches and pains; and if irony runs wild and can't be controlled any longer.

What gods will rescue us from all these ironies? The only solution is to find an irony that might be able to swallow up all these big and little ironies and leave no trace of them at all. I must confess that at precisely this moment I feel that mine has a real urge to do just that. But even this would only be a short-term solution. I fear that if I understand correctly what destiny seems to be hinting at, then soon there will arise a new generation of little ironies: for truly the stars augur the fantastic. And even if it should happen that everything were to be peaceful for a long period of time, one still would not be able to put any faith in this seeming calm. Irony is something one simply cannot play games with. It can have incredibly long-lasting aftereffects. I have a suspicion that some of the most conscious artists of earlier times are still carrying on ironically, hundreds of years after their deaths, with their most faithful followers and admirers. Shakespeare has so infinitely many depths, subterfuges, and intentions. Shouldn't he also, then, have had the intention of concealing insidious traps in his works to catch the cleverest artists of posterity, to deceive them and make them believe before they realize what they're doing that they are some-

On Incomprehensibility

what like Shakespeare themselves? Surely, he must be in this respect as in so many others much more full of intentions than people usually think.

I've already been forced to admit indirectly that the *Athenaeum* is incomprehensible, and because it happened in the heat of irony, I can hardly take it back without in the process doing violence to that irony.

But is incomprehensibility really something so unmitigatedly contemptible and evil? Methinks the salvation of families and nations rests upon it. If I am not wholly deceived, then states and systems, the most artificial productions of man, are often so artificial that one simply can't admire the wisdom of their creator enough. Only an incredibly minute quantity of it suffices: as long as its truth and purity remain inviolate and no blasphemous rationality dares approach its sacred confines. Yes, even man's most precious possession, his own inner happiness, depends in the last analysis, as anybody can easily verify, on some such point of strength that must be left in the dark, but that nonetheless shores up and supports the whole burden and would crumble the moment one subjected it to rational analysis. Verily, it would fare badly with you if, as you demand, the whole world were ever to become wholly comprehensible in earnest. And isn't this entire, unending world constructed by the understanding out of incomprehensibility or chaos?

Another consolation for the acknowledged incomprehensibility of the *Athenaeum* lies in the very fact of this acknowledgment, because precisely this has taught us that the evil was a passing one. The new age reveals itself as a nimble and quick-footed one. The dawn has donned seven-league boots. For a long time now there has been lightning on the horizon of poetry; the whole thunderous power of the heavens had gathered together in a mighty cloud; at one moment, it thundered loudly, at another the cloud seemed to move away and discharge its lightning bolts in the distance, only to return again in an even more terrible aspect. But soon it won't be simply a matter of one thunderstorm, the whole sky will burn with a single flame and then all your little lightning rods won't help you.

On Incomprehensibility

Then the nineteenth century will indeed make a beginning of it and then the little riddle of the incomprehensibility of the *Athenaeum* will also be solved. What a catastrophe! Then there will be readers who will know how to read. In the nineteenth century everyone will be able to savor the fragments with much gratification and pleasure in the after-dinner hours and not need a nut-cracker for even the hardest and most indigestible ones. In the nineteenth century every human being, every reader will find *Lucinde* innocent, *Genoveva** Protestant, and A. W. Schlegel's didactic *Elegies* almost too simple and transparent. And then too what I prophetically set forth as a maxim in the first fragments will hold true:

A classical text must never be entirely comprehensible. But those who are cultivated and who cultivate themselves must always want to learn more from it.

The great schism between understanding and not understanding will grow more and more widespread, intense, and distinct. Much hidden incomprehension will still erupt. But understanding too will reveal its omnipotence: understanding that ennobles disposition into character, elevates talent into genius, purifies one's feelings and artistic perceptions. Understanding itself will be understood, and people will at last see and admit that everyone can achieve the highest degree and that up to now humanity has been neither malicious nor stupid but simply clumsy and new.

I break off at this point so as not to profane prematurely the worship of the highest divinity. But the great principles, the convictions on which this worship depends may be revealed without profanation; and I have attempted to express the essentials by adding on something myself, by way of what the Spanish call a gloss, to one of the profound and admirable verses of the poet.† And now all I have left to wish for is that one of our excellent composers will

* Ludwig Tieck's *Leben und Tod der Heiligen Genoveva* (*Life and Death of St. Genevieve*) (1799), a play based on medieval Catholic legend.
† Schlegel's "gloss" takes off from the last stanza of Goethe's poem "Beherzigung."

On Incomprehensibility

find my lines worthy of being set to music. There is nothing more
beautiful on earth than poetry and music mingled in sweet compliance for the greater ennoblement of mankind.

> The rights of Jove are not for all.
> Don't go too far,
> Stay where you are,
> Look how you stand, or else you'll fall.
>
> One man is very humble,
> Another's cheeks swell up with pride;
> This one's brains are all a jumble,
> Another's still less well supplied.
> I love a fool, his hair and hide,
> I love it when he roars and rants,
> And love his languid, flowery dance.
> Forever will I now recall
> What in the master's heart I spied:
> The rights of Jove are not for all.
>
> To keep the mighty pyre burning
> A host of tender souls must be
> Who fresh to every labor turning
> Will make the heathen light to see.
> Now let the din grow loud and louder:
> Watch where you bite,
> Watch what you write,
> For when the fools with gun and powder
> Crawl from their lairs, think who they are:
> Don't go too far.
>
> Some few have caught and kept the spark
> That we have lighted.
> The masses still are in the dark:
> The dolts remain united.
> Lack of understanding understood
> Confers a lasting gloom
> On all that issues from the womb.
> The latest word brings lust for blood,
> The wasps fly in from near and far:
> Stay where you are.
>
> Let them talk from now till doomsday

On Incomprehensibility

They never will understand.
Some are born to go astray,
Artists buried in the sand. —
There are sparrows every season
Exulting in their song:
Does this seem wrong?
Let them live by their own reason,
Just make sure you're big and tall:
Look how you stand, or else you'll fall.

INDEX

Index

Index

Index

Novalis. *See* Hardenberg, Friedrich von

"On Incomprehensibility" (Schlegel), 17
"On Naive and Sentimental Poetry" (Schiller), 145*n*
Ovid, 181

Pindar, 175, 187, 195
Plato, 9, 63, 167, 180, 183, 198, 205, 209, 238, 240, 243
Pliny, 208

Raphael, 222
Reichardt, Johann Friedrich, 12, 12*n*
Reinhold, Karl Leonard, 157, 157*n*, 264
Richelieu, Cardinal, 233
Richter, Johann Paul Friedrich, 29, 29*n*, 148*n*, 178, 231
Robespierre, Augustin, 233
Rosa, Salvatore, 186
Rousseau, Jean Jacques, 156, 179, 188, 231, 232, 240
Rubens, Peter Paul, 185

Sachs, Hans, 252
Sallust, 180
Schelling, Friedrich von, 36, 36*n*, 173, 205
Schiller, Johann Christoph Friedrich von, 10, 12, 145*n*
Schlegel, August Wilhelm, 9, 10, 16, 16*n*, 18, 200, 269
Schlegel, Friedrich, 4, 5, 8, 16, 23, 24, 28, 29, 30, 33, 38, 39: life of, 9–10, 21–22; as a classicist, 11–12; and literary theory, 12–13, 20; and Romanticism, 14–15, 17, 18–20; concept of love, 25, 36–37; and passivity, 25–27
Schleiermacher, Friedrich, 3, 4, 4*n*, 6, 14, 16, 16*n*, 17, 18, 166
Shaftesbury, Anthony Cooper, Third Earl of, 150, 150*n*

Shakespeare, William, 12, 20, 148, 158, 159, 163, 188, 197, 198, 204, 267, 268
Socrates, 106
Sophocles, 159, 207
Spinoza, Baruch, 194, 200, 201, 204, 216, 240, 254, 256
Steen, Jan, 186, 186*n*
Sterne, Laurence, 29, 30, 143*n*, 148*n*
Stilling, Heinrich, 214, 214*n*

Tacitus, 181, 183, 191, 194
Talks on Religion (Schleiermacher), 242, 242*n*, 251, 253, 256
Thackeray, William Makepeace, 6
Thomasius, Christian, 145*n*–146*n*, 146
Thucydides, 191
Tieck, Johann Ludwig, 14, 18, 18*n*, 178*n*, 206, 230, 264, 269
Titian, 222

Veit, Dorothea, 8, 21–22
Veit, Simon, 21
Vogler, Georg Joseph, 185, 185*n*
Voltaire, François Marie Arouet, 209, 210, 222
Voss, Johann Heinrich, 157, 157*n*, 198

Wieland, Christoph Martin, 199, 238
Wilhelm Meister (Goethe), 19, 158, 190, 224, 262, 263
William Lovell (Tieck), 230, 230*n*, 231
Winckelmann, Johann Joachim, 9, 9*n*, 11, 181, 200, 206, 207, 250, 254
Woldemar (Jacobi), 12, 12*n*, 24
Wolff, Christian von, 171, 171*n*
Wordsworth, William, 3

Xenien (Goethe), 12
Xenophon, 182

277